# MYTH, DRAMA, AND THE POLITICS OF DAVID'S DANCE

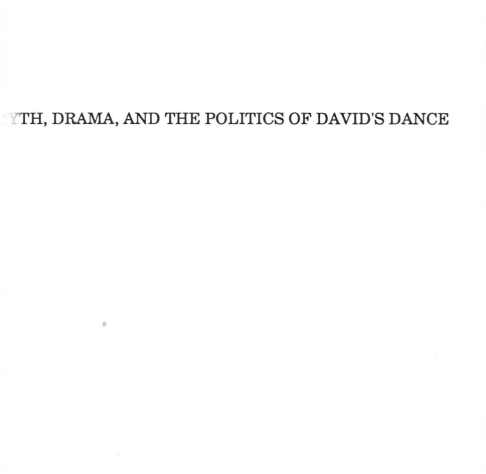

*HARVARD SEMITIC MUSEUM*

***HARVARD SEMITIC MONOGRAPHS***

edited by
Frank Moore Cross

Number 44
Myth, Drama, and the Politics of David's Dance

by
C.L. Seow

C.L. Seow

# *MYTH, DRAMA, AND THE POLITICS OF DAVID'S DANCE*

Scholars Press
Atlanta, Georgia

# Myth, Drama, and the Politics of David's Dance

by
C.L. Seow





**Library of Congress Cataloging in Publication Data**

Seow, C.L. (Choon Leong)
Myth, drama, and the politics of David's dance / C.L. Seow.
p. cm. -- (Harvard Semitic monographs ; no. 44)
Includes bibliographical references.
ISBN 1-55540-400-6 (alk. paper)
1. Ark of the law. 2. David, King of Israel. 3. Judaism--Rituals--History. 4. Jews--History--1200-953 B.C. I. Title. II. Series
BM657.A85S46 1989
296'.09'014--dc20 89-38695
CIP

CIP

Printed in the United States of America
on acid-free paper

For my beloved teacher

Frank Moore Cross

# ACKNOWLEDGEMENTS

It gives me great pleasure to thank my teachers, colleagues, and family who made the completion of this book possible.

I wish to acknowledge my gratitude to M. Douglas Nelson, who taught me access to the ancient world through the study of its languages, and Ronald L. Tyler of Pepperdine University, who first introduced me to biblical studies. I am most fortunate to have had numerous dedicated and inspiring teachers who nurtured and encouraged me over the years. In particular, I would like to mention Bernhard W. Anderson, James F. Armstrong, J. J. M. Roberts, Katharine Doob Sakenfeld of Princeton Theological Seminary, and Frank M. Cross, Michael D. Coogan, Paul D. Hanson, Thomas O. Lambdin, William L. Moran, and Piotr Steinkeller of Harvard University. This book would never have been completed without the critical and philological tools that these teachers have given me.

I am indebted to Tryggve Mettinger and William H. Propp for carefully reading the entire manuscript and saving me from much embarrasssment. Douglas Miller and Nancy Bowen proofread part or all of the manuscript, and Jeffrey Peterson tirelessly assisted me in the preparation of the indices.

None of my training in the West would have been possible without the understanding and support of my family in Singapore. For their continued faith in me I am thankful. Above all, I am grateful to my wife, Lai-King, who sacrificed the security of home and risked much more to be with me in this, sometimes difficult, sojourn in a foreign land.

C. L. Seow

Princeton Theological Seminary
Princeton, New Jersey
June, 1989

# TABLE OF CONTENTS

## ABBREVIATIONS

The abbreviations used in this work are essentially those found in the *Journal of Biblical Literature*'s "Instructions for Contributors;" *The Chicago Assyrian Dictionary;* or R. Borger's *Handbuch der Keilinschriftliteratur.* In addition, the following abreviations are used:

| | |
|---|---|
| *AbrN* | *Abr–Nahrain* |
| Akk. | Akkadian |
| *Ant.* | Josephus, *Jewish Antiquities* |
| *AP* | *Aramaic Papyri of the Fifth Century B.C.*, A. E. Cowley |
| Arab. | Arabic |
| Aram. | Aramaic |
| *Dio.* | *Diodorus Siculus* |
| DN | Divine name |
| *ECT* | *The Egyptian Coffin Texts*, A. de Buck |
| *EE* | *Enuma Elish* |
| ET | English translation |
| Fs. | Festschrift |
| GN | Geographical name |
| *HAR* | *Hebrew Annual Review* |
| Heb. | Hebrew |
| *Hist. Graec.* | Xenophon, *Historia Graeca* |
| *JNWSL* | *Journal of Northwest Semitic Languages* |
| *KS* | *Kleine Schriften*, O. Eissfeldt, 6 Volumes. |
| *KTU* | *Keilalphabetischen Texte aus Ugarit*, ed. M. Dietrich, O. Loretz, J. Sanmartín |
| LB | Late Bronze |
| LXX | "Septuagint" (the majority reading) |
| $LXX^B$ | Codex Vaticanus |
| $LXX^L$ | Lucianic Manuscripts |
| MB | Middle Bronze |
| MRS | Mission de Ras Shamra |
| OB | Old Babylonian |
| OL | Old Latin |

| | |
|---|---|
| *Pap. Anast.* | Papyri Anastasi |
| PN | Personal name |
| Praep. Evang. | Eusebius, *Praeparatio Evangelica* |
| *PRU* | *Le Palais royal d'Ugarit.* 5 Volumes, ed. C. F. A. Schaeffer |
| PS | Proto-Semitic |
| 4QDt | Deuteronomy fragments from Qumran, Cave IV, ed. P. W. Skehan |
| 1QIsa[a] | Isaiah scroll from Qumran Cave, ed. M. Burrows |
| 11QPs[a] | Psalm Scroll from Qumran, Cave 11, ed. J. A. Sanders |
| 4QSam | Samuel fragments from Qumran, Cave IV, ed. F. M. Cross |
| RS | Ras Shamra |
| *RSP* | *Ras Shamra Parallels.* 3 Volumes, ed. L. R. Fisher, *et. al.* |
| *SO* | Samaria Ostraca |
| Syr. | Syriac translation = Peshiṭta |
| Targ. | Targum |
| Targ. Jon. | Targum Jonathan |
| UBL | Ugaritisch-Biblische Literatur |
| *Urk.* | *Urkunden des ägyptischen Altertums.* ed. G. Steindorff |
| Vulg. | Vulgate |
| WBC | Word Bible Commentary |
| *WUS* | *Wörterbuch der Ugaritischen Sprache.* ed. J. Aistleitner |
| ZBAT | Zürcher Bibelkommentare Altes Testament |

# INTRODUCTION

It has long been recognized that the transfer of the ark into Jerusalem was a pivotal event in the history of Israelite religion and politics. Scholars hail David's initiative as a brilliant maneuver that effectively galvanized the loose confederation of Israelite tribes into a monarchical state. The procession was, first and foremost, of great political significance inasmuch as it legimated David and his successors. But in this event many also find the seeds of Judean dynastic ideologies and the inspiration for much of Israel's hymnody and liturgy.[1] Indeed, various notions associated with Zion as a religio-political symbol are regularly traced to this procession and to the unique encounter of the Israelite traditions associated with the ark and the Canaanite traditions native to the Jebusite cult of Jerusalem.[2]

The story of David's procession of the ark is told in 2 Samuel 6, with parallel texts in 1 Chronicles,[3] a secondary

1. See T. Ishida, *The Royal Dynasties in Ancient Israel* (BZAW 143; Berlin: de Gruyter, 1977) 121-122; H.-J. Kraus, *Worship in Israel* (trans. G. Buswell; Richmond: Knox, 1966) 201-218; idem, *Die Königsherrschaft Gottes im Alten Testament* (BHT 13; Tübingen: Mohr, 1951) 51-57.

2. See D. L. Eiler, "The Origin and History of Zion as a Theological Symbol in Ancient Israel," Unpublished Th.D. Dissertation (Princeton Theological Seminary, 1968); B. C. Ollenburger, *Zion, the City of the Great King* (JSOTSup 41; Sheffield: JSOT, 1987) 36-52.

3. 2 Sam 6:2-11 // 1 Chron 13:1-14; 2 Sam 6:12-19 // 1 Chron 15:25-29; 2 Sam 6:17-19 // 1 Chron 16:1-3; 2 Sam 6:19-20 // 1 Chron 16:4-43. The Chronicler reverses the sequence of events in the Samuel narrative, placing David's military ventures after his pious acts. This is in keeping with his portrayal of David as, first and foremost, a faithful patron of the cult.

account by Josephus,[4] and a probable allusion to it in Psalm 132. It is generally acknowledged that 2 Samuel 6 constitutes the primary source regarding the procession, with only little added in the obviously secondary accounts of the Chronicler and Josephus. Despite some dispute, Psalm 132 is commonly accepted as a liturgical text or as containing liturgical texts used in conjunction with David's procession of the ark, although some concede that the background may be Solomon's procession of the ark during the inauguration of the temple (1 Kings 8).

Yet, there is no consensus regarding the interpretation of the biblical sources. On the one hand, there have been a few who have found traces of mythological elements in 2 Samuel 6 and, hence, have regarded it as a reflex of a ritual procession in the monarchical period. Thus, in a seminal study on the enthronement festival, S. Mowinckel proposed that the ark was carried in cultic procession through the streets of Jerusalem, in much the same way that the statue of Marduk was paraded through the streets of Babylon during the autumn New Year festivals.[5] The procession of the ark, according to

---

4. *Ant.* VII.71-77, 84-86. For a convenient collocation of MT, LXX and Vulg. of 2 Samuel 6 and the parallel texts in Chronicles with the account of Josephus, see P. Vannutelli, *Libri Synoptici Veteris Testamenti* (Rome: Pontifical Biblical Institute, 1931) 44-49.

5. *Psalmenstudien* II (Skrifter utgitt av Det Norske Videnskaps-akademi i Oslo II. Hist.-Filos. Klasse 6; Oslo: Dybwad, 1922). He subsequently refined his arguments in his *Offersang og Sangoffer* (Oslo: Aschehoug, 1951) = ET: *The Psalms in Israel's Worship* (2 vols.; trans. D. R. Ap-Thomas; Nashville: Abingdon, 1967) and *Zum israelitischen Neujahr und zur Deutung der Thronbesteigungspsalmen* (Avhandlinger utgitt av Det Norske Videnskaps-Akademi i Oslo II. Hist.-Filos. Klasse 2; Oslo: Dybwad, 1953). The idea of an Israelite New Year festival was, however, earlier broached by P. Volz, *Die Neujahrfest Jahwes* (Tübingen: Mohr, 1912). But Volz made no mention of the procession of the ark during the festival.

Mowinckel, was part of a cultic drama conducted annually to celebrate the accession of YHWH as king following the defeat of his enemies in mythological combat. Mowinckel contended that narratives of the procession of the ark like 2 Samuel 6 and 1 Kings 8 should not be taken as contemporary reports of the procession, because they were actually modelled on the ritual processions of the ark in the writers' own time.

Following Mowinckel, other scholars have sought to reconstruct the ritual on the basis of its supposed mythological background in the enthronement festival. Thus, relying on a purely cultic-ritual interpretation of the Ugaritic texts of the KRT group (i.e., *KTU* 1.14-15), I. Engnell tried to explain the details of the narrative in 2 Samuel 6 as dramatizing the myth of a dying and rising god, with the king playing the role of the warrior-god and participating in hierogamy.[6] Like Mowinckel, Engnell found no real historical referent in 2 Samuel 6; the chapter was thought useful for understanding only Israelite monarchical ritual, not history. In the same vein, A. Bentzen argued for the priority of the liturgical text in Psalm 132, asserting that 2 Samuel 6 was merely a narrativizing of the ritual.[7] Indeed, Bentzen contended that the entire story of the ark in 1 and 2 Samuel is to be interpreted in the light of the combat myth.

Without denying the actuality of David's procession of the ark in history, other interpreters have accepted the idea of a cultic procession of the ark through much of the monarchical period. Notably, H.-J. Kraus spoke of an annual procession of the ark during what he believed was an annual Royal Zion Festival which served to legitimate the Davidic

6. *Studies in Divine Kingship in the Ancient Near East* (2d. ed.; Oxford: Blackwell, 1967 [1943]) 143-165.

7. "The Cultic Use of the Story of the Ark in Samuel," *JBL* 67 (1948) 37-53.

dynasty and Jerusalem as its capital.[8] The procession of the ark was not a ritual of divine enthronement, but it dramatized the election of David and Zion. As part of a comprehensive study of the biblical evidence for such regularly conducted processions in the monarchy, T. E. Fretheim examined the procession conducted by David as a historical event of great religious significance.[9] But Fretheim would accept none of the mythological interpretations espoused by the Scandinavian scholars. Indeed, he prefaced his study by stating that his was a subject concerning which "Near Eastern parallels are of no value."[10]

In a recent essay on 2 Samuel 6, P. K. McCarter defended the historicity of the procession in 2 Samuel 6.[11] Citing parallels from Mesopotamia and Syria-Palestine, he argued that the procession is to be understood as part of David's historic inauguration of the city and thus, not to be interpreted in the light of a myth and ritual approach. The procession was a unique event in Israel's history, according to McCarter, and not an annually repeated phenomenon.

It appears, then, that there are essentially two evaluations of David's procession of the ark: (1) as a religious ritual rooted in ancient Near Eastern myth and, (2) as an historical event of great political significance. But myth and history are not incompatible entities. Neither are religion and politics polarities in the social world of early Israel. Whether by design or happenstance, myth and ritual served to enhance the political legitimacy and status of individuals and nations in

8. See *Königsherrschaft*, 27-35; *Worship*, 183-185.

9. "The Cultic Use of the Ark of the Covenant in the Monarchial Period," Unpublished Th.D. dissertation (Princeton Theological Seminary, 1967).

10. Ibid., 5.

11. "The Ritual Dedication of the City of David in 2 Samuel 6," in *The Word of the Lord Shall Go Forth* (Fs. D. N. Freedman; ed. C. L. Meyers and M. O'Connor; Winona Lake, Indiana: Eisenbrauns, 1983) 273-278.

ancient Near Eastern societies.[12] So one returns to the topic of David's procession of the ark in search of a synthetic approach that attempts to understand the historic procession in the cognitive matrix of ancient Canaan.[13]

In a most provocative study, J. W. Flanagan described the procession of the ark as a kind of "rite of passage which mediated and legitimated the temporal, spatial, and social transformations" that marked the dawn of the Israelite monarchy.[14] The transfer of the ark took place in an era of transitions, according to Flanagan. The tribes of Israel were in the process of transforming into a monarchical state, political leadership was transferred from Saul to David, tribal hegemony passed from north to south, and the Israelites were emerging from years of war to become a dominant power. In this period of rapid change, Flanagan argued, the procession of the ark served to legitimate Israel's political leaders, for such rituals in any society "express, control, and regularize the allegiances of groups and individuals."[15]

But even those who do not examine the ritual in the light of sociological theories, as Flanagan does so well, recognize the socio-political significance of David's procession in Israel's history. The literature is enormous on this issue, and only the briefest sketch can be given here. J. Wellhausen, for instance, surmised that in moving the ark David was establishing his

12. Cf. W. Robertson Smith, *Lectures on the Religion of the Semites* (Edinburgh: Black, 1889) 30.

13. On the role of myth and ritual in providing society with a cognitive matrix by which to interpret events, see C. Geertz, *Interpretation of Culture* (New York: Basic, 1973) 81-82, 88-125.

14. "Social Transformation and Ritual in 2 Samuel 6," in *The Word of the Lord Shall Go Forth* (Fs. D. N. Freedman; ed. C. L. Meyers and M. O'Connor; Winona Lake, Indiana: Eisenbrauns, 1983) 361-372.

15. Ibid., 365.

ties with the religious establishment of Shiloh.[16] A. Alt pointed to the choice of Jerusalem as a brilliant tactical move: Jerusalem was a flourishing city in a militarily strategic location, and politically neutral to the Israelite tribes as well.[17] To this historically non-Israelite city, M. Noth argued, David brought the ark with all the old traditions that were associated with it, thus establishing the preeminence and legitimacy of the city that he had named for himself.[18] The successful transfer of Israel's most important cult object to his new capital greatly enhanced the political legitimacy of David.[19] Hence, the tradition of the twin-election of David and Zion was developed, with the ark linking the new regime with the Shilonite confederacy.[20] At the same time, the unique encounter of Israelite traditions with those of the Jebusites eventually produced an unprecedented synthesis of ideas, a merger of the Yahwistic traditions associated with the ark and the mythological traditions associated with the Canaanite 'Ēl 'Elyôn which supposedly dominated the cult of the Jebusite city.[21] In fact, it is sometimes suggested that the notion of

16. *Prolegomena to the History of Ancient Israel* (trans. Black and Menzies; Gloucester, Massachusetts: Smith, 1973) 20.

17. "The Formation of the Israelite State in Palestine," (1930) in *Essays in Old Testament History* (trans. R. A. Wilson; Garden City, New York: Doubleday, 1968) 217.

18. "Jerusalem and the Israelite Tradition," (1950) in *The Laws in the Pentateuch and Other Studies* (trans. D. R. Ap-Thomas; London: SCM, 1966) 134-136.

19. So, recently, J.-M. Tarragon, "David et l'arche: II Samuel, vi," *RB* 86 (1979) 517-523.

20. Kraus, *Worship*, 179-200.

21. So R. E. Clements, *God and Temple* (Oxford: Blackwell, 1965) 48-49; E. Rohland, *Die Bedeutung der Erwählungstraditionen Israels für die Eschatologie der alttestamentlichen Propheten* (D.Theol. Dissertation; University of Heidelberg, 1956) 119ff.; F. Stolz, *Strukturen und Figuren im Kult von Jerusalem* (BZAW 118; Berlin: de Gruyter, 1969).

YHWH's kingship was a by-product of this new synthesis.[22]

Given the proliferation of theories about the merger of Israelite and Jebusite traditions, it is necessary in this study first to consider the mythological traditions that may have been associated with the ark prior to its transfer to Jerusalem. No attempt is made, however, to trace the origin of the ark or to present a history of it.[23] Rather, one needs only to consider the mythological traditions that may have been associated with the two sanctuaries immediately before the transfer of the ark to Jerusalem, namely, Shiloh and Qiryat-Ye'arim. These are the only shrines that the pertinent texts either mention explicitly or to which they allude (2 Sam 6:2; Ps 132:6). The prior step of clarifying the mythological traditions will, one hopes, help clarify what aspects of the monarchical Jerusalem cultus are genuinely continuous with these earlier Israelite sanctuaries, as opposed to indigenous Jebusite traditions or Davidic-Solomonic innovations. I will attempt to demonstrate that the deity (YHWH) at Shiloh was identified with 'Ēl, the high god in the Canaanite pantheon. At Qiryat-Ye'arim, on the other hand, it was not the imagery of 'Ēl that prevailed, but the myth of Ba'l, the young god on the rise. The dominance of the respective mythological images of the deity in each case reflected the socio-political realities as Israel experienced them.

The thesis that I will set forth in the second chapter of this study is that the procession was a religio-political drama celebrating the victory of YHWH as the divine warrior of

---

22. So, e.g., L. Rost, "Königsherrschaft Jahwes in vorköniglicher Zeit?" *TLZ* 85 (1960) 721-724; Kraus, *Königsherrschaft*, 90ff.; J. Schreiner, *Sion-Jerusalem: Jahwes Königssitz* (STANT 7; Munich: Kösel, 1963); H. Schmid, "Jahwe und die Kulttraditionen von Jerusalem," *ZAW* 67 (1955) 168-197.

23. On the complex questions regarding the ark's origin and early history, see R. Schmitt, *Zelt und Lade als Thema alttestamentlicher Wissenschaft* (Gütersloh: Mohn, 1972) 52-98.

Canaanite mythology and his consequent accession as king. Although recast in a narrative form and subjected to a limited redactional process, the parts of the ancient drama are still discernible in 2 Samuel 6, and they correspond substantially to the pattern of the divine warrior myth in the ancient Near East. Inasmuch as the ark was already associated with the mythological traditions of 'Ēl and Ba'l in the earlier sanctuaries, the significance of this drama must have been immediately apprehended by those who witnessed it. Through this cultic reenactment of the myth of the divine warrior, the story of YHWH's return to prominence was told. Indeed, that mythic drama reflected the political realities as well, for the fate of David and Israel was implicitly tied to the fate of YHWH.[24]

In the third chapter of this study we will consider Psalm 132, which most commentators believe to contain an allusion to the procession of the ark under David, if it is not actually a liturgy used in conjunction with the procession of the ark. It will be argued that the present form of the psalm contains genuinely archaic liturgical material that confirms our cultic-mythological reconstruction of the procession in 2 Samuel 6 and sheds new light on the political significance of the procession for David. But the utilization of these liturgical materials in the psalm also indicates the continued significance of the procession for the descendants of David. Even as the procession served to legitimate David, so it continued in times of crisis to legitimate the Davidides.

---

24. As sociologists of religion have long asserted, the most ancient form of political legitimation was based on the notion that institutional order was a microcosm of divine order. See, P. Berger, *The Sacred Canopy* (Garden City, New York: Doubleday, 1967) 34. Cf. M. Bloch, "Symbols, Song, Dance and Features of Articulation: Is Religion an Extreme Form of Traditional Authority?" *European Journal of Sociology* 15 (1974) 55-81.

# CHAPTER ONE

## MYTHOLOGICAL HERITAGE

The ark which David transferred into Jerusalem is linked with two earlier sanctuaries: (1) Qiryat-Ye'arim, which was variously known as Ba'lah (Josh 15:9), Mount Ba'lah (Josh 15:11), Highland of Ya'ar (Ps 132:6),[1] and Qiryat-Ba'l (Josh 18:14), and (2) Shiloh.

According to 1 Chron 13:6, David and his entourage went "to Ba'lah, to Qiryat-Ye'arim which belongs to Judah" (בעלתה אל־קרית יערים אשר ליהודה). This helps clarify the problematic מבעלי יהודה in MT of 2 Sam 6:2, which is probably corrupted from original מבע<לה> ליהודה "from Ba'lah of Judah."[2] Here in Ba'lah, Qiryat-Ye'arim, the ark had been lodged for some twenty years (1 Sam 7:2). Other traditions attest to the neglect of the ark to the extent that its location had been forgotten (cf. 1 Chron 13:3; Ps 132:6). It was from this place that the ark was taken and brought to its new place (מקום) in the City of David.

The ark is, moreover, associated with the name of יהוה צבאות ישב הכרבים "YHWH *Ṣĕḇā'ôṯ* who sits (enthroned) on

---

1. See Chapter Three.

2. Cf. 4QSam$^{a}$: בעלה היא קרי[ת יערים אשר] ליהודה "Ba'lah, that is, Qirya[t-Ye'arim which] belongs to Judah." See E. C. Ulrich, Jr. *The Qumran Text of Samuel and Josephus* (HSM 19; Missoula, Montana: Scholars, 1978) 194, 198-199. LXX$^{B}$ has ἀπὸ τῶν ἀρχόντων Ιουδα ἐν ἀναβάσει, reflecting Hebrew מבעלי יהודה בעלה. Noting that Greek ἐν ἀναβάσει is probably a misconstrual of the GN בעלה, Ulrich posits that the *Vorlage* of the Greek had בעל(ה) יהודה which forms a doublet with בעלי יהודה. Cf. P. K. McCarter, *II Samuel* (AB 9; Garden City, New York: Doubleday, 1984) 162-3. One should also note the reading of LXX$^{L}$ ἐν τε ἀναβάσει τοῦ βουνοῦ "in going up to the mount," which may reflect Hebrew בעלה ההר (cf. Mic 6:2 where Greek βουνός translates Hebrew הר), properly, "Mount Ba'lah."

the Cherubim" (2 Sam 6:2),[3] a name which establishes the continuity between the Jerusalem cultus and the old cultic center of Shiloh where it had been called ארון יהוה צבאות ישׁב הכרבים.[4] The use of the full liturgical name of the ark is deliberate; its purpose is to link the ark with its past.

At the outset of the narrative regarding the procession of the ark into Jerusalem (2 Samuel 6), then, one finds allusions to these two earlier sanctuaries, Shiloh and Qiryat–Ye'arim. Inasmuch as the procession was a journey, a dramatic movement from place to place, it is necessary to consider these old ties of the ark. A thorough investigation of the mythological traditions that may have been associated with these sanctuaries is indispensable, if one is to comprehend the symbolic significance of the ark and know what ideas of divine presence might have been associated with it. Only when the mythological traditions are clearly identified may we speak, as scholars do all too readily, of the synthesis of

---

3. MT has ארון האלהים אשׁר־נקרא שׁם שׁם יהוה צבאות ישׁב הכרבים עליו, with dittography of שׁם (cf. LXX which has the shorter reading). But one could read שָׁם in the second instance (following Syr. and many Mss), thus translating the text: "the ark of God over which the name of YHWH *Ṣĕḇā'ôṯ* was proclaimed." The parallel text in 1 Chron 13:4 omits צבאות, and 4QSam[a] apparently lacks it. (See Ulrich, *The Qumran Text of Samuel and Josephus* 201). We should perhaps adopt the *lectio brevior* here, although the fuller formula suggested by 1 Sam 4:4 and Isa 37:16 is probably the original name associated with the ark.

4. 1 Sam 4:4, following the *lectio brevior* of LXX$^{B}$. MT has ארון ברית יהוה צבאות, but ברית is without doubt a deuteronomistic addition (cf. Deut 10:8; 31:9, 25, 26; Josh 3:3, 6 [*bis*]), 8, 11, 14, 17; 4:7, 9, 18; 6:6, 8; 8:33; Judg 20:27; 1 Sam 4:3, 5; 2 Sam 15:24; 1 Kgs 3:15; 6:19; 8:1, 6; Jer 3:16). On the various designations of the ark in the biblical traditions, see the survey in Schmitt, *Zelt und Lade als Thema alttestamentlicher Wissenschaft*, 128–159, and C. L. Seow, "The Designation of the Ark in Priestly Theology," *HAR* 8 (1985) 185–188.

traditions that the entry of the ark supposedly inspired. Methodologically, then, this investigation is an essential first chapter, a prelude to our study of the procession itself and its place in the history of Israelite religion.

## A. SHILOH

The association of the epithets יהוה צבאות and ישב הכרבים with the ark has long been recognized,[5] but it was Otto Eissfeldt who most persuasively established the connection of both epithets with Shiloh.[6] Significantly, the name יהוה צבאות is not mentioned in the ancestral traditions of Israel, or in connection with the exodus and occupation of the land. The name does not occur at all in the Pentateuch, or in the Books of Joshua and Judges. The earliest occurrence of it is in connection with the sanctuary of Shiloh where the ark had been kept.[7]

The designation יהוה צבאות has been the subject of intensive scholarly scrutiny in this century.[8] There is still no

---

5. Thus already E. Kautzsch, "Die ursprüngliche Bedeutung des Namens יהוה צבאות," *ZAW* 6 (1886) 17-22, and F. Seyring, "Der alttestamentliche Sprachgebrauch inbetreff des Namens der sogen. 'Bundeslade'," *ZAW* 11 (1891) 116.

6. "Jahwe Zebaoth," (1950) *KS* III, 103-123; "Silo und Jerusalem," (1957) *KS* III, 417-425; "Monopol-Ansprüche Heiligtums von Silo,' (1973) *KS* VI, 8-14.

7. 1 Sam 1:3, 11; 4:4.

8. Two dissertations have appeared on the subject: I. Gefter, "Studies in the Use of *YHWH Ṣĕbā'ôt* in its Variant Forms," Ph.D. Dissertation (Brandeis University, 1977) and B. N. Wambacq, *L'épithète divine Jahvé Ṣĕbā'ôt* (Paris: de Brouwer, 1947). For other studies, see Schmitt, *Zelt und Lade*, 145-159; T. N. D. Mettinger, "YHWH Sabaoth--The Heavenly King on the Cherubim Throne," in *Studies in the Period of David and Solomon and Other Essays* (ed. T. Ishida; Tokyo: Yamakawa-Shupansha, 1982) 109-138.

consensus on the meaning and translation of the name, but studies point to three indisputable aspects of it: (1) the military character, (2) the royal connotations,[9] and (3) the association with creation.[10] Scholars have frequently emphasized one or another of these aspects at the expense of the others. But the ideas are not mutually exclusive, in my view, if one begins with Cross' characterization of יהוה צבאות as the epithet of the divine warrior *par excellence*.[11]

---

9. The notion of YHWH's kingship antedates the establishment of the monarchy, as is evident in some of Israel's oldest traditions: Exod 15:18; Num 23:21; Deut 33:5 (for the antiquity of these texts, see F. M. Cross, Jr., and D. N. Freedman, *Studies in Ancient Yahwistic Poetry* [SBLDS 21; Missoula, Montana: Scholars, 1975] 45-65, 97-122; D. A. Robertson, *Linguistic Evidence in Dating Early Hebrew Poetry* [SBLDS 3; Missoula, Montana: Scholars, 1972]; D. N. Freedman, "Divine Names and Titles in Early Hebrew Poetry," in *Magnalia Dei: The Mighty Acts of God* [Fs. G. E. Wright; ed. F. M. Cross, W. E. Lemke and P. D. Miller, Jr.; Garden City, New York: Doubleday, 1976] 55-102). There is no need, therefore, to see this epithet, which suggest YHWH's enthronement, as a retrojection from the Jerusalem temple, as some scholars do. So, for example, J. Maier, *Das altisraelitische Ladeheiligtum* (BZAW 93; Berlin: Töpelmann, 1965) 51-60; F. Crüsemann, *Der Widerstand gegen das Königtum* (WMANT 49; Neukirchen-Vluyn: Neukirchener, 1978) 76-78; F. Stolz, *Jahwes und Israels Kriege* (ATANT 60; Zürich: Theologischer, 1972) 45-66. Thus recently B. C. Ollenburger (*Zion, the City of the Great King* [JSOTSup 41; Sheffield: JSOT, 1987] 37-41] correctly argues that both epithets יהוה צבאות and ישב הכרבים were associated with the kingship of YHWH already at Shiloh.

10. See the survey in Wambacq, *L'épithète divine Jahvé Ṣĕbā'ôt*, 1-45.

11. F. M. Cross, *Canaanite Myth and Hebrew Epic* (Cambridge, Massachusetts: Harvard University, 1973) 70; idem, "Yahweh and the Gods of the Patriarchs," *HTR* 55 (1962) 411-431; idem, "The Divine Warrior in Israel's Early Cult," in *Biblical Motifs, Origins and Transformations* (ed. A.

That is, יהוה צבאות was perceived as the divine warrior who, having fought and won cosmogonic battles, had gained ascendency in the divine council as the supreme deity, the king over all the heavenly hosts. In Canaanite mythology, this role of the victorious warrior who sits enthroned as king over the universe is typically ascribed to 'Ēl, the chief god of the pantheon.

The syntax of יהוה צבאות is notoriously thorny.[12] The occurrence of a proper name in the construct state is an anomaly in Hebrew.[13] Hence, some propose to take the second element as somehow in apposition to the name YHWH.[14] Accordingly, יהוה צבאות is rendered by W. R. Arnold as "Yahweh Militant,"[15] by O. Eissfeldt as "Jahwe, der Zebaothhafte,"[16] and by M. Tsevat as "Yahweh, the Armies."[17] An alternative solution profferred by Cross is to assume that the name יהוה צבאות was originally part of a longer formula *'*il đū yahwī ṣaba'ōt* "'Ēl who creates the (heavenly) hosts."[18] The grammatically smoother formula יהוה אלהי צבאות, which Fritz Seyring long ago proposed as the original epithet

---

Altmann; Brandeis University Studies and Texts 3; Cambridge, Massachusetts: Harvard University, 1966) 11–30.

12. See the succinct summary of Mettinger in "YHWH Sabaoth," 109–111.

13. Cf. *GKC* § 125h.

14. See P. P. Joüon, *Grammaire de l'hébreu biblique* (Rome: Pontifical Biblical Institute, 1923) §131o.

15. *Ephod and Ark* (HTS 3; Cambridge, Massachusetts: Harvard University, 1917) 142–143.

16. "Jahwe Zebaoth," 103–123, esp. 110–113. He takes צבאות as an abstract plural with the literal meaning "Kriegerischkeit" interpreted as "Mächtigkeit," or the like.

17. "Studies in the Book of Samuel, 4," *HUCA* 36 (1965) 49–58. Tsevat, citing 2 Kgs 13:14 and Num 10:36, contends that צבאות is a noun with "plural of extension".

18. "Yahweh and the Gods of the Patriarchs," 255ff; *Canaanite Myth and Hebrew Epic*, 68–72.

associated with the ark,[19] Cross argues is *lectio facilior*, introduced secondarily to ease the awkward construction of יהוה צבאות.[20] Cross adopts the view that the divine name YHWH was originally a causative verb,[21] and צבאות was the object of it.[22] The name יהוה צבאות is, according to Cross, essentially an 'Ēl epithet designating the deity as Warrior and Creator.[23]

Without accepting the philological reconstruction of Cross, Mettinger also concludes that the epithet is ultimately to be associated with 'Ēl.[24] He posits that the original name was אל צבאות, thus comparable with other 'Ēl epithets in combination with feminine plural nouns: אל דעות (1 Sam 2:3), אל נקמות (Ps 94:1); and אל גמלות (Jer 51:56).[25] Mettinger proposes that the צבאות name was a genuinely Israelite derivation created specifically for the Shiloh cultus where "the 'Ēl qualities played an important role."[26] As for the construction of יהוה צבאות, he raises the possibility that the name YHWH came to be used as a generic appellative for

---

19. "Der alttestamentliche Sprachgebrauch inbetreff des Namens der sogen. 'Bundeslade'," 116.

20. The "inserted form" (with some form of the name אלהים) occurs 21 out of 284 times, including 4 occurrences of the peculiar construction יהוה אלהים צבאות (Pss 59:6; 80:5, 20; 84:9). The form אלהים צבאות (without יהוה) occurs twice (Ps 80:8, 15).

21. Thus following his teacher W. F. Albright, in "Review of *L'épithète divine Jahvé Ṣebā'ôt*," *JBL* 67 (1948) 377–381; "Contributions to Biblical Archaeology and Philology," *JBL* 43 (1924) 370–378. cf. P. Haupt, "Der Name Jahwe," *OLZ* 12 (1909) 211–214.

22. For a critique of this view, see Mettinger, "YHWH Sabaoth," 127 n. 70.

23. *Canaanite Myth and Hebrew Epic,* 70. Cf. P. D. Miller, *The Divine Warrior in Early Israel* (HSM 5; Cambridge, Massachusetts: Harvard University, 1975) 151–155.

24. "YHWH Sabaoth," 127–138.

25. Ibid., 128, 134.

26. Ibid., 135.

"god" (cf. DN Ištar becoming synonymous with "goddess" in Akkadian) and, thus, permissible in the construct state, but he also calls attention to the epithet ᵈ*Šamaš līmīma* "Šamaš of the Thousand" in one of the Amarna letters (*EA* 205.6).[27] He cites Ugaritic *ršp ṣb'i* (*UT* 2004.15 = *KTU* 1.91.15) though not interpreting the phrase as "Rešep of the Host," thus as a close parallel of יהוה צבאות, but rather as "Rešep of the Sunset."[28] To these examples we may now add the inscriptions from Kuntillet ʻAjrud where we find reference to *yhwh šmrn* "YHWH of Samaria" and *yhwh t(y)mn* "YHWH of Teman,"[29] and the bilingual inscription from Tell Fekheriyeh, which mentions *hdd skn* "Hadad of Sikan."[30]

---

27. "YHWH Sabaoth," 135 n 109. See J. A. Knudtzon, *Die El-Amarna-Tafeln* I (VAB, Aalen: Zeller, 1964) 738-739. Here the epithet is probably synonymous with *rab līmi* "Commander of a Thousand." One should note that in peripheral Akkadian, *līmu* is closely associated with *ṣābu* (see *CAD* 9, p. 197).

28. "YHWH Sabaoth," 134-135. See W. J. Fulco (*The Canaanite God Rešep* [AOS 8; New Haven: American Oriental Society, 1976] 42), who calls attention to a reference in the Medinet Habu text of Ramses III to the prowess of "Rešep of Host(s)."

29. Z. Meshel, *Kuntillet ʻAjrud* (Israel Museum Catalogue 175; Jerusalem: Israel Museum, 1978). See the thorough treatment of J. A. Emerton, "New Light on Israelite Religion: The Implications of the Inscriptions from Kuntillet ʻAjrud," *ZAW* 94 (1982) 2-20, and P. K. McCarter, "Aspects of the Religion of the Israelite Monarchy: Biblical and Epigraphic Data," in *Ancient Israelite Religion* (Fs. F. M. Cross; ed. P. D. Miller, Jr., P. D. Hanson and S. D. McBride; Philadelphia: Fortress, 1987) 139-143.

30. A. Abou-Assaf, P. Bordreuil, and A. R. Millard, *La statue de Tell Fekheryé et son inscription bilingue assyro-araméenne* (Paris: Recherche sur les civilisations, 1982). The meaning of *hdd skn* is clarified in the Akkadian version: (Aram) *hdd yšb skn* // (Akk) ᵈ*Adad āšib sikani* "Hadad who dwells in Sikan." For other examples of the name deity in construct with GN, see McCarter, "Aspects of the Religion of

Whatever the origin and precise meaning of יהוה צבאות, it seems clear that the name denoted a victorious deity enthroned in the divine council, hence the related epithet ישב הכרבים "the one who sits enthroned on the cherubim."[31] This view of the deity is in harmony with the representation of 'Ēl in West Semitic texts and iconography. In contrast to Ba'l, who is portrayed as a feisty young god ever fighting for his kingship, 'Ēl is seen as a wise and mature ruler sitting on a throne with a footstool.[32] In the Ugaritic texts, 'Ēl is called simply *mlk* "king" (*KTU* 1.14.I.41), *mlk 'ab šnm* "the king, father of years" (*KTU* 1.1.III.23–24; 1.2.III.5; 1.3.V.8; 1.4.IV.24; 1.5.VI.2; 1.6.I.36; 1.17.VI.49),[33] and he is acknowledged by other deities as *'il mlk dyknnh* "'Ēl, the king who formed him (Ba'l)" (*KTU* 1.3.V.36; 1.4.I.5–6; 1.4.IV.48). While there are

---

the Israelite Monarchy," 140; Emerton, "New Light on Israelite Religion," 2–9.

31. Cf. G. Westphal, "צבא השמים," *Orientalische Studien* (Fs. Th. Nöldeke; ed. C. Bezold; Giesen: Töpelmann, 1906) 719–728.

32. For a comparison of the kingship of 'Ēl with that of Ba'l, see W. Schmidt, *Königtum Gottes in Ugarit und Israel* (Berlin: Töpelmann, 1966) 17–54; E. T. Mullen, Jr., *The Divine Council in Canaanite and Early Hebrew Literature* (HSM 24; Chico, California: Scholars, 1980) 1–110.

33. The meaning of *šnm* is disputed. The plural "years" is *šnt* elsewhere in Ugaritic, but it is possible that we have alternate forms in the plural, as we do in Hebrew. This remains the easiest and most attractive solution. A second view takes *šnm* as a divine name, attested almost exclusively in ritual texts and god lists with θ*kmn* who is known to be a Cassite deity. A third proposal derives the form from the root *šny* "to change, pass away," with the plural noun meaning "mortals," or the like. A variation of this view, compares the III-Weak root to Arabic *snw/y* "shine, be exalted, eminent, old," thus making *'ab šnm* as "father of the exalted/shiny ones"--an epithet of 'Ēl as chief of the divine council. See M. Pope, *El in the Ugaritic Texts* (VTSup 2; Leiden: Brill, 1955) 32–34; B. Margalit, "Lexicographical Notes on the *Aqht* Epic (Part I: KTU 1.17–18)," *UF* 15 (1983) 90–91.

sporadic references to the kingship of other gods, 'Ēl is the divine king *par excellence* in Canaanite literature.

The portrayal of 'Ēl in iconography matches the textual description of him as king.[34] The best example of this is the now famous stela published by C. F. A. Schaeffer in 1937.[35] The stela shows a bearded old god, with horns sprouting from his crown and his right-hand raised in a gesture of blessing.[36] The deity is sitting on a lion-footed-throne, with his feet upon a footstool. A similar image from Hadrumetum (Sousse) depicts a deity, presumably also 'Ēl, who is likewise bearded (cf. *KTU* 1.3.V.2, 25; 1.4.V.4; 1.18.I.12; etc.), with his right hand raised in benediction, sitting on a throne depicted with cherubim (winged-sphinxes) at the side.[37] A statue of such an old, beneficent deity sitting upon a throne has also been found.[38] Other examples are attested in scarabs, seals and coins from the Levant.[39] The cumulative evidence points to

---

34. See T. N. D. Mettinger, *The Dethronement of Sabaoth* (ConBOT 18; Lund: Gleerup, 1982) 19-37; "YHWH Sabaoth," 111-123.

35. "La stèle de l'hommage du dieu El (?)" *Syria* 18 (1937) 128-134, pl. xvii. For a recent study which supports the identification of the royal figure on this stela as 'Ēl, see N. Wyatt, "The Stela of the Seated God from Ugarit," *UF* 15 (1983) 271-277.

36. On the attributes of 'Ēl, see Pope, *El in the Ugaritic Texts*, 25-54; F. M. Cross, Jr., "אֵל *'ēl*," *TDOT* I, 244-253.

37. P. Cintas, "Le sanctuaire punique de Sousse," *Revue Africaine* 91 (1947) 180, pl. xlix and fig. 48. For other examples of cherubim-thrones see Mettinger, "YHWH Sabaoth," 128-135.

38. Cintas, "Le sanctuaire punique de Sousse," pl. ii.2.

39. Cross, *Canaanite Myth and Hebrew Epic*, 35-36; A. M. Bisi, *Le stele puniche* (Studi Semitici 27; Rome: Università di Roma, 1967) 91-103, figs. 56, 57, 58; W. Culican, "Malqart Representations on Phoenician Seals," *AbrN* 2 (1960) 41-45; idem, "The Iconography of Some Phoenician Seals and Seal Impressions," *AJBA* 1 (1968) 50-103.

the association of the divine epithet ישב הכרבים with the image of 'Ēl as king.

This kingship of 'Ēl in the divine council was accomplished by virtue of 'Ēl's prowess as a warrior. Although in Canaanite mythology it is typically Ba'l or 'Anat who is described as the divine warrior, 'Ēl is also known to have had a martial background.[40] Thus, one finds the Ugaritic personal name *'ilmhr* "'Ēl is a Warrior"[41] and other West Semitic names extolling the might or military prowess of 'Ēl.[42] In Sanchuniathon's "Phoenician History" as told by Philo Byblius, Kronos ('Ēl) waged war against Ouranos, surrounded by his σύμμαχοι "allies" who were also called Ἐλωείμ, that is, Elohim.[43] This image of 'Ēl as a warrior is not incongruous with the notion of the deity as king; יהוה צבאות is at once warrior and king in the Hebrew Bible.[44] Significantly, every occurrence of ישב הכרבים in the Hebrew Bible coincides with the idea of YHWH as divine warrior.[45] But 'Ēl is not a

---

40. See P. D. Miller, "El the Warrior," *HTR* 60 (1967) 411–431; *The Divine Warrior in Early Israel*, 48–58.

41. See F. Gröndahl, *Die Personennamen der Texte aus Ugarit* (Studia Pohl Dissertationes Scientificæ de Rebus Orientis Antiqui 1; Rome: Pontifical Biblical Institute, 1967) 156. For *mhr* meaning "warrior," see A. F. Rainey, "The Military Personnel of Ugarit," *JNES* 24 (1965) 120, and compare the personal names *b'lmhr* "Ba'l is a Warrior" and *mhryb'l* / *mhrb'l* "Ba'l is (my) Warrior."

42. See the examples cited in Miller, *The Divine Warrior in Early Israel*, 56–57.

43. Eusebius, *Praep. Evang.* I.10.17–21; see the translation in H. W. Attridge and R. A. Oden, Jr., *Philo of Byblos* (CBQMS 9; Washington, D. C.: Catholic Biblical Association of America, 1981) 48–51.

44. *Contra* J. P. Ross ("Jahwe Ṣ^e^ḇā'ôṯ in Samuel and Psalms," *VT* 17 [1967] 76–92), who denies the basic military usage of the root *ṣb'* in order to emphasize the royal imagery of the epithet.

45. The formula occurs with יהוה צבאות in 1 Sam 4:4 and 2 Sam 6:2 // 1 Chron 13:6 as part of the name of the ark

warrior in the process of becoming king. Rather, he is already the victorious warrior elevated above all other gods, a deity enthroned as celestial king. Such was the god associated with the ark at Shiloh.

But apart from the divine epithets associated with the ark, there are other indications that the deity was worshipped as ʼĒl. In the opening verses of 1 Samuel we are introduced to a certain Elqanah ben-Yeroḥam ben-Elihu, who went to Shiloh annually to worship יהוה צבאות (1:1-3). The name Elqanah is related to other West Semitic names associating the root *qny* with ʼĒl. One thinks of the name *Ilu-qa-na* in Assyrian,[46] and Punic *qnʼl*.[47] Such names recall the Ugaritic texts where the verb *qny* is associated with ʼĒl.[48] He is known in one fragmentary text as *ʼil dyqny ảdm* "ʼĒl who created the *ảdm* (mountains?)" (*KTU* 1.19.IV.57-58). In another passage, he

---

when it was brought into battle against the Philistines and when it was transferred into Jerusalem following the battle at Baʻl Peraṣim. The name occurs in Isa 37:16 // 2 Kgs 19:15 in conjunction with Hezekiah's petition for divine help in the face of Sennacherib's attack in 701 B. C. E. The martial connotation of ישב הכרבים is especially evident in Psalm 80, where the deity is asked to "shine forth" (הופיעה) and "rouse up" (עוררה) his "might," and is addressed as יהוה אלהי צבאות (vv 5, 20) and אלהים צבאות (vv 8, 15). In Ps 99:1, the name appears in conjunction with terms used of the divine warrior's march. We should also note that the royal figure in Isa 9:5 is called אל גבור. At all events, the ישב הכרבים formula is, without exception, connected with the notion of YHWH as Warrior-King and is intimately related to the צבאות name.

46. K. L. Tallqvist, *Assyrian Personal Names* (Acta Societatis Scientiarum Fennicæ 63; Helsingfors, 1918) 99.

47. *CIS* 135.5. See F. L. Benz, *Personal Names in the Phoenician and Punic Inscriptions* (Studia Pohl Dissertationes Scientificæ de Rebus Orientis Antiqui 8; Rome: Pontifical Biblical Institute, 1972) 178, 404-405.

48. See M. Pope, "The Status of El at Ugarit," *UF* 19 (1987) 219-221.

is acknowledged by the gods as *qnyn* "our Creator" and *dyknn* "the one who formed us (*KTU* 1.10.III.5-6). It was before this deity that Kirta requested that he beget (*'aqny*) children (*KTU* 1.14.II.4). Thus, 'Ēl was regarded as creator of both divine and human beings. By the same token, his consort 'Athirat is called *qnyt 'ilm* "Creatrix of the gods" (*KTU* 1.4.I.22, III.26, 30, 35; IV.32.).[49]

Among the epigraphic finds from the ancient Near East, one notes the typical association of the root *qny* with 'Ēl. In the Phoenician version of the bilingual inscription from Karatepe, a deity called *'l qn 'rṣ* "'Ēl, Creator of the Earth" is invoked together with Ba'l Šamem and other gods (*KAI* 26.A.iii.18). Interestingly, in the Hieroglyphic Luwian version,[50] *'l qn 'rṣ* is identified with Ea (Sumerian ENKI "Lord of the Earth") who is, of course, known as an old and wise god, just like 'Ēl in Ugaritic mythology (*KTU* 1.3.V.30-31; 1.4.IV.41-43; 1.4.V.3-4). Ea was known as "the Creator of the world and of humanity" and "the Begetter of humanity."[51] As is generally recognized, the name *'l qn 'rṣ* is attested already in the form Ilkunirsa from a thirteenth century Hittite adaptation of a West Semitic myth.[52] That precise formula is found again in a late Punic inscription from Leptis Magna (*KAI* 129.1), and variations of it are

49. See J. C. de Moor, "El, the Creator," in *The Biblical World* (Fs. C. H. Gordon; ed. G. Rendsburg, et. al.; New York: KTAV, 1980) 176.

50. See F. Steinherr, "Die phönizisch-hethitischen Bilinguen von Karatepe," *Münchener Studien zur Sprachwissenschaft* 32 (1974) 119.

51. E. Ebeling, "Enki (Ea)," in *RLA* II, 374-379.

52. H. Otten, "Ein kanaanäische Mythus aus Boğazköy," *MIO* 1 (1953) 125-150; H. A. Hoffner, "The Elkunirsa Myth Reconsidered," *RHA* 23 (1965) 5-16. See the translation of A. Goetze in *ANET*$^{3}$, 519. The identification of the deity is virtually certain, notwithstanding certain phonological problems arising from the translation of the name from one language to another.

attested in texts from Palmyra and Hatra.[53] In 1972, N. Avigad published an eighth century fragment of an inscription from Jerusalem containing a series of personal names and the words *qn 'rṣ* in a broken context.[54] Avigad's reconstruction of *'l* before *qn 'rṣ* seems secure in the light of the parallels.

'Ēl's epithet "Creator of the earth" corresponds to another name by which he is called, namely, *bny bnwt* "creator of creatures" (*KTU* 1.4.II.11; 1.4.III.32; 1.6.III.5, 11; 1.17.I.25).[55] So scholars are certainly correct to say that *qny* ultimately indicates 'Ēl's ownership of the earth and supremacy over the other gods.[56] Hence the connection in Gen 14:19, 22 of קנה שמים וארץ with the epithet אל עליון, that is "'Ēl, the Highest One."[57]

In light of the connection of the epithets יהוה צבאות and ישב הכרבים with creation and the kingship of the deity over the universe, it is surely no coincidence that we should find the name Elqanah ("'Ēl has Created") identifying a worshipper

---

53. See L. della Vida, "El 'Elyon in Genesis 14:18-20," *JBL* 63 (1944) 1-9; A. Caquot, "Nouvelle inscriptions araméens de Hatra," *Syria* 40 (1963) 116; cf. P. D. Miller, Jr., "El, The Creator of the Earth," *BASOR* 239 (1980) 43-46.

54. "Excavations in the Jewish Quarter of the Old City of Jerusalem, 1971," *IEJ* 22 (1972) 193-200, esp. 195-197.

55. In Akkadian, *banû* is regularly used of creation. Especially provocative are several epithets of Ea: *bān binûtu* "Creator of creatures" (*PSBA* 20, 158.14); *bān kullati bēl gimri* "Creator of all things, lord of the universe" (IV *R* 56 ii 9); *bān kala* "Creator of everything" (*Iraq* 15, 123.19); *bān šamê u erṣeti* "Creator of heaven and earth" (*LKA* 77, i 29-30).

56. So B. Vawter, "Yahweh: Lord of the Heavens and the Earth," *CBQ* 48 (1986) 461-467. But Vawter goes too far in denying that *qny* means "to create." See P. Humbert, "Qânâ en hébreu biblique," in *Festschrift für Alfred Bertholet* (ed. W. Baumgartner, et. al.; Tübingen: Mohr, 1950) 259-266; Pope, *El in the Ugaritic Texts*, 51-52; idem, "The Status of El at Ugarit," 220.

57. See R. Rendtorff, "El, Ba'al und Jahwe," *ZAW* 78 (1966) 277-292.

of the deity at Shiloh.[58] Given the remarkably consistent connection of the root *qny* with 'Ēl, the occurrence of the name Elqanah must be considered another piece of evidence for Elism at the Shiloh sanctuary. But it is only one piece among many.

The Hebrew text gives the name of Elqanah's father as Yeroḥam, but the latter is probably an abbreviated form of a longer name with a theophoric element. The Greek has Ιερεμεηλ, indicating Hebrew ירחמאל "'Ēl Gives Compassion." With this one should compare Amorite *Ya-ar-ḫa-am-AN*, *ya-ar-ḫa-mi-DINGIR*, *Ir-ḫa-mi-AN*, *Ir-ḫa-mi-la*, and *Ir-ḫa-mi-il-la*, *Ra-aḫ-mi-i-li*.[59] Amorite personal names with this verbal root are overwhelmingly Elistic. These and Hebrew ירחמאל / ירחמאלי all express confidence in the compassion of the deity as 'Ēl.[60] The reference to divine compassion is also in accord with the character of 'Ēl in Canaanite literature. Thus in the Ugaritic corpus, 'Ēl is called *lṭpn 'il dp'id* "the Kindly One, 'Ēl Who is Compassionate" (*KTU* 1.1.III.22-23, IV.18; 1.4.IV.58; 1.5.VI.11-12; 1.6.III.14; 1.15.II.13-14, etc.). This special characteristic of 'Ēl is reflected in the biblical references to YHWH as אל רחום "Compassionate 'Ēl" (Deut 4:31), אל רחום וחנון "'Ēl, Compassionate and Gracious" (Exod 34:6; Ps 86:15), or אל חנון ורחום "'Ēl, Gracious and Compassionate" (Jon 4:2; Neh 9:31). Among the epigraphic finds from Ḫirbet Beit Lei comes

58. Cf. the West Semitic PN *qnmlk* "The king ('Ēl?) has created." See Gröndahl, *Die Personennamen der Texte aus Ugarit*, 39.

59. See H. B. Huffmon, *Amorite Personal Names in the Mari Texts* (Baltimore: Johns Hopkins, 1965) 261; I. J. Gelb, *Computer-Aided Analysis of Amorite* (AS 21; Chicago: Oriental Institute, 1980) 342.

60. Cf. M. Noth, *Die israelitischen Personennamen im Rahmen der gemeinsemitischen Namengebung* (BWANT 3/10; New York: Olms, 1980) 187, 199. For extra-biblical examples, see N. Avigad, *Hebrew Bullae from the Time of Jeremiah* (Jerusalem: Israel Exploration Society, 1986) 27 no. 8.

a fragment of an inscription referring to Yah(u) as *'l ḥnn* "Gracious God".[61] The name of Elqanah's wife, Hannah, we may surmise, was also originally a name expressing confidence in 'Ēl's compassion. One cannot be certain, however, since the root *ḥnn* is also found with non-Elistic theophoric elements in the West Semitic onomastica.[62]

Elqanah and his family went to Shiloh annually to worship at the sanctuary there (1 Sam 1:3). Notwithstanding the mention of an annual חג יהוה "festival of YHWH" at Shiloh (Judg 21:19), apparently a vintage festival, M. Haran is probably correct that the זבח הימים observed by Elqanah's family (1 Sam 1:21; 2:19) was not strictly a national pilgrimage but an annual sacrifice of the clan or family (cf. 1 Sam 20:6, 29).[63] But the expression זבח הימים also finds a close parallel in the phrase *zbḥ ymm* mentioned in the Phoenician version of the bilingual inscription from Karatepe, where *'l qn 'rṣ* "'Ēl, the Creator of the Earth" was worshipped among other deities:

wylk zbḥ lkl hmskt
zbḥ ymm 'lp
wb['t ḥ]rš š
wb't qṣr š
(*KAI* 26.A.II.19–III.1–2; cf. C.IV.2–6)

---

61. Inscription B. See F. M. Cross, "The Cave Inscription from Khirbet Beit Lei," in *Near Eastern Archaeology in the Twentieth Century* (Fs. N. Glueck; ed. J. A. Sanders; Garden City, New York: Doubleday, 1970) 299–306.

62. The father of Yeroḥam (Yeraḥmeel) is called Elihu in 1 Sam 1:1, but in 1 Chron 6:27 he has the Elistic name, Eliel. The family of Elqanah is said to have descended from the Kohathite family headed by Elizaphan ben-Uzziel who was charged with care of the ark (Num 3:30–31; cf. Exod 6:22).

63. "Zeḇaḥ Hayyamîm," *VT* 19 (1969) 11–22. Cf. R. Rendtorff, *Studien zur Geschichte des Opfers im Alten Israel* (WMANT 24; Neukirchen-Vluyn: Neukirchener, 1967) 134–135.

And sacrifice was brought to all the images:
*zbḥ ymm*, one ox;
and at the [time of pl]owing, one sheep;
and at the time of harvest, one sheep.

Here the *zbḥ ymm* is associated with key events of the agricultural calendar, namely, "the time of plowing" and "the time of harvest." Indeed, all three sacrifices are subsumed under the rubric of the *zbḥ* that was brought to the images. It appears that the *zbḥ ymm* at Karatepe was an annual event, as it was for the family of Elqanah at Shiloh.[64] As an ox was sacrificed at the *zbḥ ymm* of Karatepe, so one was offered at the *zbḥ hymym* in Shiloh.[65] But there is insufficient evidence, it seems to me, to argue for a Canaanite style New Year vintage festival at Shiloh.[66] What is involved here, rather, is

64. I am not persuaded by M. Haran's efforts to distinguish the *zbḥ ymm* here, which he translates as "daily sacrifice," from the annual sacrifice known in 1 Sam 1:21; 2:19; 20:6, 29. See his "ZBḤ YMM in the Karatepe Inscription," *VT* 19 (1969) 372-373. His purpose in separating the biblical *zbḥ hymym* from the sacrifice at Karatepe is to maintain his thesis that the biblical sacrifice was a family affair, whereas it would be difficult to maintain that the *zbḥ ymm* in this inscription was such. J. C. de Moor (*New Year with the Canaanites and Israelites* [Kamper Cahiers 22; Kampen: Kok, 1972] 29 n. 121) contends that the Hieroglyphic Luwian version supports the interpretation of *zbḥ ymm* as an annual sacrifice. Cf. J. D. Hawkins and A. M. Davies, "On the Problems of Karatepe: The Hieroglyphic Text," *AnSt* 28 (1978) 112.

65. 1 Sam 1:24, following the Syr., LXX, and 4QSam. See F. M. Cross, Jr., "A New Qumran Biblical Fragment Related to the Original Hebrew Underlying the Septuagint," *BASOR* 132 (1953) 15-26.

66. So E. Olávarri, "El calendrio cúltico de Karatepe y el Zebaḥ Hayyamym en I Sam," *EstBíb* 29 (1970) 311-325; de Moor, *The Seasonal Pattern*, 58-59; *New Year with the*

an annual sacrifice for the blessing of the family, clan or wider community. Significantly, the mention of the sacrifice in the Karatepe inscriptions is immediately followed by the invocation of blessings of life, health, and strength on Azitawadda and fecundity and plenty for the people (*KAI* 26.A.III.2–10; C.IV.6–10).

For such an annual sacrifice, Elqanah's family went to the Shiloh sanctuary. There Hannah petitioned the deity to open her womb, for "Peninah had children but Hannah had no children" (1 Sam 1:2). Elqanah gave portions (*mnwt*) to his wives, but Hannah received only one portion because of her barrenness (vv 4–5). So it happened year after year at the *byt yhwh* "house of YHWH" (v 7). Taunted by her rival because of her childlessness, Hannah wept and would not eat. Thereupon, Elqanah asked:

> Why do you weep, Hannah?
> Why will you not eat?
> Why is your heart troubled?
> Am I not better to you then ten sons?" (v 8)

The family ate and drank at the sanctuary, and Hannah petitioned tearfully for a son. After some initial misunderstanding, she gained the blessing of Eli the priest (v 17). The family returned home, "Elqanah knew his wife" and she conceived a son at the turn of the year (vv 19–20).

Facets of the story echo the Ugaritic tales of Kirta and Aqhat.[67] The Legend of Aqhat opens with a scene at the sanctuary of 'Ēl, where childless Danel was offering food and drink to the gods (*KTU* 1.17.I.1–16). 'Ēl was apparently presiding over the divine banquet when Ba'l came to explain the misery of Danel:

---

*Canaanites and Israelites*, 10; Ollenburger, *Zion, the City of the Great King*, 38.

67. Cf. Mettinger, "YHWH Sabaoth," 130–131.

d'in . bn . lh . km . 'aḫh .
w . šrš . km . 'aryh
bl . 'iθ . bn . lh . k<!>m[68] . 'aḫh .
wšrš km . 'aryh
(*KTU* 1.17.I.18-21)

He has no son, as his brothers do;
no offspring, as his siblings do.
He has no son, as his brothers do;
no offspring, as his siblings do.

Ba'l appeals to the old deity, 'Ēl, who is addressed as *θr 'il* "the Bull, 'Ēl" and *bny bnwt* "Creator of Creatures"--titles suggesting 'Ēl's own virility and power over fertility:[69]

ltbrknn lθr . 'il 'aby
tmrnn . lbny . bnwt
wykn . bnh . bbt .
šrš . bqrb hklh
(*KTU* 1.17.I.23-26)

May you bless him, O Bull, 'Ēl, My Father!
May you enable him, O Creator of Creatures,
That he may produce a son in his house;
An offspring in his palace.

Infused with new passion and potency, Danel returned to his conjugal bed and impregnated his wife. He rejoiced that he could be at ease because now he had a son who, among other blessings, would supply Danel with his portion (*mnt*) in the *bt 'il* "house of 'Ēl" (*KTU* 1.17.II.12-22). The feasting at the sanctuary and the petition to the compassionate deity resulted in a son for the barren one. Just so, the feasting at

68. Instead of *k* the text has *w*, which is one wedge too many.

69. See Pope, *El in the Ugaritic Texts,* 35-42.

the Shiloh sanctuary and petition before YHWH resulted in a son for the barren Hannah. Henceforth she would receive her due portions (*mnwt*) in the "house of YHWH" (*byt yhwh*), perhaps originally "house of 'Ēl" (*byt 'l*).

In the Kirta story, the protagonist was bereaved of his family twice over; his entire family was destroyed (*KTU* 1.14.I.1-25). In a sequence that is sometimes called an "incubation," Kirta bemoaned his childlessness. He entered his chambers, wept bitterly and fell asleep in his weeping. The issue of a mortal's childlessness comes again before 'Ēl, who is called "the Bull, progenitor of humanity." So in a dream 'Ēl appeared to Kirta, saying:

mn<!>[70] krt . kybky
ydm' . n'mn . ǵlm 'il .
mlk [.] θr 'abh y'arš .
hm . drk[t] k'ab . 'adm
(*KTU* 1.14.I.40-43)

---

70. The text has *m'at*, which scholars usually compare with Hebrew מי את (Ruth 3:16), or מה אתם (Judg 18:8). So H. L. Ginsberg, *The Legend of King Keret* (BASORSup 2-3; New Haven: American School of Oriental Research, 1946) 35; J. Gray, *The Krt Text in the Literature of Ras Shamra* (Leiden: Brill, 1964) 30; J. C. de Moor and K. Spronk, "Problematical Passages in the Legend of Kirtu (I)," *UF* 14 (1982) 158. But the parallels are unconvincing. If *m'at* is correct, we must render the line literally "What's with *you*, Kirta, that *he* weeps?" The correction of *m'at* to *mn* adopted by Gordon (*UT*, 250) is followed by H. Sauren and G. Kestemont, "Keret, roi de Ḫubur," *UF* 3 (1971) 195. We compare *mīnu* "why?" in the Amarna letters: *mīnūni aššâlīšu* "why should I ask him?" (*EA* 1.83); *mīnūmi la yuddan[u]* "why was nothing given to me?" (*EA* 126.49). For the use of *mīnu* elsewhere in Akkadian, see *CAD* 10/2, 89-96. Alternatively, we may translate "What's with Kirta that he weeps?" on the basis of the use of the interrogative/indefinite pronoun *mannu* in the Amarna letters (e.g., *EA* 149.21; 286.5; 96.14).

Why does Kirta weep?
The pleasant one, lad of 'Ēl shed tears?
Does he covet the kingship
   of the Bull, his father,
Or dominion like the Father of Humanity?

The text is unfortunately broken from this point to the end of the column, with a lacuna of about eight lines, but enough is legible at the top of the next column of the tablet to allow some reconstruction on the basis of the parallel in the third column (*KTU* 1.14.III.22-26) and the movement of the story. Kirta's desire was not wealth or power, it appears, but progeny:

[tn b]nm . 'aqny
[tn n]'rm . 'am'id[71]
      (*KTU* 1.14.II.4-5)

[Grant] that I acquire [s]ons
[Grant] that I multiply [l]ads.

71. The reconstruction adopted here substantially follows Ginsberg, *The Legend of King Keret*, 36. Ginsberg reads, however: *[tn θ'a]rm 'am'id*. He cites θ'*ar* in I.15, for which translation he compares Hebrew שְׁאֵר. Apart from the fact that elsewhere in Ugaritic we have θ'*ir* (*KTU* 1.18.I.25) and *š'ir* (*KTU* 1.6.II.35, 37, etc.), it must be conceded that θ'*ar* is hardly a clear reading in I.15 (see B. Margalit, "Studia Ugaritica II: 'Studies in Krt and Aqhat'," *UF* 8 [1976] 139-140). More importantly, in II.5, an *'áyin* (unless it is part of a *š*, as *KTU* has it) is visible before *rm* in the photograph in *CTA*, and Virolleaud so represents it. Ginsberg's reading θ'*arm* must, therefore, be rejected. F. C. Fensham ("Remarks on Keret 54-59," *JNWSL* 3 [1974] 32-33) considers various options, but settles on *n'rm* on the basis of the parallelism. In an earlier essay ("The Syro-Palestinian Context of Solomon's Dream," *HTR* 77 [1984] 148 n. 28), I defended the reading assumed here, citing *n'ry* "my children" in *KTU* 2.33.29 and the frequent parallelism of *bn* and *n'r* in Hebrew and Ugaritic.

Kirta was given instructions to sacrifice to the gods and prepare for war to win the hand of the maiden Ḥurriya, through whom the blessing of progeny was to come. So he concluded that the kindly divine progenitor, 'Ēl, had indeed responded to his petition:

> dbḥlmy . 'il . ytn
> bð̆rty . 'ab . 'adm
> wld[72] špḥ lkrt
> wǵlm l'bd 'il
> (*KTU* 1.14.III.46–49)

> This has 'Ēl granted me in my dream,
> In my vision[73] the Father of Humanity.
> She will bear a family for Kirta,
> A lad for the servant of 'Ēl.

A parallel passage (*KTU* 1.15.II.7ff.) in the second tablet of the KRT series shows affinities with the Danel story. It is again a scene of feasting in the sanctuary, reminiscent of the

---

72. I am most tempted to accept the proposal of Dean McBride (*apud* Cross, *Canaanite Myth and Hebrew Epic*, 181 n. 152) to emend *wld* to *ktld*, but the same problem with *wld* occurs elsewhere in KRT cycle (*KTU* 1.14.VI.33; 1.15.III.5, 20, 21). We expect initial **w* > *y* in Ugaritic, although *w* is retained in a few personal names (*wql*, *wry*, *wrt*). It is possible that some forms of *wld* and *wpθ* may have resisted this phonological shift (so Gordon, *UT*, Glossary, no. 803, 806; S. Segert, *A Basic Grammar of the Ugaritic Language* [Los Angeles: University of California, 1984] 36), but this is far from certain. Ginsberg's reconstruction of *walādu* < **wayalādu* (see *The Legend of King Keret*, 40) is widely accepted and most recently restated in F. C. Fensham, "Remarks on Keret 136(b)–153," *JNWSL* 13 (1987) 56–57.

73. The word *ð̆rt* and a variant form, *ð̆hrt* (*KTU* 1.14.I.36) almost always appear in parallelism with *ḥlm* (*KTU* 1.6.III.4–5, 10–11; 1.14.VI.31–32), so the meaning is not in doubt, even though the etymology is debated.

cultic activity that Elqanah's family partook in at the shrine of Shiloh. There, at the convocation of the divine council before the high god, "the Kindly One, 'Ēl the Compassionate" (*lṭpn 'il dp'id)*, Ba'l again intercedes for the childless one:

> ltbrk [krt .] θ' .
> ltmr . n'mn [ǵlm .] 'il
> (*KTU* 1.15.II.14-16)
>
> May you indeed bless Kirta, the Noble One;
> Enable the Gracious One, Lad of 'Ēl.

Like Danel and Kirta, Hannah's plight came before the compassionate deity who granted fecundity to human beings. In due time she conceived and bore a son who was given the Elistic name שְׁמוּאֵל (1 Sam 1:20), a name which may have been derived from original **Šimuhu-'ilu* "His name is 'Ēl."[74]

The boy Samuel ministered under the tutelage of Eli at the Shiloh sanctuary, where the ark was kept (1 Sam 3:1-3). There the deity appeared to him in a dream at night. This phenomenon of a dream vision at the Shiloh sanctuary has been compared with the dream experiences of Danel and

---

74. Compare Amorite *Sa-mu-ú-i-la, Su-mu-i-la, Sa-mu-la-AN, Su-mu-la-AN* (Huffmon, *Amorite Personal Names*, 247-249). The interpretation of the name as bearing a third person pronominal suffix is evidenced in the additional *ú* syllable in names like *Sa-mu-ú-i-la, Ya-si-im-su-mu-ú, Ṭà-ab-su-mu-ú, Ḫa-ya-su-mu-ú*, etc. So J. Aistleitner, "Studien zur Frage der Sprachverwandtschaft des Ugaritischen, II," *Acta Orientalia Academiae Scientiarum Hungaricae* 7 (1957) para. 12f-h; A. Goetze, "Remarks on Some Names Occurring in the Execration Texts," *BASOR* 151 (1958) 32. For *šm* with the 3 ms pronominal suffix, compare Old South Arabic *smh'mr, smh'pq, smhwtr, smhkrb, smhsm', smh'ly, sms'mn, sms'mr* in G. Ryckmans, *Les noms propres sud-sémitiques* I (Bibliothèque du Muséon 2; Louvain: Muséon, 1934) 266. A Liḥyanite name *šm'l* is attested (ibid., 251), but it is probably not etymologically related to Hebrew *šmw'l*.

Kirta.[75] This manner of divine appearance is typical of 'Ēl in Canaanite mythology.[76] Whereas Ba'l's appearance is typically in a storm theophany, 'Ēl's will is made known through dreams and visions, and through intermediaries by the spoken word.[77] So it is significant that at Shiloh the deity appeared to Samuel in a dream and spoke through intermediaries like Eli and Samuel. According to the narrator: "YHWH continued to appear in Shiloh, for YHWH was revealed to Samuel in Shiloh through the word of YHWH."[78]

The connection of 'Ēl to the cult of Shiloh is further suggested by the tradition of the deity's tent-dwelling there. The destruction of Shiloh, now apparently confirmed by excavations at Ḫirbet Seilun,[79] is remembered thus:

ויטשׁ משׁכן שׁלו
אהל שׁכן בארם
(Ps 78:60)

He forsook the tabernacle of Shiloh,
the tent where he tabernacled among humans.

Again referring to the Shiloh shrine, the text speaks of the "tent of Joseph" (אהל יוסף) which the deity rejected in

75. So recently R. K. Gnuse, *The Dream Theophany of Samuel* (New York: University Press of America, 1984) 142–149. But see also E. L. Ehrlich (*Der Traum im Alten Testament* [Berlin: Töpelmann, 1953] 45–51), who sees this as a classic example of an incubation scene in the Hebrew Bible.

76. So Mettinger has noted in "YHWH Sabaoth," 130–131.

77. Cross, *Canaanite Myth and Hebrew Epic*, 177–186.

78. 1 Sam 3:21.

79. See I. Finkelstein, S. Bunimovitz, and Z. Lederman, "Excavations at Shiloh 1981–84. Preliminary Report," *Tel Aviv* 12 (1985) 123–180; I. Finkelstein, *The Archaeology of the Israelite Settlement* (Jerusalem: Israel Exploration Society, 1988) 220–234.

favor of David and Zion (Ps 78:67). In contrast to the Shiloh "tabernacle" or "tent," the shrine on Mount Zion is characterized as a sanctuary (מקדש) that was built "like the heavens" and its foundation deep as the netherworld forever (Ps 78:69).[80] Unlike the transient "tabernacle" or "tent" of Shiloh, the temple of Jerusalem would be a permanent base of YHWH.

This vocabulary of YHWH's dwelling at Shiloh is in accord with Nathan's Oracle (2 Sam 7:6), which claims that YHWH had not remained in a house, but had wandered about "in a tent and tabernacle" (באהל ובמשכן).[81] According to Josh 18:1, the whole congregation of Israel gathered at Shiloh and pitched the אהל מועד "tent of Assembly" there.[82] It was before this "tent of Assembly" at Shiloh that the territories

80. The idiom is reminiscent of Akkadian royal propaganda, where the kings would boast of their building activities. Similar diction is evident in an inscription of Nabopolassar (625-605 B. C. E.), who speaks of his plan to build the temple Etemenanki, "in order to found its base firmly as deep as the netherworld, its top to equal the heavens" (*išissa ina irat kigalle ana šuršudam rēšīša šamami ana šitnuni*). See S. Langdon, *Die neubabylonischen Königsinschriften* (VAB 4; Leipzig: Hinrichs, 1923) 60, col. I, ll. 36-37.

81. Cf. Ps 132:6-8, where the pre-Davidic sanctuary is described as a tabernacle (משכן).

82. The vocabulary of this verse is typical of P, whose reliance on archaic terminologies and traditions is well documented. See Cross, *Canaanite Myth and Hebrew Epic*, 321-325; R. J. Clifford, "The Tent of El and the Israelite Tent of Meeting," *CBQ* 33 (1971) 221-227. Although most of the occurrences of אהל מועד occur in P, the tent-shrine cannot be assumed to be a late concoction. It is associated with Moses already in Exod 33:7-11 (JE) which, despite G. von Rad's influential essay ("The Tent and the Ark," [1931] in *The Problem of the Hexateuch and Others Essays* [London: SCM, 1966] 103-124), does not indicate that the ark and tent were originally separated. Cf. also Num 11:16; 12:4; Deut 31:14-15.

were apportioned to the tribes (Joshua 18–19).[83] An anti-Elide polemic about the illicit activities of Phinehas and Hophni at the entrance of the אהל מועד (1 Sam 2:22), though secondary,[84] probably reflects an authentic tradition about the tent-shrine at Shiloh.[85]

The tradition of the אהל מועד at Shiloh is most intriguing in light of the evidence of Elism there. In the Ugaritic texts, 'Ēl presides over the convocation of the divine council, called *pḫr m'd*, at the sacred mountain where he dwelled (*KTU* 1.2.I.14-16, 19–24).[86] Elsewhere in Ugaritic literature, the abode of 'Ēl is designated *ḏd 'il* "dome-tent of 'Ēl" and *qrš* "tent-shrine" (*KTU* 1.1.III.21–24; 1.3.V.5–9; 1.4.IV.20–24; 1.6.I.32–36; 1.17.VI.46–49).[87] The language

83. Cf. Deut 32:8–9, where 'Elyôn supposedly apportioned the territories to the nations. The apportionment of land before the אהל מועד at Shiloh is most provocative if Clifford is correct that אהל מועד originally meant "Tent of the (Divine) Assembly" (see "The Tent of El and the Israelite Tent of Meeting," 226). Since 'Ēl was perceived as the chief deity of the divine assembly, it would have been appropriate for the territories to be alloted at the central shrine, the abode of the deity.

84. MT ואת אשר־ישכבון את־הנשים הצבאות פתח אהל מועד is not reflected in LXX$^{B}$ and 4QSam$^{a}$. See Ulrich, *The Qumran Text of Samuel and Josephus*, 57.

85. So Cross, *Canaanite Myth and Hebrew Epic*, 201–203.

86. Cf. Hebrew *hr mw'd* where the divine asssembly convened in the far north (Isa 14:13). On 'Ēl's abode, see R. J. Clifford, *The Cosmic Mountain in Canaan and the Old Testament* (HSM 4; Cambridge, Massachusetts: Harvard University, 1972) 43–48; Mullen, *The Divine Council*, 128–129.

87. My translation of *ḏd* follows Cross (*Canaanite Myth and Hebrew Epic*, 55 n. 43), who accepts the argument of Clifford ("The Tent of El and the Israelite Tent of Meeting," 222; *The Cosmic Mountain*, 51–54) from "intra-Ugaritic evidence" that *ḏd* is a synonym of *qrš* and *'ahl* (cf. *KTU* 1.19.IV.50–52). It must be admitted, however, that *ḏd* does not always refer to "tent" in Ugaritic. In

pertaining to this abode of 'Ēl is formulaic: in every instance someone uncovers (*gly*) the *d̉d* of 'Ēl and enters (*bw'*) the *qrš*.[88] In the Hittite mythological fragment of Ilkunirsa, the god is said have resided in a tent (*GIŠ.ZA.LAM.GAR* = Akk. *kuštāru* "tent") at the source of the Māla River.[89]

The traditions about YHWH's tent-dwelling at Shiloh,

---

*KTU* 1.23.59, 61, *d̉d* refers to "breast," whereas in *KTU* 1.19.IV.58 *d̉dm* are the objects of 'Ēl's creation, perhaps "mountains." For further discussion, see Margalit, "Studia Ugaritica II," 184; "Lexicographical Notes on the Aqht Epic," 88-89.

88. The etymology of *qrš* is unknown. M. Dijkstra and J. C. de Moor ("Problematical Passages in the Legend of Aqhâtu," *UF* 7 [1975] 192) suggest Akkadian *karāšu* "camp" as a cognate, but the proposal is problematic. They do not establish the phonological equivalence of Ugarit *q* and Akkadian *k*, or explain the exclusively military use of *karāšu*. They do not consider the presence of the root *qrš* in Akkadian, or the inevitable connection of the Ugaritic word with Hebrew *qrš*. In the Hebrew Bible, *qèreš* is used almost exclusively in P, in connection with the construction of the tabernacle. The word is probably related to Akkadian *qiršu* < *qarāšu* (Arabic *qaraša* "to cut in pieces;" see *AHW* III, 903; *CAD* 13, 128). The *qršym* used for the tabernacle in the Bible were strips of acacia wood, but Akkadian *qiršu* may refer to strips of leather or fabric (see *CAD* 13, 270). Perhaps one should think of Ugaritic *qrš* as the material of 'Ēl's canopy which, by extension, may refer to the canopy itself. Thus Hebrew יריעה "tent-flap" may refer to the tent itself (cf. Isa 54:2; Jer 4:20; 10:20; 49:29; Hab 3:7, where יריעה // אהל), and the ark is said to have been placed within a יריעה (2 Sam 7:2; 1 Chron 17:1). Aistleitner (*WUS*, no. 2461) takes *qrš* to mean a precinct, or district--i.e., a strip of (holy) land. But there is no evidence for this meaning anywhere.

89. Otten, "Ein kanaanäischer Mythus aus Boğazköy," 126, 1.7. The Māla River is to be identified as the Euphrates (Akk. *Purattu*), as two bilingual tablets from Boğazköy have confirmed. See J. Garstang and O. R. Gurney, *The Geography of the Hittite Empire* (London: British Institute of Archaeology in Ankara, 1959) 48-49.

then, are in accord with the 'Ēl imagery there. But they also appear to contradict allusions to the Shiloh sanctuary as היכל (1 Sam 1:9; 3:3) and בית (1 Sam 1:7, 24; Judg 18:31), both presumably referring to a permanent structure. These allusions are, of course, commonly assumed to be anachronistic.[90] But the apparently conflicting terms of 'Ēl's abode are present already in the Ugaritic texts. Although the 'Ēl's dwelling in the major mythological texts is described as a tent, he is known to have had a "palace" (*hkl*), also called a "house" (*bt*). Thus, when ʻAnat came to 'Ēl's mountain home at "the source of the double deep," he heard her voice from the "seventh chamber // eighth enclosure" (*KTU* 1.3.V.11-12). In a conversation that ensued, ʻAnat referred to 'Ēl's *bht* and *hkl* (ll. 19-21). Moreover, in several texts one finds mention of *bt 'il* (*KTU* 1.17.I.33, II.5, 22; 1.5.IV.21, etc.), and in the Rephaim texts,[91] 'Ēl is seen inviting the other gods to his *hkl // bt* for a banquet:

> lk [.] bty [rp'im .]
> [rp'im . b]ty . 'aṣḥkm [.]
> 'iqr'a[km . 'ilnym bh]kly .
> (*KTU* 1.21.II.1-3, cf. 8-11; 1.22.II.1-4, 8-10)

> Come to my house, [O Hale Ones!]
> [O Hale Ones,] I call you to my [ho]use!
> I invite [you, O Gods, into] my [pa]lace!

The invitation to the *rp'im* is most intriguing in light of our earlier references to the stories of Danel and Kirta. The

---

90. So Cross, *Canaanite Myth and Hebrew Epic*, 73 n. 114; M. Haran, "Shiloh and Jerusalem: The Origin of the Priestly Tradition in the Pentateuch," *JBL* 81 (1962) 14-24; idem, *Temples and Temple Services in Ancient Israel* (Oxford: Clarendon, 1978) 201-202; Mullen, *The Divine Council*, 173-174.

91. See C. E. L'Heureux, *Rank Among the Canaanite Gods* (HSM 21; Missoula, Montana: Scholars, 1979).

former is called *mt rp'i* "a *rp'*-man"--i.e., one of the Rephaim (*KTU* 1.17.I.2, 18, 36-38, etc.) and is, indeed, mentioned by name in one of the Rephaim banquet texts (*KTU* 1.20.II.7-8). The latter is hailed "exalted one in the midst of the *rp'i 'arṣ* (*KTU* 1.15.III.2-3, 13-14). It may be that Danel and Kirta were both regarded as belonging to the guild or class of beings who were invited to the ritual feasting at the *hkl // bt* of 'Ēl.

At all events, we know that 'Ēl had a *hkl // byt* where he played the host at divine feasts. In one particularly interesting banquet text, we find the deity in his palace (*hkl // bt*) preparing a feast for the gods:

'il dbḥ . bbth . mṣd .
ṣd . bqrb hkl[h]
ṣḥ . lqṣ . 'ilm .
tlḥmn 'ilm . wtštn .
tštn y<n> ʻd šbʻ
trΘ . ʻd . škr
(*KTU* 1.114.1-4)[92]

'Ēl slaughtered game in his temple,
Victuals within [his] palace.
He called the gods to dine.[93]

---

92. See J. C. de Moor, "Studies in the New Alphabetic Texts from Ras Shamra I," *UF* 1 (1969) 167-175; M. Pope, "A Divine Banquet at Ugarit," in *The Use of the Old Testament in the New and Other Essays* (Fs. W. F. Stinespring; ed. J. M. Efird; Durham, North Carolina: Duke University, 1972) 170-203.

93. The root is *qṣṣ* "to cut." Hence, de Moor ("Studies in the New Alphabetic Texts," 168-169) translates "for carving," citing *CTA* 3.A.8; 4.III.42, VI.57; 5.IV.14 (= *KTU* 1.3.I.8; 1.4.III.42, VI.57; 1.5.IV.14). I. Al-Yasin (*The Lexical Relation Between Ugaritic and Arabic* [Shelton Semitic Monograph Series I; New York: Shelton College, 1952] 69) cites Arabic *qaṣṣ*, which is used of a cut of meat.

The gods ate and drank.
They drank wi<ne> till sated,
New wine till drunk.

At this banquet 'Ēl sat enthroned like a king, presiding over the banquet for the divine beings.[94] It was at the "palace" (*hkl*) or "house" (*bt*) of 'Ēl that the divine assembly convened to feast. One is reminded here of the ritual performed by Danel, who gave the gods to eat and drink at the sanctuary (of 'Ēl?) where the gods had gathered. We may also note in passing that at Shiloh the family of Elqanah "ate and drank" at the *hykl* (1 Sam 1:9), and Hannah was thought to be *škrh* "drunk" with wine (1 Sam 1:13-14).

While the depiction of YHWH's dwelling at Shiloh as a tent is in agreement with the typical description of 'Ēl's abode in Canaanite mythology, it seems that the terms suggesting some kind of permanent structure, namely *hykl* and *byt*, cannot be dismissed. They are entirely appropriate to the image of the deity as divine king, and are in accord with the picture in several Ugaritic texts. Indeed the narrative in 1 Samuel suggests, in language reminiscent of 'Ēl's banquet at Ugarit, that Elqanah's family was dining in the temple precinct--as the high priest Eli sat down על־מזוזת היכל יהוה "by the door-posts of the temple of YHWH" (1 Sam 1:9). This picture is consistent with the results of recent excavations of Shiloh, that is, Ḫirbet Seilun.

The excavators report that Shiloh had a long history as a cultic center.[95] In MB II contexts they uncovered evidence of a cultic installation where several cultic objects were found, including a bull-shaped zoomorphic vessel--perhaps symbolizing virility and fecundity. Shiloh continued as a cultic site through the Late Bronze period, even though the site

94. So Mullen, *The Divine Council*, 261-267.

95. Finkelsten, Bunimovitz and Lederman, "Excavations at Shiloh 1981-1984," 163-165.

appears to have been uninhabited then.[96] Most significantly, in the Iron I stratum, several buildings have been uncovered, which the excavators have identified as storerooms and other annexes of "a larger building complex that extended eastwards in the direction of the summit."[97] Though they were unable to excavate the summit, the archaeologists are convinced that the well-planned buildings on the western slopes of the tell are continued in that direction. The evidence is not conclusive, but there is enough to indicate the probability of a permanent structure in Shiloh at precisely the time that the *hêkāl* or *bêt yhwh* was supposed to be there. The site appears to have been a central sanctuary with a permanent structure. This fits well with the image of the deity as king "who sits enthroned upon the cherubim" (ישׁב הכרבים). But what about the indication that there was a tent-shrine in Shiloh?

The idea of a cultic complex, suggested by the terms *hykl* and *byt*, is not necessarily incompatible with the notion of a tent-shrine. The people of ancient Ugarit and Israel did not appear to have been troubled by what modern people perceive to be an inconsistency. Apart from the terminology, one notes the report in 1 Kgs 8:4 (cf. 2 Chron 5:5) that Solomon brought the ark into the temple together with the אהל מועד. This reference is, again, usually dismissed as a priestly gloss.[98] But one must ask if the tolerance of it in the traditions is not a testimony to the probability of an ancient reality. Indeed, Jewish traditions suggest that the ark was removed from the temple together with the tent when the Jerusalem temple was sacked.[99] Josephus also reports that the ark was brought into the temple together with the tent, and adds that the cherubim were covering the ark "as under a tent

96. Ibid., 166–167.

97. Ibid., 169.

98. So J. Gray, *I & II Kings* (OTL; Philadelphia: Westminster, 1976) 209.

99. 2 Macc 2:4–8; cf. Bab. Talm., Yoma 53b.

or dome" (ὑπὸ σκηνῇ τινι καὶ θόλῳ).[100] Finally, in the only description of the ark in the NT, the ark is said to have been in a tent "behind the second curtain" (Heb 9:4).

Now one could argue that the terminology of the tent-dwelling or of the temple is reflected only in language and has no historical reflex. That is, a permanent sanctuary could have been called a "tabernacle" or "tent" and a tent-shrine could have been dubbed a "temple."[101] But, it seems more plausible in this case that the tent-shrine and temple *both* represented historical realities. That is, the ark was housed in a tent-shrine, particularly when it was transported from place to place, but it was also located in the temple precincts.

There are parallels for such moveable shrines elsewhere in the Levant. Diodorus Siculus testifies that the Carthaginians had a "holy tent" (ἱερὰ σκήνη) housing the image of a deity which they carried with them to battle.[102] Philo Byblius, quoting Sanchuniathon's "Phoenician History" (*Praep. Evang.* I.10.12) speaks of an animal-drawn shrine (ναὸν συγαφορούμενον) which the Phoenicians had for a deity called "the Hero of the Field" (ὁ Ἀργοῦ Ἥρως), who may be identified with Semitic *'Ēl Šadday*,[103] and who was also known as "Rustic" (Ἀγρότης).[104]

One may invoke again the old analogy that scholars have

100. *Ant.* VIII.101–103.

101. So, for example, one may note that *mškn* is used of temples elsewhere in the Levant. See D. R. Hillers, "*Mškn* 'temple' in Inscriptions from Hatra," *BASOR* 206 (1972) 54–56.

102. *Dio.* XX.65. Note how the Philistines equated the coming of the ark with the presence of the Israelite god (1 Sam 4:7–8).

103. See Attridge and Oden, *Philo of Byblos*, 85 n. 71.

104 Perhaps also to be identified with 'Ēl, as L. R. Clapham ("Sanchuniathon: The First Two Cycles," Unpublished Ph.D. Dissertation [Harvard Universiy, 1969] 119–123) has suggested.

made with the *qubbâ*, a dome shaped tent-shrine of some pre-Islamic Arab bedouin.[105] The *qubbâ* was carried from place to place by the nomads, led the tribes in their search for water and campsites, was used for divination, and functioned as a war-palladium. It was made of red leather and contained two sacred stones (betyls). Several Palmyrene texts mention the *qubbâ*, and a relief from a temple of Bel at Palmyra of around the first century B. C. E. shows a camel in a procession, carrying such a tent-shrine whose red color is still faintly visible in the drawing.[106]

By such analogies, one may see the ark as an emblem of divine presence that was sheltered in a tent-shrine, sometimes mounted on an animal-drawn cart (cf. 1 Sam 6:7, 11; 2 Sam 6:3).[107] The old alternative posed between a tent-shrine of desert origin and a temple of Canaanite origin is a false one. The tent-shrine was the dwelling of the deity in transition, whereas the temple was a permanent base. When the ark was transported from place to place, or when there was no durable permanent structure to house it, the tent-shrine was

105. See F. M. Cross, Jr., "The Priestly Tabernacle," (1947) *Biblical Archaeologist Reader* I (ed. D. N. Freedman and G. E. Wright; Garden City, New York: Doubleday, 1961) 217–219; J. Morgenstern, "The Ark, the Ephod, and the 'Tent of Meeting," *HUCA* 17 (1942–43) 155–171; K. Koch, "אֹהֶל *'ōhel;* אָהַל *'āhal,"* *TDOT* I, 122--123. Variations of this cult object survived in the *'uṭfâ* (also called *markab*) and *maḥmal* of later Muslim bedouin.

106. H. Seyrig, "Bas-reliefs monumentaux du temple de Bêl à Palmyre," *Syria* 15 (1934) 159–165, pl. xix; H. Ingholt, "Inscriptions and Sculptures from Palmyra, I," *Berytus* 3 (1936) 85–88; R. de Vaux, "Arche d'alliance et tente de réunion," in *Bible et Orient* (Paris: Cerf, 1967) 262–265. It is interesting to note that a קֻבָּה is closely associated with the אהל מועד in Num 25:8.

107. Cf. V. W. Rabe, "Israelite Opposition to the Temple," *CBQ* 29 (1967) 228–233; J. Milgrom, *Studies in Levitical Terminology*, I (Berkeley: University of California, 1970) 68–70.

used. Thus, the tent-shrine housed the emblem of the god in transition and is, as such, not inconsistent with the presence of a temple. In this reconstruction, Nathan's Oracle (2 Samuel 7) does not provide evidence against the existence of a permanent structure at Shiloh *per se.* Rather, the polemic there is against the complete replacement of the old tradition of a patriarchal god with a deity that is permanently limited to one location.[108]

At Shiloh, the presence of a temple did not preclude the notion of a deity who also moved about in a tent. Whether the tent-shrine remained pitched even in a permanent sanctuary is a matter of speculation beyond the scope of this study.[109] My purpose here is simply to argue for the compatibility of the tent-dwelling and the temple at Shiloh, and to demonstrate that both are appropriate to the imagery of 'Ēl.

Beyond the Samuel narratives, some evidence for Elism at Shiloh is found in Psalm 78.[110] The psalm contains a recitation

---

108. That is, a complete replacement of 'Ēl ideology with the ideology of Ba'l's kingship. See Cross, "The Priestly Tabernacle in the Light of Recent Research," in *Temples and High Places in Biblical Times* (ed. A. Biran; Jerusalem: Hebrew Union College, 1981) 43.

109. See provisionally O. Eissfeldt, "Kultzelt und Tempel," (1973) *KS* VI, 1-7.

110. A tenth century date for this psalm was advocated by O Eissfeldt, *Das Lied Moses Deuteronomium 32,1-43 und das Lehrgedicht Asaphs Psalm 78 samt einer Analyse der Umgebung des Moses-Leides* (Berichte über die Verhandlungen der Sächischen Akademie der Wissenschaft zu Leipzig. Phil.-Hist. Klasse, 104/5 [Berlin: Akademie, 1958] 31-41 and more recently defended by A. F. Campbell, "Psalm 78: A Contribution to the Theology of the Tenth Century Israel," *CBQ* 41 (1979) 51-79. Robertson (*Linguistic Evidence*) places it in the late tenth or early ninth century, as does Freedman ("Divine Names and Titles," 80-82, 96). Apart from the language, there is also no knowledge of the destruction of Samaria--only of Shiloh. A date in the early divided

of history which culminates in the abandonment of the north and the election of the south. It is clear that the poem refers to the destruction of the Shiloh sanctuary and the consequent capture of the ark by the Philistines in the eleventh century (vv 52–64). That historic event is interpreted as a rejection of the northern sanctuary at Shiloh in favor of Jerusalem:[111]

וימאס באהל יוסף
ושבט אפרים לא בחר
ויבחר את־שבט יהודה
את־הר ציון אשר אהב
(Ps 78:67–68)

He rejected the tent of Joseph
The tribe of Ephraim he did not choose.
But he chose the tribe of Judah,
Mount Zion which he loved.

The deity associated with the northern sanctuary is repeatedly called 'Ēl (vv 7, 8, 18, 19, 34, 41), 'Elyôn (vv 17, 56), and 'Ēl 'Elyôn (v 35). In this Elohistic psalm, אלהים occurs 8 times, but it is frequently in parallelism to 'Ēl (vv 7, 19) or 'Elyôn (vv 35, 56).[112] YHWH occurs only in the introduction (v 4), and once in the recitation proper (v 21). This recurrence of 'Ēl and 'Elyôn in a historical recitation leading to the destruction of Shiloh adds to our contention that YHWH was worshipped as 'Ēl in that sanctuary. At least to the composer of the poem, the deity worshipped at Shiloh was known as 'Ēl and 'Elyôn.

---

monarchy seems most likely. For other perspectives, see W. H. Propp, *Water in the Wilderness* (HSM 40; Atlanta: Scholars, 1987) 46 n. 46.

111. But see R. J. Clifford, "In Zion and David a New Beginning: An Interpretation of Psalm 78," in *Traditions in Transformation* (Fs. F. M. Cross; ed. B. Halpern and J. D. Levenson; Winona Lake, Indiana: Eisenbrauns, 1981) 121–141.

112. Cf. Freedman, "Divine Names and Titles," 80–82.

In support of the association of ‘Elyôn with the cult of Shiloh, one may further point to the name of the High Priest, Eli (עלי). His name is probably an abbreviated form of a PN with the theophoric element *'ly*, in turn an abbreviated or alternate form of ‘Elyôn.[113] One may compare such theophorous names as *yḥw'ly* "May the Most High Give Life," attested in the Samaria ostraca,[114] and *yhw'ly* "Yahu is the Most High," attested at Elephantine.[115] The name of the High Priest at Shiloh, then, may suggest that YHWH was worshipped as the supreme deity, "the Most High"--an appropriate epithet for ’Ēl.

The context of the Song of Hannah also implies that YHWH was acknowledged as *‘Ēlî / ‘Elyôn* (Most High) already at Shiloh:

---

113. See H. S. Nyberg, "Studien zum Religionskampf im Alten Testament," *ARW* 35 (1938) 329-387; M. Dahood, "The Divine Name ‘Ēlî in the Psalms," *TS* 14 (1953) 452-457; A. Cooper, *RSP* III, 451-458.

114. *SO* 22.2. See W. F. Albright, *Archaeology and the Religion of Israel* (Baltimore: Johns Hopkins, 1942) 202 n. 18; idem, "The Old Testament and Canaanite Language and Literature," *CBQ* 7 (1945) 31 n 89. See A. Lemaire, *Inscriptions hébraïques* I (Littératures anciennes du Proche-Orient; Paris: Cerf, 1977), 52-53.

115. A. E. Cowley, *Aramaic Papyri of the Fifth Century B. C.* (Oxford: Clarendon, 1923) 70 no. 22.105. M. Silverman (*Religious Values in the Jewish Proper Names at Elephantine* [AOAT 217; Neukirchen-Vluyn: Neukirchener, 1985] 165) takes *'ly* as a stative but cites, *inter alia*, *yḥw'ly* where *'ly* must be a divine name or title. Other pertinent examples include: *'lyw*, *'lyhw*, *yw'ly*. See N. Avigad, "The Contribution of Hebrew Seals to an Understanding of Israelite Religion and Society," in *Ancient Israelite Religion* (Fs. F. M. Cross; ed. P. D. Miller, P. D. Hanson, and S. D. McBride; Philadelphia: Fortress, 1987) 200, 207 n. 9; *Hebrew Bullae from the Time of Jeremiah* 45, 93-94.

יהוה יחתו מריבו[116]
עלי[117] בשמים ירעם
(1 Sam 2:10a)[118]

YHWH, his enemies are shattered;
The Most High thunders in heaven.

The parallelism of יהוה and עלי here indicates that the latter is an epithet of the deity. If this poetic fragment may indeed be linked with Shiloh, as its context suggests, we may conclude that at that sanctuary עלי was an epithet of YHWH as 'Ēl, the most high god of the Canaanite pantheon. One may compare the pairing of יהוה // עלי with the parallelism of יהוה and עליון in another text from the approximately the same period, that is, the early monarchy:[119]

ירעם מן־שמים יהוה
ועליון יתן קולו
(2 Sam 22:14//Ps 18:14)

YHWH thunders from heaven,
The Most High gives forth his voice.

---

116. 4QSam$^a$ reads יהוה יחת מר[י]בו, as do LXX, Syr., Targ., but the reading of MT is *lectio difficilior*.

117. MT has עלו, which probably arose when the divine name or epithet עלי had been forgotten. Cf. Nyberg, "Studien zum Religionskampf im Alten Testament," 372; D. N. Freedman, "Psalm 113 and the Song of Hannah," *EI* 14 (1975) 70.

118. Here, as elsewhere in this book, no attempt is made to reconstruct the original orthography of the archaic poems. Historical forms will be reproduced only to explain a confusion or otherwise clarify the meaning of the text.

119. See Freedman, "Psalm 113 and the Song of Hannah," 56–70; "Divine Names and Titles," 75–77; F. M. Cross and D. N. Freedman, *Studies in Ancient Yahwistic Poetry* (SBLDS 21; Missoula, Montana: Scholars, 1975) 125–158.

Although the imagery of YHWH thundering from heaven belongs properly to the tradition of Ba‘l,[120] this hymn probably originated when no distinction was made between the attributes of the deity as Ba‘l and ’Ēl in Israelite theology. Hence it is not surprising to find the deity identified as ’Ēl in this poem (vv 31, 32, 33, 48).

It may be argued, of course, that since the Song of Hannah and this hymn stem from the monarchical period, the association of עליון / עלי with Shiloh is anachronistic, being a retrojection from the Jerusalem temple. Indeed, it is common to assume that the worship of YHWH as ‘Elyôn is derived from the Jebusite cult of ’Ēl ‘Elyôn in the pre-Israelite city.[121] But the solitary piece of evidence adduced for this elaborate hypothesis is the enigmatic passage of Abram's encounter with Melkiṣedeq, the priest-king of Salem (Gen 14:18-22).[122] Apart from this text, there is nothing to indicate that there was a cult of ’Ēl ‘Elyôn in the Jebusite city. The identification of Salem with Jerusalem, though probable, is not beyond dispute. It is based primarily on the parallelism of Salem and Zion in Ps 76:3. But even if one assumes the correctness of the equation of Salem and Jerusalem, one must still ask if the text may be used to demonstrate the existence of a pre-Israelite cult of ’Ēl ‘Elyôn. The name of the city itself, attested in Egyptian Execration texts and the Amarna letters, links it with Šalim, an astral

---

120. Cf. *KTU* 1.16.III.5-9, where Ba‘l who gives rain is called *‘ly* "Most High," and the language of Ba‘l's thunder in *KTU* 1.4.VII.29: *qlh . qdš [.] b‘l [.] ytn* "Ba‘l gives forth his holy voice."

121. The bibliography is extensive here, the most influential works being, H. Schmid, "Jahwe und die Kulttraditionen von Jerusalem," *ZAW* 67 (1955) 168-197; Rohland, *Erwählungstraditionen Israels*, 119ff.; Clements, *God and Temple* 43-48; Stolz, *Strukturen und Figuren im Kult von Jerusalem*.

122. The best treatment of this text is still J. A. Emerton, "The Riddle of Genesis XIV," *VT* 21 (1971) 403-439.

deity known elsewhere in the ancient Near East.[123] Among the Amarna letters, one from ʻAbdi-Ḫepa in Jerusalem says the city was called *Bīt-NIN.IB*, which has been interpreted as *bīt Šulmāni* "House of (the god) Šulmān."[124] As for the PN ʻAbdi-Ḫepa, B. Maisler (Mazar) has argued that it is a theophorous name related to the Hittite goddess Ḫebat, whom he equates with Šulamit,[125] the consort of Šalim.[126]

Besides Šalim, there is some evidence of the worship of the West Semitic deity *Ṣdq* in Jerusalem. The Amorite king of Jerusalem whom Joshua encountered was named 'Adoniṣedeq ("My Lord is Ṣedeq")[127], which must be compared with the name Melkiṣedeq ("My king is Ṣedeq"). This deity appears in Sanchuniathon's history as Συδύκ, who is mentioned with Μισώρ, the pair being West Semitic equivalents of Mesopotamian ᵈ*Kittu* and ᵈ*Mīšaru*, who are identified as astral

123. See J. J. M. Roberts, *The Earliest Semitic Pantheon* (Baltimore: Johns Hopkins University, 1972) 51; E. Weidner, "Neue Entdeckungen in Ugarit," *AfO* 18/1 (1957) 170; M. Dahood, "Ancient Deities in Syria and Palestine," in *Le antiche divinità semitiche* (edited by S. Moscati; Studi Semitici 1; Rome: Università di Roma, 1958) 88, 91.

124. The text says: *māt ú-ru-sa-lim*ᵏⁱ *šu-mu-ša(!)* ᵁᴿᵁ*bīt* ᵈ*NIN.IB* "Jerusalem whose name was Bīt NIN.IB" (*EA* 290.15; cf. Knutdson, *Die El-Amarna Tafeln* I, 876-877). *NIN.IB* has been identified by J. Lewy ("The Šulmān Temple in Jerusalem," *JBL* 59 [1940] 519-522) as Ninurta, who is identified with the planet Saturn in Akkadian mythology, but the equation is uncertain. See J. J. Schmitt, "Pre-Israelite Jerusalem," in *Scripture in Context* II (PTMS 34; Pittsburgh: Pickwick, 1980) 109.

125. "Das vordavidische Jerusalem," *JPOS* 10 (1930) 189.

126. Cf. F. Boehl. "Ältteste keilinschriftliche Erwähnungen der Stadt Jerusalem und ihrer Göttin?" *AcOr* 1 (1922) 76-80.

127. Cf. PN *'adnṣdq* in *KTU* 4.129.8.

deities.[128] Although the precise relationship between Šalim and Ṣedeq is unclear, it is highly probable that they were both astral deities in the pre-Israelite cult in Jerusalem. Some have attempted to identify these deities with 'Ēl 'Elyôn, or to take them as hypostases of him, but the connections are tenuous at best.[129] Astral deities were regarded as subordinate to 'Ēl in Canaanite mythology, as is evident in the Ugaritic myth of Šalim and Šaḥar, where the twins are designated *bn 'ilm* "sons of 'Ēl" (*KTU* 1.23.49-52). Indeed, the traditions in Israel are all about their demise, as in the allusion to the attempt of Helel ben-Šaḥar to rise above the "stars of 'Ēl" to usurp the throne of 'Elyôn in the far-reaches of Ṣaphon (Isa 14:12-15; cf. 24:21-23). In Ugaritic mythology, the astral deity 'Athtar is likewise seen as inadequate to assume the position of the divine king in Ṣaphon (*KTU* 1.6.I.54-66).[130] The astral deities can, therefore, hardly be equated with the "Most High," a designation that is entirely suitable for the high god, 'Ēl. And since the evidence points only to the worship of astral deities in pre-Israelite Jerusalem, any hypothesis about the priority of the putative cult of 'Ēl 'Elyôn there needs to have greater support than the problematic tradition in Gen 14:18-22, which probably had its origin *after* David's capture of Jerusalem.[131]

The earliest occurrence of *'Elyôn* in the Hebrew Bible is in the Balaam Oracles, where it is parallel to *'Ēl* and

---

128. See R. A. Rosenberg, "The God Ṣedeq," *HUCA* 36 (1965) 161-177; M. C. Astour, "Some New Divine Names from Ugarit," *JAOS* 86 (1966) 282-283.

129. So Schmid, "Jahwe und die kulttraditionen in Jerusalem," 177; Nyberg, "Studien zum Religionskampf im Alten Testament," 356; G. Widengren, *Sakrales Königtum im Alten Testament und im Judentum* (Stuttgart: Kohlhammer, 1955) 47; Mowinckel, *The Psalms in Israel's Worship* 132-133.

130. See P. C. Craigie, "Helel, Athtar, and Phaeton (Jes 14:12-15)," *ZAW* 85 (1973) 223-224.

131. See Emerton, "The Riddle of Genesis XIV," 414-426.

*Šadday* (Num 24:16).[132] The association of the oracles with 'Ēl is supported by the inscriptions from Deir 'Allā, where the vision of Balaam is said to be an "oracle of 'Ēl."[133] The connection with Šadday in the Balaam Oracles of the Bible and Deir 'Allā is also intriguing, since the epithet occurs in the oldest poetic texts and appears to have been eschewed in the Israelite traditions of the monarchical period.[134] Significantly, *Šadday* appears in Jacob's blessing of the tribe of Joseph, where it is mentioned together with אביר יעקב "The bull of Jacob," a divine epithet of the northern

---

132. On linguistic and prosodic grounds, the poems have been dated to the eleventh or tenth century. See W. F. Albright, "The Oracles of Balaam," *JBL* 43 (1944) 207–233. Freedman ("Divine Names and Titles," 66–67) would also date it to this general period on the basis of his typology of divine names. I am inclined to accept the early dating, despite the recent challenge of M. D. Coogan, "Canaanite Origins and Lineage: Reflections on the Religion of Ancient Israel," in *Ancient Israelite Religion* (Fs. F. M. Cross; ed. P. D. Miller, P. D. Hanson, and S. D. McBride; Philadelphia: Fortress, 1987) 116–118. Coogan wants to date the oracles with the Deir 'Allā texts to the late eighth century, explaining the conservative features as evidence of archaizing; but, given the unusually large amount of archaic features in the poems, it seems better to explain the non-archaic elements as attempts at *standardizing* the poetry.

133. Combination I, l. 2. See J. Hoftijzer and G. van der Kooij, *Aramaic Texts from Deir 'Alla* (OrAnt 19; Leiden: Brill, 1976) 188–189. I follow the reading of J. A. Hackett in *The Balaam Text From Deir 'Allā* (HSM 31; Chico, California: Scholars, 1980) 27, 33. For an alternate reconstruction, see A. Caquot and A. Lemaire, "Les textes araméens de Deir 'Alla," *Syria* 54 (1977) 194; P. K. McCarter, Jr. "The Balaam Texts from Deir 'Allā: The First Combination," *BASOR* 239 (1980) 51–52.

134. See Cross, *Canaanite Myth and Hebrew Epic*, 59–60; Freedman, "Divine Names and Epithets," 68.

cultus probably connected with the ark (Gen 49:22–25).[135] In addition, there is the name *'ēl 'āḇîḵā* "'Ēl, your Father" (v 25a), an epithet which together with the epithet "Bull of Jacob" certainly cannot be separated from Ugaritic *θr 'il 'abk* "the Bull, 'Ēl, your father" invoked by Kirta and for Danel in their quests for blessings from 'Ēl--not an insignificant datum in view of the context of the *blessing* of Joseph. D. N. Freedman, who reconstructs a divine epithet *gibbōr wĕ'al* "the Exalted Warrior" in v 26, posits that this passage has its origins in "the 'Ēl-worshipping community in the Shechem area in pre-Mosaic times."[136] Freedman, however, dates the Testament of Jacob as a whole to the eleventh century. Considering the archaeological indications of Shiloh's prominence as a central sanctuary in the eleventh century, the probable connection of the epithet אביר יעקב with the ark, and the evidence of Elism there, I would contend that Shiloh is a better candidate for the origin of the Blessing of Joseph, which I would date with most of the Testament of Jacob to

---

135. The name אביר יעקב occurs in connection with the ark in Ps 132:2, 5. It appears to be an epithet of 'Ēl as divine warrior and, hence, is an alternate of יהוה צבאות. It occurs in Isa 49:26 and 60:16, both times concerning YHWH's military intervention to deliver his people. The only occurrence of אביר ישראל is in Isa 1:24, where it is parallel to יהוה צבאות. It is pertinent to mention that אבירים in Ps 78:25 is translated by the LXX as "angels"--that is, members of the heavenly hosts. See A. Kapelrud, "אָבִיר *'ābhîr;* אַבִּיר *'abbîr,*" *TDOT* I, 42–44, and the literature cited therein, to which we must add only N. M. Sarna, "The Divine Title *'abhir ya'aqobh,*" in *Essays on the Occasion of the Seventieth Anniversary of the Dropsie University* (ed. A. I. Katsch and L. Nemoy; Philadelphia: Dropsie University, 1979) 389–396. The connection of this epithet to the ark at Shiloh has been defended recently by Ollenburger, *Zion, the City of the Great King*, 41–42.

136. "Divine Names and Titles," 66.

the late eleventh century.[137]

As for the parallelism of Šadday and 'Elyôn in the Balaam Oracles, it is impossible to avoid comparison with the inscriptions from Deir 'Allā. There, the *šdyn* appear as *'lhn* "gods" and members of the divine council headed by 'Ēl.[138] In this connection, Jo Ann Hackett has argued plausibly that Šadday is "an epithet of El in his position as chief of the [divine] council."[139] This is supported in part by the parallelism of Šadday and 'Elyôn in the Balaam Oracles and in Ps 91:1.[140] It is also not amiss to note that the epithet is most commonly translated in LXX as παντοκράτωρ, which is precisely the Greek equivalent for צבאות in over a hundred instances.[141]

I am inclined to agree with Cross, that 'Elyôn is an early epithet of 'Ēl, although we must concede that *'lyn* and the related epithet *'ly* are not limited to 'Ēl in the non biblical sources.[142] Indeed, עלי/עליון may even have been used of 'Ēl already at Shiloh. In the Hebrew Bible, the epithet is used regularly of YHWH as the supreme deity in the divine

---

137. It is tempting to point to the explicit mention of שילה in v 10, but that is a notorious *crux interpretum*. M. Bar-Magen ("The Shiloh Sanctuary," *Beth Mikra* 29 [1983/1984] 149-153) has recently defended the reading of in MT, connecting the reference to the festival of Judges 21, but problems remain.

138. Combination I, ll. 5-6.

139. *The Balaam Text From Deir 'Allā*, 85-89.

140. See O. Eissfeldt, "Jahwes Verhältnis zu 'Elyon und Schaddaj nach Psalm 91," (1957) *KS* III, 441-447.

141. Cf. T. N. D. Mettinger, *In Search of God* (trans. F. H. Cryer; Fortress: Philadelphia, 1988) 69-72.

142. F. M. Cross, "Yahweh and the God of the Patriarchs," *HTR* 55 (1962) 243; *Canaanite Myth and Hebrew Epic*, 51. See also the discussions in R. Lack "Les origines de 'ELYON, le Très-Haut, dans la tradition cultuelle d'Israel," *CBQ* 24 (1962) 44-66; R. du Mesnil du Buisson, *Nouvelles études sur les dieux et les mythes de Canaan* (Leiden: Brill, 1973) 40-43.

council, with YHWH functioning like ʾĒl in the Canaanite pantheon. This is evident in several texts from the Psalter:[143]

כי אתה יהוה עליון על־כל־הארץ
מאד נעלית על־כל־אלהים
(Ps 97:9)

For you, YHWH, are ʿElyôn over all the earth;
You are greatly elevated above all the gods.[144]

כי יהוה עליון נורא
מלך גדול על־כל־הארץ
(Ps 47:3)

Indeed, YHWH is the awesome ʿElyôn,
The great king over all the earth.[145]

וידעו כי אתה שמך יהוה
לבדך עליון על־כל־הארץ
(Ps 83:19)

And let them know that your name is YHWH;
You alone are ʿElyôn over all the earth.

אודה יהוה כצדקו
ואזמרה שם־יהוה עליון
(Ps 7:18)

---

143. On these texts, see J. J. M. Roberts, "The Religio-Political Setting of Psalm 47," *BASOR* 221 (1976) 129–130.

144. The word play here of עליון // נעלית suggests the meaning of the epithet.

145. As Roberts ("The Religio-Political Setting of Psalm 47," 130–131) has pointed out, the traditional interpretation of עליון as appositional to YHWH and נורא as the predicate misses the point of the parallelism of the epithet to מלך גדול.

I will confess YHWH
 according to his righteousness,
I will sing the name of YHWH, (the) 'Elyôn.

The use of עליון in reference to a human king in Ps 89:28 would further confirm that it is an epithet, and not a proper name.[146]

According to Sanchuniathon's cosmogony, Elioun was called Ὕψιστος "the Most High" and he was the Father (πατήρ) of Ouranos (Heaven) and Ge (Earth).[147] So in the Song of Moses, YHWH as 'Elyôn is also called אביך קנך "your Father who created you" and עשך ויכננך "the one who made

146. It is sometimes suggested that *'Elyôn* should not be interpreted as an epithet since we have in one of the Sefîre inscriptions *'l w'lyn* following a series of divine names occurring in pairs (*KAI* 222.A.11), thus supposedly implying that *'l* and *'lyn* are separate deities. So, for example, R. Rendtorff, "The Background of אל עליון in Gen 14," *Fourth World Congress of Jewish Studies* I (Jerusalem: Magnes, 1967) 168. This argument does not hold, since (1) the pairs mentioned are couples (i.e., god and consort), whereas *'lyn* certainly cannot be interpreted as the consort of *'l*, (2) the pairs are separated from *'l w'lyn* by other expressions which break the pattern of divine pairs, (3) we are dealing with a different pantheon in this portion of the inscription than the deities of Barga'yah. I am inclined to take *w* as *wāw explicativum*, and thus to interpret *'l w'lyn* as "'Ēl, that is, (the) 'Elyōn." One should compare the West-Semitic deities with double names: *Kθr-w-Ḫss, Mt-w-Šr, Qdš-w-'Amrr* and so forth. L'Heureux (*Rank Among the Canaanite Gods*, 45–47), who also sees *'lyn* as an epithet of 'Ēl, suggests plausibly that the pairing of *'l w'lyn* is in imitation of the pairing of other deities, but it actually refers to the same god. See further J. A. Fitzmyer, *The Aramaic Inscriptions of Sefîre* (Rome: Pontifical Biblical Institute, 1967) 37–38.

147. *Praep. Evang.* 1.10.15. W. H. Propp has suggested to me that the Progenitor in Sanchuniathon is to be related to the function of 'Ēl as "Creator" (*qny*) of heaven and earth, the root *qny* being used regularly of procreation.

you and formed you" (Deut 32:6), and is portrayed as the high god who parcelled out the land, "according to the number of the gods."[148] The passage reflects the climax of an ancient cosmogony, when the victorious deity distributed the territories of the world to the lesser gods. The language of creation, especially the use of the verbs *qny* and *kwn*, echoes Canaanite mythology, where 'Ēl is seen as the progenitor and creator.[149] In v 9 of the poem, some see a primitive subordination of YHWH to 'Elyôn, but this is too literal an interpretation of a mythopoeic text. It seems more likely to me that 'Elyôn is an epithet of YHWH and *kî* in v 9 should be taken as an asseverative particle: "Indeed! YHWH's own portion is his people, Jacob is the territory of his fief." At all events, this archaic poem suggests that the epithet 'Elyôn in Israelite tradition antedates the occupation of Jerusalem.[150]

---

148. Deut 32:8, reconstructed on the basis of LXX and 4QDt. See P. W. Skehan, "A Fragment of the 'Song of Moses' (Deut. 32) from Qumran," *BASOR* 136 (1954) 12-15; J. Hempel, "Zu IVQ Deut. 32:8," *ZAW* 74 (1962) 70.

149. Note the deity is identified as 'Ēl in Deut 32:4, 8, 12, 18, 21.

150. Eissfeldt (*Das Lied Moses*) dates the poem to the eleventh century on the basis of its content. Mainly on linguistic grounds, W. F. Albright ("Some Remarks on the Song of Moses in Deuteronomy XXXII," *VT* 9 [1959] 339-346) dates the poem to the same general period, as does Robertson (*Linguistic Evidence*, 146, 155) for vv 8-20. See also G. E. Mendenhall ("Samuel's 'Broken Rib': Deuteronomy 32," in *No Famine in the Land* [Fs. J. L. McKenzie; ed. by J. W. Flanagan and A. W. Robinson; Missoula, Montana: Scholars, 1975] 63-74) and Freedman ("Divine Names and Titles," 77-80), who places the poem between the late tenth or early ninth century. The linguistic arguments are the strongest, although they cannot be sustained for the entire poem. It is likely that an archaic poem, including but not limited to vv 6-9, was reworked in the exilic or post-exilic period. See S. M. Olyan, *Asherah and the Cult of Yahweh in Israel* (SBLMS 34; Atlanta: Scholars, 1988) 72 n. 7.

This portrayal of deity in Deuteronomy 32 is found also in Psalm 82, where YHWH is the chief of the divine council (עדת־אל, v 1), the ʻElyôn who determines the fate of divine and human beings alike. Not insignificantly, this and the majority of the references to ʻElyôn in the Psalter--Pss 50:14; 73:11; 77:11; 78:11, 17, 35, 56; 83:19--belong to the collection of the Psalms of Asaph which, some have argued, are of northern provenance.[151] So the people of ʻElyôn are called "the children of Jacob and Joseph" (Ps 77:16), "Joseph" (Ps 78:9), and "the children of Ephraim" (Ps 78:9), suggesting that the epithet *ʻElyôn* was at home among the northern tribes.

It is striking that the earliest texts and a significant number of the references in the hymnic material connect ʻElyôn with the northern tribes, and point to the relation of these tribes with ʻElyôn prior to the establishment of the monarchy. While one may not be able to trace the precise origin of ʻElyôn as a divine epithet in the history of Israelite religion, one can reject any theory that emphasizes the priority of pre-Israelite Jerusalem as the source for the epithet in Israelite theology. Even if one grants that there was a cult of ʼĒl ʻElyôn in the Jebusite city--and that is dubious--one cannot simply trace the origin of the Israelite identification of YHWH as ʻElyôn to the Jebusites. ʻElyôn was merely an epithet for any deity in the position of supremacy over against other deities in the divine council. It is, therefore, most appropriately used of ʼĒl in Israel's earliest traditions. Given the images of ʼĒl as creator and king at Shiloh and the indications of Elism there, including the suggestive name of the high priest ʻĒlî, I would venture to suggest that YHWH was already venerated as ʼĒl ʻElyôn "ʼĒl, the Most High" at that sanctuary. This was the deity associated with the ark at Shiloh: יהוה צבאות ישב הכרבים "YHWH of Hosts, the One Enthroned on the Cherubim." This was the god of Elqanah, Samuel and Eli.

151. M. J. Buss, "The Psalms of Asaph and Korah," *JBL* 82 (1963) 382-392.

## B. QIRYAT-YE'ARIM

The ark remained in Shiloh until it was seized by the Philistines in battle around the middle of the eleventh century. The story of the ark's capture and its fate following the battle are recorded in 1 Samuel 4-6. Indeed, virtually everything we know of the fate of the ark in the years following its removal from Shiloh is found in these chapters. After this narrative, there is no explicit mention of the ark again until the account of its transfer to Jerusalem in 2 Samuel 6.[152] This is in accord with the tradition of the ark's neglect in the years preceding the rise of David (1 Chron 13:3; Ps 132:1-6).

The provenance of the story of the ark is controverted. In an influential study published in 1926, Leonhard Rost argued that 1 Sam 4:1b-7:1 together with 2 Sam 6:1-20 constituted a single "Ark Narrative" (*Ladeerzählung*) composed in Jerusalem in the eighth century as the *hieros logos* for the sanctuary where the ark was kept.[153] The purpose of this narrative, according to Rost, was to instruct pilgrims about the significance of the ark and to explain how it came to be in Jerusalem.

For half a century this notion of a unified "Ark Narrative" dominated scholarly opinion in a way that few

---

152. MT of 1 Sam 14:18 mentions the ark twice, but most comentators follow LXX$^{BL}$ to read אפוד instead of ארון, citing 1 Sam 23:9; 30:7 and the tradition about the ark's location in Qiryat-Ye'arim during the reign of Saul. An attempt to defend the reading of MT has been made, however, by P. R. Davies ("Ark or Ephod in 1 Sam. XIV. 18?" *JTS* 26 [1975] 82-87), who dismisses the tradition of the ark in Qiryat-Ye'arim as legendary and the reading of אפוד in the Samuel passages as secondary.

153. *Die Überlieferung von der Thronnachfolge Davids* (BWANT 3/6; Stuttgart: Kohlhammer, 1926), now translated into English as *The Succession to the Throne of David* (Historic Texts and Interpreters in Biblical Scholarship 1; trans. M. D. Rutter and D. M. Gunn; Sheffield: Almond, 1982) 6-34.

theories have. At least three dissertations have appeared explicitly on the "Ark Narrative" essentially as Rost delineated it.[154] But the unity of the narrative in 1 Samuel with the account of the procession of the ark in 2 Samuel 6 has been intensely challenged in recent years.[155] The stylistic, literary, and form-critical arguments adduced by these critics have, in my view, completely laid to rest any presumption of literary coherence of the ark narrative in 1 Samuel with 2 Samuel 6.[156]

The study of Miller and Roberts is particularly persuasive. Following a lead by M. Delcor that the ark was analogous to the divine image in Mesopotamia,[157] they posit that the ark narrative of 1 Samuel corresponds in genre to the accounts of the capture of divine images in the ancient Near East.[158] 2 Samuel 6, on the other hand, properly belongs with

---

154. A. F. Campbell, *The Ark Narrative (1 Sam 4-6; 2 Sam 6)* (SBLDS 16; Missoula, Montana: Scholars, 1975); J. J. Jackson, "The Ark Narratives. An Historical, Textual, and Form-Critical Study of 1 Samuel 4-6 and II Samuel 6," Unpublished Th.D. Dissertation (Union Theological Seminary, New York, 1962); R. Ficker, *Komposition und Erzählung: Untersuchungen zur Ladeerzählung 1 Sam 4-6; 2 Sam 6 und zur Aufstieg Davids 1 Sam 15-2-Sam 5* (D.Theol. Dissertation; University of Heidelberg, 1978).

155. Notably by F. Schicklberger, *Die Ladeerzählungen des ersten Samuel-Buches* (FB 7; Würzburg: Echter, 1973) 129-149; P. D. Miller and J. J. M. Roberts, *The Hand of the Lord* (JHNES 8; Baltimore: Johns Hopkins University, 1977); J. T. Willis, "An Anti-Elide Narrative Tradition from a Prophetic Circle at the Ramah Sanctuary," *JBL* 90 (1971) 288-308.

156. Nothwithstanding the rejoinder of A. F. Campbell in "Yahweh and the Ark: A Case Study in Narrative," *JBL* 98 (1979) 31-43.

157. "Jahweh et Dagon ou le Jahwisme face à la religion des Philistins, d'après 1 Sam. V," *VT* 14 (1964) 136-154.

158. *The Hand of the Lord*, 9-17.

the texts of the return of divine images.[159] Accordingly, the aim of the narrator in 1 Samuel was to account for the loss of the ark and to offer a theological response to the crisis. Following older critics, Miller and Roberts include 2:12–17, 22–25, 27–36 with the narrative, arguing that these verses introduce the Elides to whom culpability for the ark's demise was traced. The ark was captured because of the sins of the Elides, but the narrator also wanted to argue that the loss of the ark did not mean the defeat of YHWH. In fact, the story of the ark's sojourn in Philistine territory vindicates Israel's god, for YHWH ultimately triumphed over Dagon the god of the Philistines on their home turf.

According to the narrative in 1 Samuel 4, the Israelites were engaged in battle against the Philistines. The former were encamped at Ebenezer, modern Izbet Ṣartah; the latter at Aphek. Initial skirmishes resulted in defeat for Israel and the death of four thousand soldiers. Puzzled over what they perceived was YHWH's smiting of his own people, they sent for the ark to be brought from Shiloh. The purpose of that move they stated explicitly: "that [YHWH] may come into our midst and deliver us from the power (*kp*) of our enemies" (1 Sam 4:3). So it was that the ark was brought into battle and, with it, Eli's sons Hophni and Phinehas. Thus the ark functioned as a war palladium, the presence of which was supposed to guarantee victory for those who followed YHWH.

This close association of the ark with the presence of YHWH in battle is also reflected in Num 14:39–45, which is generally attributed to the Old Epic (JE).[160] According to that account, the Israelites were warned not to go up against the Amalekites and the Canaanites because YHWH was not going

---

159. Ibid., 16–17. While accepting their form-critical analysis of the narrative in 1 Samuel and their isolation of 2 Samuel 6, McCarter has challenged the precision of their characterization of the latter. See his "The Ritual Dedication of the City of David in 2 Samuel 6," 273–278.

160. See P. J. Budd, *Numbers* (WBC 5; Waco, Texas: Word, 1984) 154.

with them and they would be defeated by their enemies (vv 42–43). They proceeded despite the warning, though "neither the ark of the covenant nor Moses departed from the camp" (v 44), and so they were defeated in battle.[161] The ark symbolized the presence of YHWH as the divine warrior.

The use of the ark as a war palladium has precedent in Israel's early history. This is suggested by two fragments of an ancient liturgy used in conjunction with Israel's holy wars (Num 10:35–36).[162] The first may have been the incipit of a song chanted when the ark was brought forth into battle.[163] According to the narrative context, it was proclaimed whenever the ark travelled:

קומה יהוה ויפצו איביך
וינסו משנאיך מפניך
(Num 10:35)

Arise, YHWH, let your enemies scatter,
Let your foes flee from your presence.

A second incipit is evidently the remnant of an old liturgy associated with the return of the ark from battle:

---

161. On the ark as a war palladium, see Schmitt, *Zelt und Lade als Thema alttestamentlicher Wissenschaft*, 139–144; Maier, *Das altisraelitische Ladeheiligtum*, 47 n. 54; Schicklberger, *Die Ladeerzählungen*, 45 n. 105.

162. See G. H. Davies, "The Ark of the Covenant," *ASTI* 5 (1966/67) 30–47. There is some consensus that Num 10:29–36 belongs to J, but vv 35 and 36 are probably adapted from an old ark liturgy. Similarities with Psalm 68, universally accepted as an archaic piece, would tend to confirm the antiquity of the poetic fragment, as would its prosody and language. I cannot accept Tarragon's contention that the presence of the ark in Num 10:35–36 is unhistorical. See "David et l'arche," 519.

163. Cf. Miller, *The Divine Warrior in Early Israel*, 145–146.

שׁובה יהוה [ברכב] רבבות
אלפי [שׁנני] ישׂראל
(Num 10:36)[164]

Return,[165] YHWH, [with chariotry] by myriads,
[With] thousands of [the archers of] Israel.

These ancient fragments suggest the mythological and ritual background of the ark as a war palladium in early Israel. The picture here is of YHWH as a divine warrior who marches forth to battle and returns with his entourage, no doubt represented in ritual by the armies of Israel. It has been observed that the vocabulary of the first incipit (Num 10:35)

---

164. The text is corrupt; perhaps hopelessly so. My tentative reconstruction here is based in part on Ps 68:18, which may have been part of a liturgy of the ark's return, thus corresponding to Ps 68:2 (// Num 10:35). The loss of ברכב is due to homoiarkton, *bêt* and *rēš* being graphically similar in the palaeo-Hebrew script. I take *šnn* to be a cognate of Ugaritic θ*nn*, Alalakh *šanannu* and Egyptian *snn*. See W. A. Ward, "Comparative Studies in Egyptian and Ugaritic," *JNES* 20 (1961) 39; R. O. Faulkner, "Egyptian Military Organization," *JEA* 39 (1953) 43. Cf. W. F. Albright, "Notes on Psalms 68 and 134," *NorTT* 56 (1955) 2-4. The Peshiṭta of Ps 68:18 has *ḥyl'*, suggesting some kind of military personnel. The pairing of אלפים // רבבת is common in Hebrew and Ugaritic poetry (see S. Gevirtz, *Patterns in the Early Poetry of Israel* [SAOC 32; Chicago: The University of Chicago, 1973] 15-18), not infrequently in military contexts (Deut 32:30; 1 Sam 18:7; Ps 91:7; *KTU* 1.14.II.39-40, III.17-18). Note the occurrence in *Pap. Anast.* III, 6.3-4 of the expression *snn n t-nt ḥtr* "archer of the chariotry."

165. M. Dibelius (*Die Lade Jahwes* [FRLANT 7; Göttingen: Vandenhoeck & Ruprecht, 1906] 10-11) read *šēḇâ* "be seated (enthroned)" (instead of MT *šûḇâ*). This is unnecessary, as R. Smend has noted, for שׁוב belongs with the vocabulary of return from war. See *Yahweh War and Tribal Confederation* (trans. M. G. Rogers; Nashville: Abingdon, 1970) 79 n. 11.

has an intriguing parallel in the language of Ba'l's theophany in Ugaritic mythology, when Ba'l advances against his foes:[166]

'ib . b'l . t'iḫd y'rm
šn'u . hd . gpt ǵr
(*KTU* 1.4.VII.35-37)

The enemies of Ba'l took to the forests,
The foes of Hadd to the edges of the mountain.

In the lines immediately preceding, the divine warrior Ba'l issued his voice (thunder), whereupon the earth shook, the mountains trembled, and the peoples from afar were afraid (*KTU* 1.4.VII.29-35).[167] The enemies of Ba'l were in dismay, for they feared "the weapons of *Dmrn*."[168] Ba'l's "hand" (*yd*) was poised to strike; he wielded his lightning tree in his right hand (ll. 40-41).

It is most suggestive, then, that when the ark was brought into the battlefield, the Israelites gave a great shout (קול תרועה גדולה), whereupon the earth shook, and the people

166. Miller, *The Divine Warrior in Early Israel*, 146.

167. B. Margalit (*A Matter of Life and Death* [AOAT 206; Neukirchen-Vluyn: Neukirchener, 1980] 59, 62 n. 2) reconstructs *[yt]r 'arṣ* in l. 31, citing *KTU* 1.17.VI.46; cf. also Hab 3:5-6.

168. *Dmrn* is mentioned in *KTU* 1.92.30 as an epithet of Ba'l the warrior (cf. PNs *ảmrb'l, ảmrhd*). It corresponds to Sanchuniathon's Δημαροῦς, who is also called Ἄδωδος, i.e., Hadad (*Praep. Evang.* 1.10.31). See O. Eissfeldt, "Adrammelek und Demarus," (1966) in *KS* III, 335-339. I cannot accept Margalit's rendering of *dmrn* as "Perdition" on the basis of Arabic *damara* "perish" (see *A Matter of Life and Death*, 63-66). Margalit rejects the identification of *dmrn* as an epithet of Zeus but makes no mention of its connection with Ba'l/Hadad. His purpose in arguing for this interpretation of the term is to support his hypothesis that this Ugaritic passage concerns the storming of the mountain of Ba'l by Mot, a hypothesis that he does not demonstrate.

were afraid (1 Sam 4:5–6).[169] When the Philistines heard the shout, they trembled, for they reckoned that the gods of the Israelites had entered the battlefield (v 7).[170] They cried (v 8): "Woe to us! Who will deliver us from the power (*yd*) of these mighty gods? These are the ones who smote the Egyptians with every scourge <and> with plague!"[171] The allusion to the Exodus here, as Miller and Roberts have observed, "calls to mind the march of the divine warrior Yahweh in Israel's earliest history to deliver her and destroy her enemies."[172] One may further argue that the reference to האלהים האדירים alludes not only to the Exodus but to YHWH's victory over the Sea in mythological combat. Although the unruly waters were called מים אדירים (Exod 15:10), YHWH was acknowledged to be "mightier" (אדיר) than the mighty breakers of the sea (Ps 93:4).

If the mythological march of the divine warrior lies behind this narrative, the mention of the plague (דבר) is provocative, for elsewhere Deber accompanies the divine warrior in his march to battle. Thus an ancient poem depicts the warrior's march from the south:

---

169. On the association of the *tĕrûʿâ* with the institution of holy war, see especially P. Humbert, *La 'Terouʿa'* (Neuchâtel: Université de Neuchâtel, 1946) 7–9; G. von Rad, *Der heilige Krieg im alten Israel* (Göttingen: Vandenhoeck & Ruprecht, 1951) 11.

170. Reading באו האלהים with LXX and v 8.

171. The reference to the smiting of the Egyptian in the wilderness (per MT) makes no sense. J. Wellhausen (*Der Text der Bücher Samuelis* [Göttingen: Vandenhoeck & Ruprecht, 1871] 55), followed by Driver (*Notes on the Hebrew Text and Topography of the Books of Samuel*, 37) and others, read וּבַדֶּבֶר instead of במדבר "in the desert," thus restoring the copula with LXX. We should probably follow M. Dahood ("Hebrew-Ugaritic Lexicography II," *Bib* 45 [1964] 401–402) to read במ<ו>־דבר, and assume the archaic preposition במו, for which, see *RSP* I, 136.

172. *The Hand of the Lord*, 35.

לפניך ילך דבר
< >יצא רשף לרגליך
עמד וי[נ]דד ארץ
ראה ויתר גוים
(Hab 3:5–6)[173]

Before him Deber marched,
Rešep went forth at his feet.
He stood and shook the earth,
He looked and caused nations to tremble.

The image of the divine warrior's march here has been compared with Ba'l's advance to battle in Ugaritic mythology. Although Deber is not mentioned in conjunction with the advance of Ba'l, J. Day has proposed on the basis of *PRU* 2.1.3 ( = *KTU* 1.82.3) that Rešep was part of Ba'l's entourage in his advance to battle with the dragon.[174] Other scholars commenting on the pair of Rešep and Deber have connected the allusion to the divine warrior's entourage with the occurrence of plagues and pestilences in 1 Samuel 5.[175]

In any case, the issue in the ark narrative here is power and dominion. So the Philistines were exhorted to brace themselves to fight, "lest you become *slaves* to the Hebrews as they have been *slaves* to you" (1 Sam 4:9). But it turned out that it was the Israelites who were defeated and it was they who had to flee. The defeat (מכה) that the Philistines feared

173. See the careful treatment of T. Hiebert, *God of My Victory* (HSM 38; Atlanta: Scholars, 1986) 5, 19–20, 92–94.

174. "New Light on the Mythological Background of the Allusion to Resheph in Habakkuk III 5," *VT* 29 (1979) 143–151.

175. A. Caquot, "Sur quelques démons de Ancien Testament (Reshep, Qeṭeb, Deber)," *Sem* 6 (1956) 57–58; F. Vattioni, "Il dio Resheph," *AION* 15 (1965) 67–68. One may further note that Plague and Pestilence marched at the side of Marduk. See J. Hehn, *Hymnen und Gebete an Marduk* (Leipzig: Hinrichs, 1905) 314, ll. 4–5.

did not come to pass, but the מכה suffered by the Israelites was very great (v 10).

A Benjaminite messenger brought the news to Shiloh that day, with his clothes rent and earth upon his head, obviously as a sign of mourning (v 12). When he arrived, he found Eli sitting "on the seat" (*'l hks'*) by the way, his heart trembling for the ark (v 13). The whole city cried out (vv 13, 14). Curiously, the narrator calls the messenger מבשר, a term used elsewhere of bearers of good news. Eli died when he heard the report of Israel's defeat and the capture of the ark (v 17). The pregnant wife of Phinehas was, likewise, devastated when told the news. She bore a child on her death-bed whom she named *'Î-kāḇôḏ*, commemorating the exile of the ark.

The apparent set-back that the ark suffered at the hands of the Philistines is, however, a setup for the exaltation of YHWH in chapters 5 and 6. This pattern has already been noticed by commentators. But it needs also to be said that the pattern of demise followed by victory is paralleled in the adventures of Ba'l in Ugaritic mythology. As in the ark narrative in 1 Samuel, the issue is power and dominion in the tale of Ba'l's battle with Yamm, deified Sea, also known as Nahar (River).[176] Yamm sent an embassy to the divine council to demand the surrender of Ba'l and his retinue. The gods of the assembly were afraid; they bowed their heads to their knees. Even 'Ēl was quick to concede:

> 'bdk . b'l . yymm .
> 'bdk . b'l [nhr]m .
> bn . dgn . 'a[s]rkm .
>
> (*KTU* 1.2.I.36-37)

> Ba'l is your slave, O Yamm,
> Ba'l is your slave, [Nahar]
> The son of Dagan is your pr[ison]er.

176. *KTU* 1.2.

Ba'l is to be subservient to Yamm, that is, to be a slave. He, too, must pay homage and bring tribute to Yamm like one of the lesser gods. The divine council was prepared to surrender Ba'l to Yamm. But Ba'l himself would not concede defeat. He prepared himself for battle against his enemies. Kothar, the craftsman among the gods, cheered him on, urging him to defeat his enemies and establish his dominion forever. Kothar made two magical weapons called Yagarriš ("May It Drive Away") and 'Āy-yamarrī ("May It Indeed Overwhelm") to help Ba'l in battle. The clubs struck Yamm on his head and between the eyes.

> yprsḥ . ym . yql l'arṣ .
> tnǵṣn . pnth . wydlp . tmnh .
> (*KTU* 1.2.IV.22-26)

> Yamm collapsed; he fell to the ground.
> His joints shook; his frame collapsed.

So in the climax of the tale, Yamm is completely annihilated and Ba'l is proclaimed king. The initial set-back that Ba'l suffered did not tell the whole story; Ba'l eventually triumphed over his enemies.

In a variation of the story, Ba'l was confronted by Mot, personified death, who scorched the earth and destroyed its vegetation.[177] Mot's appetite was insatiable; even Ba'l, "the rider of the clouds" and giver of life, was in danger of being swallowed up by Mot. Ba'l was afraid. He sent messengers to Mot, agreeing to be Mot's *slave ('bd)* forever. The fate of Ba'l's people hung in a balance.

The text is badly damaged at this point, and the sequence of events is not entirely clear. Apparently Ba'l tried repeatedly to appease Mot, but to no avail. Mot taunted him. Ba'l's attempts to escape were unsuccessful, and he was defeated by Mot.

---

177. *KTU* 1.5.II.

News of Ba'l's demise was brought to 'Ēl by two messengers:

mǵny . lb'l .
npl . l'arṣ .
mt . 'al'iyn . b'l
ḫlq . zbl . b'l .'arṣ
(*KTU* 1.5.VI.8-10)

We came upon Ba'l:
He had fallen to the ground.
Mighty Ba'l is dead!
Perished is the Prince, Lord of the Earth.

The announcement was made to 'Ēl who, like Eli, was found sitting on a seat (*ks'i*). Upon hearing the news, 'Ēl poured earth on his head in mourning, covered himself in sackcloth, and cried:

b'l . mt . my . l'im .
bn dgn . my . hmlt .
(*KTU* 1.5.VI.23-24)

Ba'l is dead! What of the people?
The Son of Dagan! What of the multitudes?

Ba'l's consort, 'Anat, searched everywhere for him. She, too, found him "fallen to the ground" (*npl l'arṣ*).[178] In another tablet, we find her performing the same mourning ritual as 'Ēl, grieving over the death of Ba'l and lamenting the plight of his people (*KTU* 1.6.I.1-7). Ba'l's existence on earth was a blessing for his people; the prospect of his continued absence from earth was frightening. Instead of fertility, there would be drought. The earth would become cracked and dry. So 'Anat lamented:

---

178. *KTU* 1.5.VI.30-31.

'iy . 'al'iyn . b'l
'iy . zbl . b'l . 'arṣ
(*KTU* 1.6.IV.4–5, 15–16)

Where is Mighty Ba'l?
Where is the Prince, the Lord of the Earth?

'Anat confronted Mot in battle and defeated him. She seized him, split him with a sword, winnowed, burnt, ground, and scattered him in the fields (*KTU* 1.6.II.30–38). But in another battle scene, it is Ba'l himself who fought the battle:

y'iḫd . b'l . bn . 'aΘrt
rbm . ymḫṣ . bktp
dkym[179] . ymḫṣ . bṣmd
ṣǵrm[180] ymṣḫ . l'arṣ
py['l .] b[']l . lks'i mlkh
[lnḫt] . lkḥθ . drkth
(*KTU* 1.6.V.1–6)

Ba'l seized the sons of 'Athirat.
The mighty ones he smote with a mace,[181]
The leaders he smote with a club.[182]

---

179. The attempt of J. W. Wesselius ("Three Difficult Passages in Ugaritic Literary Texts," *UF* 15 [1983] 312) to read *tkym* must be categorically rejected. The suggestion that we have just one wedge (*t*) written over an erasure of a *d* seems contrived, as is the putative noun *tkym*, supposedly meaning "middle ones."

180. The new collation of *KTU* is certainly to be preferred over the reading *ṣḥr mt* in *CTA*, and it is now generally accepted by scholars.

181. Cf. R. T. O'Callaghan, "The Word *ktp* in Ugaritic and Egypto-Canaanite Mythology," *Or* 21 (1952) 27–46.

182. The *ṣmd* is a weapon used by Ba'l in his defeat of Yamm (*KTU* 1.2.IV.15). R. M. Good ("Some Ugaritic Terms

The youths he smote to the ground.[183]
B[a'] as[cended] his royal throne,
[The comfort] of his seat of dominion.

The adversaries of Ba'l here are probably members of Mot's retinue, thus comparable with the entourage of Yamm (cf. *KTU* 1.3.III.40–43). The identity of *ṣǵr* is unclear, but I am inclined to take it as a military title. In a fragment of the Ba'l–Yamm combat, the epithet *ṣǵr hdd* is closely associated with or parallel to *zbl b'l* "Prince Ba'l" and *ǵlm* "Lad" (*KTU* 1.9.17–18). In another instance, *ṣǵr* is a synonym of *n'r* (*KTU* 1.107.38, 41). Since *ǵlm* and *n'r* may refer to military personnel in Ugaritic,[184] it is also possible that *ṣǵrm* here should be interpreted as military personnel.[185] In this regard, J. MacDonald has observed that Akkadian *ṣuḫārū* refers to military personnel in the Shemshara and Mari tablets.[186] Since the term *ṣuḫārū* is used regularly of apprentices or assistants, one may translate *ṣǵrm* as "cadets," or the like, though I have rendered it as "youths" here to preserve the ambiguity. One may also point to a class of military personnel known as the *ṣiḫrūtu*, mentioned after *dannūtu* "the mighty ones," and *šanûtu* "the lieutenants," in a Neo-Assyrian letter (*ABL* 1285 rev. 19). Here the *ṣiḫrūtu* may be low ranking military officers

---

Relating to Draught and Riding Animals," *UF* 16 [1984] 29) conjectures that its association with *ktp* comes from its shape being like a shoulder-blade.

183. Cf. Zech 13:7, where YHWH Ṣĕḇā'ôṯ summons weapons against his shepherd and his hand turns against the *ṣ'rym*.

184. See B. Cutler and J. MacDonald, "Identification of the *na'ar* in the Ugaritic Texts," *UF* 8 (1976) 27–35; Rainey, "The Military Personnel of Ugarit," 24ff.

185. Belonging to Ba'l's entourage are "seven *ǵlm*" and "eight *ḫnzr* (*KTU* 1.5.V.6).

186. "The Role and Status of the *Ṣuḫārū* in the Mari Correspondence," *JAOS* 96 (1976) 57–68, esp. 58–60. See *ARM* XIV 70.5–6; XIV 2.20–31.

or apprentices in the military. The *dkym* should, likewise, be taken as a military title.[187] The root is *dky*, thus corresponding to Akkadian *dekû/dakû*, a verb which is used most frequently of troop movements.[188] I take *dkym* as a participle, referring to officers who lead the attack, or muster the troops for battle.[189]

At all events, Ba'l defeated the allies of Mot and claimed his kingship. Mot lamented his own demise. Because of Ba'l, Mot had to be split, burnt with fire, ground, winnowed and scattered. Thus, notwithstanding his initial set-back, Ba'l vanquished his enemies and established his dominion.

There is a similar movement from set-back to victory in the ark narrative of 1 Samuel. Chapter 4 chronicles the disaster of the ark's capture, when the god of the Philistines apparently triumphed over YHWH. It paints a gloomy picture for the people of YHWH. Defeated in battle, they fled and were slaughtered. But the movement in the narrative from set-back to victory, imitating the myth of Ba'l, allowed the narrator to accept the fact of the ark's capture and, indeed, to turn the attention of the audience to the ultimate and decisive triumph of YHWH. Yet, the narrator did not appropriate the mythic pattern without significant theological reworking. Nowhere in the gloomy story is there an admission of YHWH's defeat. There is certainly no hint that the god of Israel might have died, like Ba'l. Rather, the capture of the ark and the defeat of Israel are conceded without admission of YHWH's defeat.

---

187. G. Del Olmo Lete ("Notes on Ugaritic Semantics V," *UF* 14 [1982] 57-69) considers *dkym* "an epiexegetical expansion," that is, a gloss on *rbm*. He interprets *dkym* as *d-k-ym* "those who are like Yammu." But the battle is with Mot, not Yamm, and *dkym* should parallel *ṣǵrm*.

188. See *CAD* 3, 123-128.

189. Cf. Akkadian *dēkû* "the ones who initiate (the attack)." In Enuma Elish, Tiamat is said to have exalted Kingu above others in her entourage to lead her forces, and "to launch the attack" (*EE* I.149).

Nevertheless, there was death aplenty among the people of YHWH. In fact, the death toll in the second battle far exceeded the first: four thousand died in the first battle, thirty thousand in the second. In particular, the narrator singles out the deaths in Eli's family, beginning with the deaths of Hophni and Phinehas, who came with the ark from Shiloh. The deaths of Hophni and Phinehas are mentioned in vv 11, 17, of Eli in v 18, of Eli and Phinehas in vv 19, 21, and of the wife of Phinehas in v 20.[190] In the myth of Ba'l, the fate of his people hung in a balance in the face of his absence. So here in the narrative of the ark, the fate of YHWH's people is in question. The people of the city (i.e., Shiloh) cried aloud. In preserving the mythic pattern of demise-victory, the narrator was able to speak of the ark's capture without ever compromising the sovereignty of YHWH. Whereas in the myth of Ba'l, the deity was defeated and struck dead, here only humans died. Thus, a theological rationale was provided for the tragedy, namely, the sins of the Elides at Shiloh.

Significantly, the chapter ends with the wife of Phinehas lamenting the capture of the ark. She named the child whom she bore on her deathbed *'Î-kābôd*, whose name, whatever it might have meant originally,[191] calls to mind the cry of 'Anat in the face of her husband's death:

'iy . 'al'iyn . b'l
'iy . zbl . b'l . 'arṣ

(*KTU* 1.6.IV.4–5, 15–16)

Where is Mighty Ba'l?
Where is the Prince, the Lord of the Earth?

---

190. The loss of the ark and the deaths are closely connected. Indeed, one may even say that the loss of the ark marked the end of the Elide era. So F. Stolz, *Das erste und zweite Buch Samuel* (ZBAT 9; Zürich: Theologischer, 1981) 43.

191. Cf. Hebrew איזבל, איתמר; Ugaritic *'iyb'l, 'iy'dm, 'iyθr*.

The cry of absence is a setup for the liturgical response, namely, the affirmation of Ba'l's existence:

> kḥy . 'al'iyn . b'l
> k'iθ . zbl [.] b'l [.] 'arṣ
> (*KTU* 1.6.III.2–3, 20–21)

> Verily, Mighty Ba'l lives!
> Verily, the Prince, Lord of the earth exists!

Recognizing this mythic pattern, one cannot accept the proposal of Schicklberger to separate the narrative of the disaster in chapter 4 from the chapters that follow.[192] To do so is to truncate the story. Rather, following the pattern in the myth of Ba'l, we expect the narrative to continue on to the triumph of YHWH over Dagon. And so it does.

The captured ark was brought into the temple of Dagon in Ashdod and set up beside the image of the Philistine god (1 Sam 5:2). The purpose of this was probably to present the Israelite god as tribute to Dagon and to demonstrate Dagon's superiority over the god of Israel. Captured images are treated in like manner in Mesopotamia.[193] But on the following day the Philistines found the statue of their god fallen before the ark. The Hebrew is especially provocative here: והנה דגון נפל לפניו ארצה לפני ארון יהוה "Lo! Dagon was falling before him to the ground, before the ark of YHWH."[194] The use of the participle (נֹפֵל) suggests an ongoing act (of worship)--Dagon was falling before YHWH in obeisance.

---

192. *Die Ladeerzählungen*, 25–73.

193. See M. Cogan, *Imperialism and Religion* (SBLMS 19; Missoula, Montana: Scholars, 1974) 22–34.

194. 1 Sam 5:3, cf. v. 6. LXX has Dagon falling ἐπὶ πρόσωπον αὐτοῦ "upon his face." So Wellhausen (*Der Text der Bücher Samuelis*, 58), Driver (*Notes on the Hebrew Text of the Books of Samuel*, 40) and many commentators prefer to read על־פניו or לאפיו.

The language of Dagon's prostration is remarkably similar to the account of Joshua's act of submission and penitence before YHWH following the defeat of Israel at Ai: ויפל על־פניו ארצה לפני ארון יהוה "he fell upon his face, to the ground, before the ark of YHWH" (Josh 7:6). Because the people of Israel had violated the ban in holy war, YHWH had allowed them to be slaughtered. And so Joshua tore his garments and fell before YHWH to plead for mercy on the people's behalf. Not insignificantly, this parallel text belongs to the tradition of ritual conquest and ark procession at Gilgal, a tradition which betrays influences of the Ba'l myth.[195] Not only are the motifs of the drying of the river and driving out of the enemies reminiscent of Ba'l's victory over Prince Sea *alias* Judge River (*KTU* 1.2.IV), the deity is called the "living god" (*'l ḥy*) and "lord of all the earth" (*'dwn kl h'rṣ*).[196] Both names recall the proclamation of Ba'l's victory over his enemies: *ḥy 'al'iyn b'l // 'iθ zbl b'l 'arṣ* "Mighty Ba'l lives! // The Prince, Lord of the Earth exists!"[197] Especially pertinent to our exegesis of the ark narrative in 1 Samuel is the expressed purpose of the ritual conquest, "so that all the people may know that *the hand of YHWH* (יד יהוה) is mighty, that they may fear YHWH your god all the days" (Josh 4:24).[198]

The reference to Dagon's fall may allude to yet another motif in the Ba'l myth, namely, the defeat of a god in

---

195. The connection of this narrative with the Gilgal tradition has been noted by A. Schulz, *Der Bücher Samuel* II (EHAT 8; Münster: Aschendorffsche, 1920) 330.

196. Josh 3:10, 11, 13. The epithet *'dn kl 'rṣ* is attested of Ba'l in Arslan Tash, if the restoration of A. Caquot is correct. See his "Observations sur la première tablette Magique d'Arslan Tash," *JANES* 5 (1973) 45–57.

197. Cf. *KTU* 1.6.III.2–3, 20–21.

198. MT has יְרָאתֶם "you shall fear," but we should probably read יִרְאָתָם, that is, the inf. cs. with 3 mp suffix. So, F. Langlamet, *Gilgal et les récits de la traversée du Jourdain (Jos., III–IV)* (CahRB 11; Paris: Gabalda, 1969) 54.

mythological combat.[199] The language pertaining to the discovery by the Philistines of their fallen god echoes the news of Ba'l's demise. 'Anat and the two messengers of 'Ēl reported that they found Ba'l "fallen to the ground" (*npl l'arṣ*).[200] But the tables were later turned, and Ba'l's enemies were vanquished instead. So it is in the tale of Ba'l's battle with Sea. The weapons of Ba'l struck Sea on the head (*qdqd*) and between the eyes, and Sea collapsed and "fell to the ground" (*yql l'arṣ*).[201]

The allusion in 1 Sam 5:3, then, is to the subjugation of Dagon before YHWH. The Philistines erected the statue again, but on the next day the statue of Dagon was once more prostrate before the ark, this time with Dagon's head (*r'š*) and both his hands (*kpwt ydyw*) cut off (v 4). The expression רק דגון נשאר עליו "only Dagon was left upon him" in MT makes no sense. The versions suggest רק גו דגון "only the trunk of Dagon," or the like.[202] Comparison may be made here to the defeat of the Philistine champion, Goliath, who "fell on his face to the ground" (ויפל על־פניו ארצה) and who had his head cut off ignominiously (1 Sam 17:49–51). Miller and Roberts point to 'Anat's dismemberment of her enemies whose heads (*r'išt*) and hands (*kpt*) she hung on herself as trophies of her victory.[203] They note that the verb used is *ḫṣb*, which is also found in the Hebrew Bible of the slaughter of the sea-monsters (Isa 51:9–10). In this connection, one should also mention the destruction of Mot, who is split by the sword and whose flesh and limbs are scattered in the fields (*KTU* 1.6.II.30–38; cf. Ps 74:12–14). Later in the same tablet,

---

199. See Miller and Roberts, *The Hand of the Lord*, 43–46.

200. *KTU* 1.5.VI.8–9, 31.

201. *KTU* 1.2.IV.23–27.

202. So LXX πλὴν ἡ ῥάχις Δαγων; Vulg. *Dagon truncus solus;* Syr. *wgwšmh ddgwn;* Targ. רק גופיה.

203. *The Hand of the Lord*, 46. Cf. *KTU* 1.3.II.9–13. The connection has also been noticed by L. Fisher, *apud* Campbell, *The Ark Narrative*, 86 n. 1.

Mot concedes that it is on account of Ba'l that he has experienced the humiliation and destruction (*KTU* 1.6.V.11–19). The point in 1 Sam 5:1–5, in any case, is the absolute victory of YHWH in divine combat. In spite of the apparent set-back of the ark's capture, YHWH has been proven the superior deity. Dagon is vanquished!

The story of the ark continues with its journey through the Philistine cities.[204] As in the Gilgal tradition, where the drying of the Jordan in the ritual crossing of the ark was to make known the "*hand (power) of YHWH*" (יד יהוה),[205] so the travel of the ark from city to city manifested the *yd* of YHWH. The narrator mentions *yd yhwh* "hand of YHWH" (5:6, 9), *yd h'lhym* "hand of God" (5:11), and *ydw* "his hand" (5:7; 6:3, 5, 9). J. J. M. Roberts has called attention to similar idioms elsewhere in the ancient Near East.[206] In particular, Roberts notes that the Akkadian idiom *qāt DN* (or *qātum ša DN*) is used frequently of diseases and plagues.[207] The divine hand is regularly described as "strong" (*dannatu*) or "heavy" (*kabtu*) upon the victim(s), inflicting diseases or death. Similar idioms are found in a Ugaritic letter reporting that "the hand of the god(s) is very strong here like death."[208] So the hand of YHWH is said in the ark narrative to be "heavy" (*tkbd* [5:6]; *kbdh* [5:11]) and "severe" (*qšth*, [5:7]).[209] But the manifestation of the hand of YHWH in this part of the narrative has already been anticipated in the response of the Philistines to the entry of the ark into the battlefield: "Who can deliver us from the hand of these mighty gods? These are the ones who smote the Egyptians with every scourging <and> with

---

204. See G. W. Ahlström, "The Travels of the Ark: A Religio-Political Composition," *JNES* 43 (1984) 143–149.

205. Josh 4:24.

206. "The Hand of Yahweh," *VT* 21 (1971) 244–251.

207. Ibid. For additional examples, see *CAD* 13, 186–187.

208. *CTA* 53.11–13 (= *KTU* 2.10.11–13), cited and translated by Roberts, "The Hand of Yahweh," 247–248.

209. In Josh 4:24, it is said to be "strong" (*ḥzqh*).

plague."[210] The presence of the ark, representing the divine warrior, caused "a very great panic" (מהומה גדולה מאד, v 9) and a "panic of death" (מהומת מות, v 11), for the Philistines perceived that the ark was brought to slay them (vv 10–11).[211] The effect of YHWH's hand brought terror upon the Philistines, their leaders, and their gods (cf. *KTU* 1.4.VII.32–41). Hence, they were told to follow a certain prescription that "perhaps [YHWH] might lighten his hand from upon you, upon your gods and upon your land" (1 Sam 6:5).

It is clear that the image of YHWH in this ark narrative is quite different from the picture we have of the deity at Shiloh. Whereas at Shiloh the deity was portrayed in terms reminiscent of 'Ēl--as a creator and divine king firmly established as supreme god in the divine council, in 1 Samuel 4–6 YHWH is described in a manner that recalls the myth of Ba'l. The journey of the ark appears to parallel the rise of Ba'l in Canaanite mythology. After an initial set-back, when it fell into the hands of the enemy, the ark's presence in Philistine territories caused the demise of the Philistines and their gods. Through deadly plagues and pestilences, which the presence of the ark brought, the hand of YHWH was made manifest.

As Miller and Roberts have shown, the narrative is a theological treatise as well.[212] It explains why it was that the ark fell into enemy hands in the first place: the sins of the Elides had caused the tragedy! But the narrative is not concerned only with the end of an era, it is concerned also with the beginning of another. The story climaxes with the return of the ark to the Israelites, this time to be in the custody of the house of Abinadab in Qiryat-Ye'arim. The

---

210. 1 Sam 4:8. See n. 171 above.

211. It is interesting that 4QSam[a] reads מהומת יהוה in v 11, for that precise expression is found in Zech 14:13, in the context of the divine warrior's battle against the nations.

212. *The Hand of the Lord*, 69–75.

story begins with the worthless, sinful sons of Eli; it concludes with the consecration of the son of Abinadab who was charged with the care of the ark.

It would appear that the ark narrative in 1 Samuel served to legitimate the new sanctuary at Qiryat-Ye'arim. Inasmuch as Qiryat-Ye'arim was the home of the ark for some twenty years, it is not surprising that there should be an account explaining how the ark got there. The ark narrative in 1 Samuel is not, therefore, the *hieros logos* for the sanctuary in Jerusalem, as Rost posited, but for Qiryat-Ye'arim. As Miller and Roberts have argued, the narrative probably had its genesis in Qiryat-Ye'arim some time shortly after the events that it reports.[213] Some scholars believe that it was an actual plague in Philistia that prompted the return of the ark,[214] and the return prompted the theological polemic.

So the ark was returned to the Israelites at Qiryat-Ye'arim which, though nominally under Israelite control, was still within the Philistine sphere of influence. The city was, moreover, a relatively neutral site where the boundaries of Dan, Benjamin and Judah converged.[215] The old central sanctuary at Shiloh having been destroyed, the ark had to remain at the relatively obscure site of Qiryat-Ye'arim, modern Deir al-Azhar.

We do not know very much about religion at Qiryat-Ye'arim. Connection with the traditions of Ba'l is

---

213. Ibid.

214. Ibid., 74. See also M. C. Lind, *Yahweh is a Warrior* (Scottdale, Pennsylvania: Herald, 1980) 94. Lind links the plague with the one at Ba'l Pe'or (Josh 22:17), citing extra-biblical evidence of a deadly plague in the region in the early Iron Age. Cf. G. Mendenhall, *The Tenth Generation* (Baltimore: Johns Hopkins, 1973) 106-107. It is both impossible and unnecessary, however, to reconstruct the historical details. See L. I. Conrad, "The Biblical Tradition for the Plague of the Philistines," *JAOS* 104 (1984) 281-287.

215. See J. Blenkinsopp, *Gibeon and Israel* (SOTSMS 2; Cambridge: Cambridge University, 1972) 9.

suggested by its various names: Qiryat-Ba'l, that is, the City of Ba'l (Josh 15:60; 18:14), Ba'lah (Josh 15:9), Mt. Ba'lah (Josh 15:11), and Ba'lah of Judah (2 Sam 6:2; cf. 1 Chron 13:6).[216] It is sometimes suggested that the name Ba'lah refers to one of the goddesses Asherah, Astarte, or 'Anat.[217] This is most unlikely, in my judgment. Rather, the feminine form is simply an abbreviated reference to Qiryat-Ba'l, the word for city being feminine. At all events, the name of the city suggests ancient connections with Ba'l. It is hardly surprising, therefore, that the *hieros logos* originating from there should be influenced by images from the myth of Ba'l. Having to account for the demise of the ark at the hands of the Philistines, the custodians of the ark at Qiryat-Ba'l (Qiryat-Ye'arim) told the story of the ark's initial set-back but ultimate and decisive triumph over its enemies, using a tradition already well established in the city and known to the residents. Even though the narrative does not concede the defeat of YHWH, it is not difficult to see that the myth of Ba'l had been adapted. The myth chosen reflects the political realities for Israel at the close of the eleventh century. The picture of YHWH as 'Ēl, which was dominant at Shiloh, was obviously inappropriate in the light of Israel's defeat and the subsequent destruction of the temple at Shiloh.[218] At that sanctuary, YHWH was the supreme deity, firmly enthroned on the cherubim as divine king, and creator who gave fecundity to his people and fertility to the land. But Qiryat-Ye'arim was a different reality. Although the ark was somehow returned to the Israelites, their political future was still in question. Their god was more like the feisty young god Ba'l, fighting for dominion against the forces of chaos that constantly threatened to oust him.

---

216. See n. 2 above.

217. So R. G. Boling and G. E. Wright, *Joshua* (AB 6; Garden City, New York: Doubleday, 1982) 369.

218. The destruction is not mentioned in 1 Samuel, but Jer 7:12-15 and Ps 78:60-61 suggest it and recent excavations confirm it.

## C. SUMMARY OF RESULTS

At Shiloh, YHWH had come to be identified with 'Ēl, the supreme deity of the Canaanite pantheon. Personal names like Elqanah, Yeroḥam (Yeraḥme'el), and Samuel provide some evidence of Elism at Shiloh in the eleventh century. The deity was also known by the epithet YHWH Ṣĕḇā'ôṯ, an epithet of the deity as the victorious divine warrior, creator, and king. Like 'Ēl, YHWH appeared to people in dreams and spoke through intermediaries. He responded to the plight of the barren Hannah, granting fecundity as 'Ēl did to Danel and Kirta. Like 'Ēl, YHWH was depicted at once as an itinerant, tent-dwelling deity and a king enthroned in his palace. The image of YHWH as 'Ēl is in accord with the biblical and archaeological indications that Shiloh functioned as a central sanctuary in that period. In any case, the association of YHWH with 'Ēl, the Most High god of the Canaanite pantheon, is found already at Shiloh, as suggested by the name of the High Priest, Eli. That tradition was not bestowed on Israelite religion from a putative cult of 'Ēl 'Elyôn of the Jebusite sanctuary, as is often supposed.

At Qiryat-Ye'arim, however, the Elistic model of YHWH seems to have given way to the model of the deity as the feisty warrior-god, Ba'l. The appropriation of the Ba'l myth, again, reflects the socio-political realities, for the dominant position of the deity at Shiloh had been betrayed by the ignominy of defeat. The ark was captured by the Philistines and the sanctuary at Shiloh was destroyed. The supremacy of the Israelite god was called into question. Hence the elaborate story of the adventures of the ark, which is based on the mythic pattern of the rise of Ba'l from defeat to victory. Like Ba'l, the ark suffered an initial set-back. The demise of the ark was marked by mourning, even as the defeat of Ba'l was marked by mourning. The absence of the ark prompted the lament "Where is Glory?" (*'Îḵāḇôḏ*), even as the absence of Ba'l led 'Anat to ask "Where is Ba'l?" (*'iy b'l*). But as Ba'l eventually triumphed over his enemies, so the presence of the ark in the temple established the dominion of YHWH over Dagon.

There is insufficient information to allow the historian to know how the tradition of YHWH as 'Ēl was handled along with the tradition of YHWH as Ba'l. The ark narrative of 1 Samuel 4-6 gives no hint of YHWH being associated with 'Ēl. This is in stark contrast to the evidence of Elism at Shiloh, as evident in 1 Samuel 1-3. The story of the ark's fate among the Philistines is clearly analogous to the myth of Ba'l. Obviously both traditions were known to the Israelites at Qiryat-Ye'arim. But the tradition of YHWH as 'Ēl appears to have been suppressed in favor of the myth of Ba'l because the latter mirrored the socio-political realities after the fall of Shiloh more precisely. Despite the triumphalistic tone of the ark narrative, the sojourn of the ark in the relatively obscure site of Qiryat-Ye'arim was an embarrassment for the Israelites. According to biblical traditions, the ark was forgotten (Ps 132:6) and neglected (1 Chron 13:3), and the Israelites "lamented after YHWH" for two decades or so, when the ark was at Qiryat-Ye'arim (1 Sam 7:2). There it remained until David brought it in triumphant procession into Jerusalem.

## CHAPTER TWO

# RELIGIO-POLITICAL DRAMA

The primary account of David's procession of the ark is 2 Samuel 6 which, unlike the ark narrative of 1 Samuel 4-6, is concerned with the presence of the ark in the new monarchical capital of Jerusalem. While the tales of the ark's sojourn at Shiloh and Qiryat-Ye'arim provide an indispensable backdrop for understanding the cognitive matrix of the procession and certain literary allusions in the chapter,[1] recent scholarship is correct in its emphasis on the continuity of 2 Samuel 6 with the preceding and following units of thought. T. N. D. Mettinger, for instance, argues that the chapter belongs to the History of David's Rise (HDR) which, he maintains against Grønbæk and others, does not end in 5:10 but continues through chapter 7.[2] 2 Samuel 6 is not to be lifted from its present literary context, but must be interpreted as a sequel to the victory of YHWH in chapter 5 and preceding the attempt to construct the temple in chapter 7, thus in accordance with ancient Near Eastern mythic pattern of the divine warrior's rise.[3]

---

1. At least to some extent the chapter must have been intended as a necessary conclusion to the adventures of the ark in the narrative of 1 Samuel 4-6. So recently, K. A. D. Smelik, "De intocht van de Ark in Jerusalem," *Amsterdamse Cahiers* 4 (1983) 26-36.

2. *King and Messiah* (ConBibOT 8; Lund: Gleerup, 1976) 33-47. Cf. J. H. Grønbæk, *Die Geschichte vom Aufstieg Davids* (Acta Theologica Danica 10; Copenhagen: Prostant apud Munksgaard, 1971).

3. Cf. T. W. Mann, *Divine Presence and Guidance in Israelite Traditions* (JHNES 9; Baltimore/London: Johns Hopkins University, 1977) 213-214. For the pattern of the conflict myths, see *RSP* III, 233-284 and the literature cited therein.

## A. THE BATTLES

As a prelude to our study of the procession, it is imperative to consider the place of the battles with the Philistines in 2 Sam 5:17-25. This passage is properly to be regarded as "a necessary introduction" to the account of the procession of the ark in 2 Samuel 6.[4] Yet, this text has not usually received due attention, the spotlight being focused on the proverbially impossible capture of Jerusalem (2 Sam 5:6-10). But no battle is reported in the account of the taking of Jerusalem, the Jebusite stronghold that had apparently earned a reputation for its impregnability.[5] Rather, the passage focuses on the Jebusite boast of the city's inviolability, noting only that David took it nevertheless and named it after himself.[6] One might have expected the sensational capture of the city to be followed immediately by the victorious procession into the city. Instead, the passage about the battles with the Philistines is found before the report on the induction of the ark. It is as if the combat element, specifically the combat with the Philistines, had to be introduced to provide the necessary framework to understand the procession.

---

4. McCarter, *II Samuel*, 143. Other scholars note that the word *'ôd* "again" in 6:1 links the transfer of the ark with the victory in chapter 5. So Mettinger, *King and Messiah*, 42.

5. The boast may have been justified, for the stronghold is listed in Josh 15:63 and Judg 1:21 as one of the Canaanite cities that could not be conquered. Indeed, Jerusalem appears to have remained in Jebusite hands until David's conquest of it. See Ishida, *The Royal Dynasties in Ancient Israel*, 118-136.

6. It is probable that the stronghold was taken without a fight. See G. Brunet, "David et le *ṣinnôr*," in *Studies in the Historical Books of the Old Testament* (VTSup 30; ed. J. A. Emerton, Leiden: Brill, 1979) 73-86; S. Bakon, "How David Captured Jerusalem," *Dor le Dor* 15 (1986/87) 43-44. *Contra* V. Scippa, "Davide Conquista Gerusalemme," *Bibbia et Oriente* 27 (1985) 65-76.

The renewed battles with the Philistines immediately recall previous skirmishes, not least of which was the battle that resulted in the ignominious capture of the ark, the destruction of YHWH's temple in Shiloh, and the sojourn of the ark in Qiryat-Ye'arim for twenty years thereafter. The sensational capture of Jerusalem alone appears to have been an insufficient setup for the vindication of YHWH and the triumphant return of the ark from Qiryat-Ye'arim; the decisive victory over the Philistines and their gods had first to be established.

When the Philistines heard that David had been made king, they scattered about (וינטשו) in search of him (2 Sam 5:17-18). The issue is, once again, power and dominion. As expected in a holy war, David sought an oracle from the deity, asking if the enemies would be delivered into his power (*yāḏ*). Then, having received assurance that they would, he fought them at Ba'l-Peraṣim in the Valley of Rephaim, that is, the plain of al-Baq'a, south-west of Jerusalem.[7] There David defeated the Philistines, whereupon he concluded: פרץ יהוה את־איבי לפני כפרץ־מים "YHWH has broken my enemies before me like the breaking of waters."[8]

In the interpretation of this verse, commentators without exception take מים as the subject of פרץ. That is, YHWH's breaking of the Philistines is likened to water breaking through a wall, a fence, a dam, or the like.[9] But פרץ is never

7. Josh 15:8; 18:16; 2 Sam 23:13; 1 Chron 11:15; 14:9.

8. The typical translation of פרץ as "breach" or "break through" is inadequate. The cognate in Arabic means "to cut, slit, smite, or open." W. von Soden (*AHW* II, 832) associates Akkadian *parāṣu* with *parāsu* "to split, sever, divide," a verb used of cosmogonic battles.

9. Thus already Targ. Jon. likens the event in 2 Sam 5:20 to the breaking of a clay vessel that is filled with water. Among the modern commentators, H. W. Hertzberg's imagination is typical: "the water which pours down sweeps through and carries away any obstacles which may be in its path, banks of earth, hedges, walls, even a house built on the

so used in the Hebrew Bible. The verb פרץ regularly pertains to the breaching of walls (e. g., Neh 3:35; Pss 80:13; 89:41), but the subject of the breaching is never water, or any other liquid for that matter.[10]

The translation of this verse cannot be isolated from the remarkably similar reference to the incident at Pereṣ-'Uzzah in 2 Sam 6:8: פרץ יהוה פרץ בעזה, literally, "YHWH broke a breaking on/against 'Uzzah." Both texts are aetiological. David smote his enemies at a location (ויכם שם, 2 Sam 5:20), and so that place was called Ba'l-Peraṣim (קרא שם־המקום ההוא בעל פרצים, 2 Sam 5:20). God smote 'Uzzah at a location (ויכהו שם, 2 Sam 6:7), and so that place was called Pereṣ-'Uzzah (ויקרא למקום ההוא פרץ עזה, 2 Sam 6:8). The similarities are striking:

| | |
|---|---|
| 2 Sam 5:20 | ויכם שם דוד |
| 2 Sam 6:7 | ויכהו שם האלהים |
| 2 Sam 5:20 | פרץ יהוה את־איבי לפני כפרץ מים |
| 2 Sam 6:8 | פרץ יהוה פרץ בעזא |

The meaning of the GN פרץ עזה (Pereṣ-'Uzzah) is clarified in the construction פרץ בעזא "the breaking on/against 'Uzzah"--the preposition ב here indicates that 'Uzzah is the *object* of the breaking, not the subject. As the above juxtaposition of the texts suggests, the construction פרץ מים is analogous to פרץ בעזא "the smiting of Uzzah," supposedly the original meaning of GN פרץ עזה (Pereṣ 'Uzzah). Hence, if עזה in the construction פרץ עזה is the *object* of the smiting, then מים in the phrase פרץ מים must

---

sand." See *I & II Samuel* (OTL; trans. J. S. Bowden; Philadelphia: Westminster, 1964) 274.

10. The closest analogy we have to liquid breaking forth is in Prov 3:10, where we have wine vats bursting forth with new wine (תירוש) and barns being filled with plenty. The image there is not a military or violent one, as is the case with the use of פרץ in 2 Samuel 5.

also be the *object* of the smiting. The Greek rendering of פרץ מים as διακόπτεται ὕδατα, probably "water is broken through," supports this interpretation.[11]

The verb פרץ occurs several times in the Hebrew Bible with YHWH as the subject. It is employed thrice in a manner akin to the usage in the Pereṣ-'Uzzah incident--that is, of God's retribution for failing to observe the boundaries between the sacred and the profane.[12] Related to this is the outbreak (פרץ) of a plague against the Israelites at Ba'l Pe'or (Ps 106:29; cf. Num 25:1-13).[13] YHWH's own people is the object of his breaking in Ps 60:3, and his land is said to have been rent; it quaked and tottered like the enemies of the divine warrior in Canaanite mythology. In 1 Chron 20:37, ships that are bound for Tarshish are destroyed (פרץ) by YHWH and wrecked (וישברו).[14] The verb is attested with the noun פֶּרֶץ in Job 16:14. Here again we note the military language:

---

11. Greek διακόπτω is attested in the active or passive voice; the middle meaning required by the image of water itself breaking through, if correct, would be exceptional. The verb is regularly used in military contexts: e.g., διακόπτειν ὅτῳ ἐντυγχάνοιεν "to cut in pieces whatever they encountered" (Xenophon, *Anabasis* I.viii.10; cf. also *Hist. Graec.* VII.5); διέκοψαν τὴν φάλαγγα τῶν Μακεδόνων "they cut to pieces the Phalanx of the Macedonians" (Plutarch, *Phyrrus* VII.5). The subject of the verb is never water or any other liquid. Interestingly, διακόπτω is used to translate Hebrew חצב "cut down, hew" (Ps 29:7) and נקב "pierce" (Hab 3:14) in connection with the divine warrior's slaying of his mythological enemies.

12. Exod 19:22, 24; 1 Chron 15:13.

13. Cf. Lind's reference to the bubonic plague at Ba'l-Pe'or (Josh 22:17) that may have been connected with the plagues that the Philistines suffered in 1 Samuel 5-6, plagues inflicted by YHWH as divine warrior. See Lind, *Yahweh is a Warrior*, 97.

14. This is reminiscent of YHWH's breaking of Tarshish-bound ships in Ps 48:8.

יפרצני פרץ על־פני־פרץ ירוץ עלי כגבור

He breaks me, breaking upon breaking;[15]
He charges against me like a warrior.

The martial connotation of פרץ must be retained in our translation of 2 Sam 5:20, for the text speaks of the divine warrior in combat. Here the analogy is not with the bursting forth of water, but with the shattering of the unruly waters and watery monsters.[16] This motif is well attested in the Hebrew Bible, although admittedly, not with the verb פרץ. It is attested with the related root פרר in the following text:

אתה פוררת בעזך ים
שׁברת ראשׁי תנינים על־המים
אתה רצצת ראשׁי לויתן
(Ps 74:13-14a)

You have broken Sea with your might,
Shattered the heads of the Dragon on the waters.
You have crushed the heads of Leviathan.

---

15. A. C. M. Blommerde (*Northwest Semitic Grammar and Job* [BibOr 22; Rome: Pontifical Biblical Institute, 1969] 28) follows Dahood in assuming the second פרץ as the conjunction *pa* + the inf. abs. *rōṣ*, but we should probably take על־פני as an idiom like Akk. *ana pāni* "in addition to" (so É. Dhorme, *A Commentary on the Book of Job* [trans. H. Knight; New York: Nelson, 1984] 237; R. Gordis, The Book of Job [New York: Jewish Theological Seminary, 1978] 177). Thus in *EA* 189.4 one reads: *7-šu a-na pa-ni 7-ta-an am-qut* "I fall seven times and seven times more."

16. On the containment of unruly waters and the defeat of sea-monsters, see U. Cassuto, *Biblical and Oriental Studies* II (trans. I. Abrahams; Jerusalem: Magnes, 1975) 69-109; P. Reymond, *L'eau, sa vie, et sa signification dans l'Ancien Testament* (VTSup 6; Leiden: Brill, 1958) 182-189; *RSP* III, 369-383 and the literature cited therein.

The language in this passage is reminiscent of two texts of divine combat in Ugaritic mythology. The first concerns ‘Anat's battle with Yamm and his entourage:

lmḫšt . mdd ’il ym .
lklt . nhr . ’il . rbm
l’ištbm . tnn . ’ištm[l]h[17]
mḫšt . bṯn . ‘qltn
šlyṭ . d. šb‘t . r’ašm
(*KTU* 1.3.III.38-42)

I have smitten the beloved of ’Ēl, Sea;
I have annihilated the River of ’Ēl, the Mighty.
I snared[18] the Dragon, I trapped (?) it.
I smote the slithery Serpent[19]
Šlyṭ, the one with seven heads.[20]

---

17. *KTU* has a word divider after *m*, but D. Pardee ("Will the Dragon Never be Muzzled?" *UF* 16 [1984] 253-254) denies that the divider is there. So he reconstructs *’ištm[d]h*, citing *šmd* "to destroy" in Hebrew, Aramaic, and Akkadian. But *šmd* never occurs in the infixed-t stems in Hebrew or Akkadian. Aramaic has forms in Nt, but these are reflexives. I would read, tentatively, tD 1 cs of *šml* (Herdner, Virolleaud and many others also read *l* here), a verb related to Arabic *šamala* "to envelope, enclose" (cf. Hebrew שמלה).

18. The verb is related to *šbm* in *KTU* 1.83.7-9: *ảnbtm tn<!>n lšbm tšt*, for which, see S. E. Loewenstamm, "Anat's Victory Over the Tunannu," *JSS* 29 (1975) 22-27. But the etymology of *šbm* is debated (J. Barr, "Ugaritic and Hebrew ‘šbm’?" *JSS* 18 [1973] 17-39; M. Dietrich and O. Loretz, "*šb*, *šbm* und *udn* im Kontext von KTU 1.3 III 35b-IV 4 und KTU 1.82.8," *UF* 14 [1982] 77-78).

19. Cf. Isa 27:1 and see U. Cassuto, *The Goddess Anath* (trans. I. Abrahams; Jerusalem: Magnes, 1971) 49-50.

20. Most scholars connect *Šlyṭ* with the root *šlṭ* "to be powerful," while others assume a *šqṭl* form of a middle weak root. See J. C. de Moor, "Contributions to the Ugaritic Lexicon," *UF* 11 (1979) 641 and the literature cited therein.

The second Ugaritic passage is of Ba'l's combat with the watery monsters:

ktmḫṣ . ltn . bθn . brḥ
tkly . bθn . 'qltn .
šlyṭ . d . šb't . r'ašm
(*KTU* 1.5.I.1–3)

When you smote Lôtān,
the fleeing serpent,[21]
Annihilated the slithery serpent,
Šlyṭ, the one with seven heads.

A close parallel to the latter is in the little Apocalypse of Isaiah, where YHWH is expected to smite "Leviathan the fleeing serpent" (לויתן נחש ברח), also called "Leviathan the slithery serpent" (לויתן נחש עקלתון).[22] But elsewhere in the Hebrew Bible, it is simply the waters that are smitten and flee (Pss 77:16; 114:3, 5). Most frequently, in the hymnic texts from the south, the cosmogonic *Chaoskampf* is politicized and transformed into a *Völkerkampf*, where the enemies of the deity are not just cosmic chaos but YHWH's historical

---

21. The translation of *brḫ* is disputed. C. Rabin ("BĀRI$^{A}$H," *JTS* 47 [1946] 38–41) argues that the basic meaning of *brḫ* is "to twist, to be hairless, smooth." He cites Akkadian *barāḫu, barīḫu, burāḫu*, all of which are, however, of uncertain meaning. Gordon (*UT* §19.515) and Aistleitner (*WUS*, 577) among others, point to Arabic *barḥ* to suggest "evil" as the appropriate translation. Most scholars, however, assume the meaning "to flee"--a meaning present in Hebrew (Judg 9:21; 1 Sam 19:12; 22:20; Isa 22:3; etc; cf. *HALAT*, 149), Phoenician (*KAI* 1.2; 89.4; see *DISO*, 43 on *brḥ I*), and indeed in Ugaritic (*KTU* 1.19.III.48, 55). So K. Aartun, "Beiträge zum ugaritischen Lexikon," *WO* 4 (1969) 282–284.

22. Isa 27:1, for which, see *RSP* III, 33–36 and the bibliography cited therein. 1QIsa[a] has בורח "fleeing" (cf. LXX φεύγοντα).

enemies.[23] Thus, the enemies of YHWH (that is, the enemies of Israel) are said to be smitten, even as the unruly waters and watery monsters are smitten in mythology. This *Völkerkampf* motif is one of the hallmarks of the Zion tradition, and it is nowhere more blatantly stated than in the following oracle of Isaiah:[24]

הוי המון עמים רבים
כהמות ימים יהמיון
ושאון < >[25] ישאון לאמים
כשאון מים רבים ישאון
(Isa 17:12-13a)

Ho! The thunder of many peoples--
Like the thundering of the seas do they thunder!
The people roar a roar;
Like the mighty waters do they roar!

---

23. See T. N. D. Mettinger, "Fighting the Powers of Chaos and Hell--Towards the Biblical Portrait of God," *ST* 39 (1985) 27-28.

24. I cannot accept the contention of G. Wanke (*Die Zionstheologie der Korachiten* [BZAW 97; Berlin: Töpelmann, 1966] 73-92) that the *Völkerkampf* motif in Zion theology originated only in the post-exilic period. See the critiques of R. de Vaux, "Jerusalem et les prophètes," *RB* 73 (1966) 508-509 and J. J. M. Roberts, "The Davidic Origin of the Zion Tradition," *JBL* 92 (1973) 338-339.

25. Omit לאמים כשאון מים כבירים in MT as a variant. The choice of כבירים may have been influenced by the expression מים כבירים in 28:2. LXX has καὶ νῶτος ἐθνῶν πολλῶν ὡς ὕδωρ ἠχήσει, reflecting Hebrew ושאון עמים רבים כמים ישאון (ἐθνῶν πολλῶν precisely repeats the same expression in 12a), but it is perhaps a paraphrase of ושאון ישאון לאמים. Many commentators prefer to omit 13a, but this makes nonsense of the prosody. H. Wildberger (*Jesaja* II [BKAT 10; Neukirchen-Vluyn: Neukirchener, 1978] 664) reckons with the metre, but comes up with a rather awkward translation: "und die Gebraus von Nationen, wie das Brausen."

Mythological allusions are contained in delightful word play. The nations that besieged Jerusalem (*'ammîm*) are likened to the waters that threatened to inundate the earth (*yammîm*; *máyim*). But the *'ammîm rabbîm* will be silenced as surely as the *máyim rabbîm*.[26] The nations would be rebuked, even as the chaotic waters in mythology are rebuked by the divine warrior. And the enemies will flee from the warrior in history as in myth.

It is not impossible that Isaiah remembered the battles with Philistines in Davidic times as a decisive victory for the divine warrior. He speaks of the annihilation of YHWH's enemies in terms of a harvest at the Valley of Rephaim (Isa 17:4–6). He also refers to YHWH's rising up in battle as on "Mount Peraṣim" (Isa 28:21) and how the warrior will cause quaking as in "the valley in Gibeon."[27]

As in the texts of Zion, so in 2 Samuel 5, the historical victory of Israel is seen as a victory for YHWH. The vanquished Philistines abandoned their divine images--"their gods," as the Greek translators and the Chronicler (1 Chron 14:12) would have it. The Israelites carried away the Philistine images, thus reversing the result of the battle near Ebenezer where the ark was carried away by the Philistines.

Before a second battle at the Valley of Rephaim, David again sought divine approval for battle. The divine reply is suggestive:

---

26. The equation is even more explicit in Greek: ὡς ὕδωρ πολὺ ἔθνη πολλά.

27. Reading יַרְגִּז against יִרְגַּז in MT. The verb רגז regularly refers to the convulsion of nature in the face of the divine warrior's march (2 Sam 22:8 // Ps 18:8; Isa 5:25; 64:1; Joel 2:10; Pss 77:17, 19) or to the trembling of the nations because YHWH sides with his people (Exod 15:14; Deut 2:25; Ps 99:1; Jer 33:9; Joel 2:1; Mic 7:17; Hab 3:7). With YHWH as subject, the verb never occurs in the G-stem; it is always in the causative, with nations (Isa 23:11; Jer 50:34) or heaven and earth (Isa 13:13; Job 9:6) as the objects of YHWH's shaking.

> You shall not go up. Go around to their rear and go to them opposite Beka'im.[28] When you hear a sound of marching (קול צעדה) above the *bākā'*-trees,[29] get set![30] For then YHWH will go forth before you to smite the Philistine camp.
>
> (2 Sam 5:23–24)

Most striking in this oracle is the allusion to YHWH's celestial army. John S. Holladay includes this oracle in the "holy-war tradition," along with references to the heavenly hosts in the Elisha cycle (2 Kgs 6:11ff.) and the Song of Deborah (Judg 5:20).[31] It is reminiscent of Joshua's encounter with the שר־צבא־יהוה "the commander of YHWH's army" in a prelude to holy war (Josh 5:13–15). The celestial host is

---

28. MT has no definite article with בכאים, but cf. v 24 and 1 Chron 14:14–15. The site may be identified with the Valley of the Baka' (עמק הבכא) through which pilgrims processed *en route* to Zion to celebrate the theophany and enthronement of YHWH *Ṣĕḇā'ôṯ* (Ps 84:7). Beka'im/Baka' was probably named for the abundance of *bākā'*-trees there.

29. McCarter (*II Samuel*, 152) emends MT קול צעדה בראשי הבכאים to קול <ה>סערה באשרי הבכאים "the sound of the wind in the asherahs (sacred groves) of Bachaim." But this reconstruction is problematic for several reasons: (a) it ignores the parallel in 1 Chron 14:15 and the evidence of the versions there, (b) the expression "asherah of GN" is without parallel anywhere, (c) the retroversion of the Greek τοῦ ἄλσους or τῶν ἀλσῶν is uncertain. The traditional understanding of the *bĕḵā'îm* as trees of some sort (so already Targ. Jon. reads אילניא) must be retained.

30. The meaning of תחרץ here is "to be ready (cf. Akk. *ḫarāṣu*) for battle." Hence the Chronicler (1 Chron 14:15) paraphrased: תצא במלחמה "you shall go forth into battle" (cf. *inter alia*, LXX$^{L}$).

31. "Assyrian Statecraft and the Prophets of Israel," *HTR* 63 (1970) 33 n. 21.

gathered at the command of "YHWH of Hosts" to fight the forces of chaos. The command to wait for divine accompaniment in our passage also recalls the battle of the Israelites with the Amalekites, which the Israelites lost because YHWH was not among them and the ark did not depart from their camp (Num 14:41–44). The context, then, is clearly the holy war, with YHWH taking the lead in combat. Moreover, as Miller has observed, the march of the divine warrior is suggested by the vocabulary.[32] The root צעד is typically used of the deity's advance to battle in Judg 5:4; Ps 68:8; Hab 3:12; Isa 63:1,[33] whereas יצא functions the same way in Judg 5:4; Ps 68:8; Hab 3:13; Zech 14:3. When used in tandem, צעד and יצא *always* concern the divine warrior's advance.

So David acted as YHWH had instructed, and he defeated the Philistines "from Geba to Gezer" (2 Sam 5:25).[34] The narrator understood the victory to be decisive and complete. If there had been any doubt about the end of Philistine hegemony over Israelite territories, that issue is settled once and for all. Israel had come full circle in their encounter with the Philistines. The expected smiting of the Philistines in combat at Ebenezer–Aphek (1 Samuel 4), which did not materialize, is now accomplished under David. The story of YHWH's defeat of Dagon (1 Samuel 5–6) is given political and historical substance on the eve of YHWH's entry into Jerusalem. Not only in myth, but also in history, the divine warrior had decisively defeated his enemies. YHWH had triumphed in his battle with the unruly forces of chaos.

---

32. *The Divine Warrior in Early Israel*, 132.

33. Emending MT צעה with most commentators.

34. Most commentators follow LXX and 1 Chron 14:16 to read גבעון (Gibeon) instead of גבע (Geba), but for a defense of the reading in MT, see A. Demsky, "Geba, Gibeah, and Gibeon--an Historico-Geographical Riddle," *BASOR* 212 (1973) 26–31.

B. THE VICTORY CELEBRATION

The defeat of the Philistines was properly followed by a victory parade. Once again (עוד), David gathered[35] all the elite troops of Israel--thirty thousand of them (את־כל־בחור בישראל שלשים אלף). The language is of the mustering of troops for warfare, suggesting a continuation of the combat scene from the previous unit of thought--only now the advance of YHWH with his troops would be dramatized in the victory parade. It is perhaps no coincidence, too, that the vocabulary is reminiscent of Saul's mustering of "three thousand elite troops from all Israel" (שלשת אלפים איש בחור מכל־ישראל) in pursuit of David (1 Sam 24:3). But now, David the fugitive was in control of Israel's elite troops--only he had ten-fold more at his command. And the narrator adds that "all the people were with him" (6:2). Furthermore, it should be noted that the situation here reverses the tragedy in 1 Samuel 4. Defeated at Ebenezer-Aphek, the Israelites were scattered and *thirty thousand* fell; but now they are triumphant and *thirty thousand* are mustered again.

The contingent brought the ark from Qiryat-Ye'arim, here called Ba'lah of Judah.[36] The name of the ark again recalls the battle near Ebenezer-Aphek and brings to mind images of YHWH's role as the triumphant warrior-king at Shiloh. The connection is deliberate.[37] The procession will dramatize the triumphant return, the ascension of the divine warrior from Qiryat-Ye'arim to his rightful place as king.

So the ark was mounted on a new cart (2 Sam 6:3-4).[38] One is reminded here of the animal-drawn carts that were

35. Assuming with the versions that וַיֹּסֶף (presumably for וַיֹּאסֶף) in MT is a misinterpretation of וַיֶּאֱסֹף.

36. See Chapter One, n. 2. above.

37. See A. Strivoski, "The History of the Name Ṣĕḇā'ôt in the Book of Samuel," *Beth Mikra* 49 (1972) 183-192.

38. Omitting (with LXX and 4QSam$^a$) חדשה וישאהו מבית אבינדב אשר בגבעה from the end of v 3 on as dittography.

used for the procession of the divine statue in Mesopotamia.[39] In particular, Ningirsu the storm-god is said to have had a war-chariot which Gudea was ordered to build and then to bring in joyous procession into the temple, celebrating the kingship of the god.[40] The procedure, moreover, echoes the return of the ark from Philistine territory in 1 Samuel 6. Smitten by the plagues because of presence of the ark, the Philistines asked how it might be returned "to its place" (למקומו, 1 Sam 6:2). Accordingly, they were instructed to place the ark on a "new cart" (עגלה חדשה) to be drawn by animals that have never been yoked (1 Sam 6:7). But, whereas in the ark narrative of 1 Samuel the ark was ultimately brought *to* "the house of Abinadab on the hill" (1 Sam 7:1), in 2 Samuel 6 it is led *from* the same "house of Abinadab on the hill,"[41] accompanied by ʻUzza and ʼAḥyo (or "his brother[s]"),[42] "the sons of Abinadab." And so the ark was eventually brought into Jerusalem and put "in its place" (במקומו, 2 Sam 6:17). The account of the victory procession recalls the earlier return of the ark from Philistine territory (1 Samuel 6). The victory over the Philistines and their gods, which was told and retold in the ark narrative of Qiryat-Yeʻarim (1 Samuel 4–6) and given substance at Baʻl-Peraṣim, is now dramatized in a triumphant parade. But the procession also underscores the

39. See A. Salonen, "Prozessioneswagen der babylonischen Götter," *StudOr* 13 (1946) 3–10.

40. Gudea Cylinder A, VI.14–VII.30. See A. Falkenstein and W. von Soden, *Sumerische und akkadische Hymnen und Gebete* (Die Bibliothek der alten Welt; Zürich: Artemis, 1953) 143–145. The procession of David has already been compared with the politically significant journey of Ningirsu to Lagash by Mann (*Divine Presence and Guidance*, 216–218) and Ahlström ("The Travels of the Ark: A Religio-Political Composition," 147–149.

41. The hill (גבעה) here is probably to be identified with גבעת קרית <י>ערים of Josh 18:28 (LXX).

42. LXX has οἱ ἀδελφοί (i.e., Heb. אחיו), prompting many commentators to to read אֶחָיו instead of אַחְיוֹ in MT. But MT also has PN אַחְיוֹ in 1 Chron 8:14, 31; 9:37.

dawn of a new era for the ark. It was taken from the temporary and relatively obscure sanctuary in Qiryat-Ye'arim to David's newly won mount.

According to the text, "all the house of Israel" (כל־בית ישׂראל) revelled (משׂחקים) before YHWH.[43] J. M. Sasson has argued that the term משׂחקים means "play-acting," or the like.[44] He compares the activity with the command performance by Samson before the Philistines (Judg 16:25-26), the wrestling contest between the followers of Joab and Abner (2 Sam 2:12-17), and the dancing in the golden calf episode (Exod 32:6). But one may be even more specific about the nature of the performance in 2 Samuel 6.

In an earlier victory parade, again celebrating David's defeat of the Philistines, dancers came forth from the cities to meet the victor in joy, with timbrels and lutes (1 Sam 18:6-7). The women, called המשׂחקות, chanted:

הכה שׂאול באלפו
ודוד ברבבתיו
(1 Sam 18:7)

Saul has defeated his thousands,
And David, his myriads.

---

43. McCarter (*II Samuel*, 163), citing LXX and 4QSam[a], reads כל בני ישׂראל instead of כל בית ישׂראל per MT. But the latter occurs in 1 Sam 7:2. The ark sojourned in Qiryat-Ye'arim for twenty years and all Israel mourned for it. In spite of the triumphalistic theological claims of the ark narrative in 1 Samuel, the tragedy of the ark's demise could not be forgotten. Qiryat-Ye'arim remained only nominally in Israelite hands. Thus the mourning of "all the house of Israel." But with the decisive victory of David "from Geba to Gezer," and with the transfer of the ark from its place of sojourn, mourning is turned to rejoicing. So "all the house of Israel" now revel in the triumphant return of the ark.

44. "The Worship of the Golden Calf," in *Orient and Occident* (Fs. C. H. Gordon; AOAT 22; Neukirchen-Vluyn: Neukirchener, 1973) 155-156.

Although interpreted in its present context as a taunt of Saul, it is likely that in the original couplet the object of derision was not Saul but the Philistines. "Thousands" and "myriads" constituted a fixed pair in Canaanite poetry; they were never meant to be contrastive. The original couplet must have been a part of a victory song in praise of Israel's leaders, Saul and David alike. But in the context of 1 Samuel 18, it appears that Saul's paranoia had prompted the distortion of the parallelism; a song of victory over the Philistines was jealously interpreted as a comparison with a political rival.[45]

The association of שׂחק with victory is evident in a promise of a new procession to Zion that will mark the end of the exile:[46]

עוד תעדי תפיך
ויצאת במחול משחקים
(Jer 31:4b)

Once again, you shall parade
(with) your timbrels;[47]
You shall go forth in the dance of revellers.

In Zechariah 8, we have an oracle of devastated Jerusalem brought back to life as YHWH delivers his people from their enemies once and for all. The text speaks of the return of the divine warrior (YHWH *Ṣĕḇa'ōṯ*) to Mount Zion

---

45. Cf. Gevirtz, *Patterns in the Early Poetry of Israel*, 14–24.

46. On laughter and rejoicing in cultic contexts, see D. W. Harvey, "Rejoice Not, O Israel!" in *Israel's Prophetic Heritage* (Fs. J. Muilenburg; ed. B. W. Anderson and W. Harrelson; New York: Harper and Row, 1962) 116–127.

47. MT "you shall adorn timbrels" is strange and the parallelism with יצא makes no sense. I take the verb to be related to Syriac and Aramaic *'dy* "cross over, pass" (used in the Targ. to translate Hebrew *'br*), and *'dw* in Ethiopic and Arabic. The root is found in Job 28:8 where it parallels *drk*.

amidst revelry (משחקים) in the streets (v 5).

In conjunction with the role of human participants in the revelry celebrating YHWH's victory, one should note also YHWH's own laughter at the expense of his enemies. The motif of YHWH's laughter is evident in Ps 59:5-9. Here, again, we find the *Völkerkampf* motif. YHWH is urged to rise up (עורה) against the nations, who yelp (יהמו) like dogs that prowled/surrounded (ויסובבו) the city. But, says the psalmist, YHWH would laugh (תשחק) at the nations and mock them.

Elsewhere in the Psalter, the raging and plotting of the nations are ridiculed:

יושב בשמים ישחק
אדני ילעג־למו
אז ידבר אלימו באפו
ובחרונו יבהלמו
ואני נסכתי מלכי
על־ציון הר־קדשי
(Ps 2:4-6)

The one enthroned in heaven laughs;
Adonay mocks them.
Then he speaks to them in his anger,
and in his rage he terrifies them.
"I, I have installed my king
Upon Zion, my holy mountain!"

The connection of laughter and revelry with victory in divine combat is evident in Ugaritic, as it is in Hebrew.[48] Thus, following the report of ʻAnat's destruction of her enemies in combat, we find her marching home to her palace (*KTU* 1.3.II.17-18). The text says "she was not satisfied with her fighting in the valley (*bʻmq*), her cutting down between the two cities" (lines 19-20). So the battle continued in some

48. Cf. H. H. Hvidberg, *Weeping and Laughter in the Old Testament* (Leiden: Brill, 1962).

kind of ritual, which was apparently dramatized by the arranging of tables and chairs. Then:

> m'id . tmtḫṣn . wt'n
> tḫtṣb . wtḥdy 'nt
> tǵdd . kbdh . bṣḥq[49] .
> yml'u lbh . bšmḫt .
> kbd . 'nt tšyt .
>
> (*KTU* 1.3.II.23-27)

> Vigorously she fought and chanted;
> 'Anat battled and looked.
> Her liver swelled with *laughter*,
> Her heart was filled with joy,
> 'Anat's liver, with victory.

'Anat's laughter and rejoicing accompanied the ritual combat celebrating her victory over her enemies. She fought till she was satisfied with her battle "in the house/temple" and "between the tables" (lines 29-30). Revelry (*ṣḥq*) followed the defeat of the enemies in battle.

In another tablet, 'Anat petitioned 'Ēl to have a house built for victorious Ba'l.[50] When her request was granted she rejoiced (*šmḫ*) and laughed (*ṣḥq*); she stomped her feet, making the earth quake (*KTU* 1.4.V.20, 26). She marched toward the "height of Ṣaphon" to bring the good news to Ba'l that a temple would be built for him and to call Ba'l to summon a caravan (*ḫrn*) to his house. Thereupon, the victorious Ba'l rejoiced (*šmḫ*) and called the caravan to his house, where a banquet was prepared for the gods (*KTU* 1.4.V.35-48). The revelry of 'Anat was part of the

49. There is no semantic difference between *śḥq* and *ṣḥq* in Hebrew, as evident in the interchangeability of PN יצחק/ישחק and the verbs ויצחק/וישחק (Judg. 16:25). The sibilant *ś* is simply assimilated to the two emphatic radicals. Cf. the shift of *t* > *ṭ* in נצטרק ( < *נצתרק < נתצרק).

50. *KTU* 1.4.IV.

victory celebration following Ba'l's defeat of his enemies and leading to the divine banquet on Ba'l's mount of victory.

Suggestively, the revelry (משחקים) in 2 Samuel 6 follows the victory of the divine warrior over his enemies and anticipates the establishing of an abode for the deity in the newly won mount where a feast was hosted. It was a victory celebration, accompanied by all kinds of musical instruments and, perhaps, incense as well.[51]

## C. THE SMITING OF 'UZZAH

According to present account, an accident happened that caused the procession to be temporarily aborted. The party came to גרן נכון, "a prepared threshing floor."[52] Here an

---

51. MT of v 5 has בכל עצי ברושים, a notorious crux. Following LXX, 4QSam[a] and 1 Chron 13:8, most commentators emend the text to read בכל ע<זו> ובשירים "with all <his> might and with songs," or the like. McCarter (*II Samuel*, 163), citing 2 Chron 30:21, reconstructs בכל<י> ע<ז> "with sonorous instruments." But עז in the *Vorlage(n)* of these sources clearly anticipates v 14, and MT is *lectio difficilior*. Thus, a few scholars adhere to the interpretation of D. Kimḥi of עצי ברושים as instruments of pine-wood (clappers?). So J. A. Soggin, "'Wacholderholz' 2 Sam VI 5a gleich 'Schlaghölzer,' 'Klappern'?" *VT* 14 (1964) 374–377; A. Cooper, "The Life and Times of King David According to the Book of Psalms," in *The Poet and the Historian* (HSS 26; ed. R. E. Friedman; Chico, California: Scholars, 1983) 127. This is purely conjectural, however. In my judgment, the qualification בכל both isolates עצי ברושים from the rest of the list and makes it unlikely that it refers to a musical instrument. Rather, I would take ברושים as a cognate of Akkadian *burāšu* "crushed wood" or wood shavings used in rituals, particularly in connection with the *akītu* festival. See the references in *CAD* 2, 327–328.

52. My translation follows Targ. and Syr. in assuming נכון to be a participle. The textual witnesses are confusing. 4QSam[a] has either נורן or נירון; LXX[B] νωδαβ; 1 Chron 13:9

accident supposedly happened when 'Uzzah stretched out his hand to secure the ark when the calf drawing the cart stumbled. The event is portrayed as a historical incident: the violation of a taboo resulted in death.[53] But it is difficult to know precisely what happened during the procession, to extricate any historical kernel from the narrative.

The text says that "YHWH was angry with 'Uzzah" (ויחר־אף יהוה בעזה, v 7), and so the deity smote him. The

---

כידון (cf. Josephus, *Ant.* VII.8). The problem exists probably because *kap* and *nūn* were sometimes confused (being graphically similar in various periods), as were *wāw* and *yōḏ*. See F. M. Cross, Jr., "The Development of the Jewish Scripts," in *The Bible and the Ancient Near East* (Fs. W. F. Albright; ed. G. E. Wright; Winona Lake, Indiana: Eisenbrauns, 1979) 133–202, *passim*. If the word is a PN, as is most commonly assumed, then the threshing floor must have been fairly well known. Besides this text, there are two threshing floors that are sometimes thought to be associated with proper names: (1) גרן האטד, Gen 50:10–11, and (2) גרן (ה)ארונה, 2 Sam 24:16, 18 (cf. LXX$^L$ of 2 Sam 6:6). In the first instance, האטד cannot be a personal name; the definite article suggests the translation "The Threshing Floor of the Bramble," or the like. As for ארונה, it has often been noted that the word is related to Hurrian *iwirne* "lord, chief" or Hittite *arawa(nni)* "free person, aristocrat." So it is הארונה (!) "the *Arawna*" in 2 Sam 24:16. See I. J. Gelb, P. M. Purves and A. A. McRae, *Nuzi Personal Names* (OIP 57; Chicago: University of Chicago, 1943) 210; H. B. Rosen, "Arawna--nom Hittite?" *VT* 5 (1955) 318–320; Gröndahl, *Die Personennamen der Texte aus Ugarit*, 224–225, 272; N. Wyatt, "'Araunah the Jebusite' and the Throne of David," *ST* 39 (1985) 39–53. If האטד and (ה)ארונה are not personal names, "the threshing floor of PN" in 2 Sam 6:6 would be unique in the Bible. Indeed, as a PN נכון is without parallel in Semitic onomastica.

53. Cf. the warning in the Instruction of Any: "Do not question his images, do not accost him when he appears, do not jostle him in order to carry him...." (M. Lichtheim, *Ancient Egyptian Literature* II (Berkeley: University of California, 1976) 41.

passage is closely tied to the battle of Ba'l-Peraṣim. There YHWH smote the Philistines like "the breaking of Waters," and so the place was called Ba'l-Peraṣim "Ba'l/Lord of the Breaking" (i.e., Ba'l = YHWH); here YHWH smote 'Uzzah (ויכהו), and so the place of the smiting was called Pereṣ-'Uzzah, "the Breaking of 'Uzzah" (2 Sam 6:7). The connection of this "breaking" with the "breaking of the Waters" at Ba'l-Peraṣim cannot be missed. This "breaking" is analogous to that "breaking." Thus, if the mythological combat of the divine warrior lies in the background of the historical battle at Ba'l-Peraṣim, perhaps one ought to consider the possibility of a dramatization of that combat--indeed, the mythological combat--in this incident. Such reenactments of cosmogonic battles were carried out in state sponsored rituals in Mesopotamia. Some of these are explicated in a series of Standard Babylonian explanatory texts.[54] In some cases the role of the divine warrior is played by the king, and the defeat of the enemy is dramatized by the slaughter of animals, by the crushing, winnowing and scattering of grain, and the like.[55]

In this connection, it is difficult to resist comparison with the agricultural process through which vanquished Mot, the enemy of Ba'l, was subjected by 'Anat:

---

54. See A. Livingstone, *Mystical and Mythological Explanatory Works of Assyrian and Babylonian Scholars* (Oxford: Clarendon, 1986) 115-170.

55. So a sheep roasting in the oven symbolized the burning of Kingu (*K* 3476, obv. 6), an ox and sheep thrown alive to the ground represented Kingu and his seven sons (*VAT* 8917, rev. 17-19), a dove was used to represent the splitting of Tiamat (*VAT* 8917, rev. 17-19), the binding of reeds is equated with the binding of rebellious enemies (*VAT* 10099), the splitting of *zarê* (crushing of seeds?) is called the stirring of battle (*VAT* 9947, obv. 10), and so forth. See Livingstone, *Mystical and Mythological Explanatory Works*, *passim*.

t'iḫd bn . 'ilm . mt .
bḥrb tbq'nn .
bḫθr . tdrynn .
b'išt . tšrpnn .
brḥm . tṭḥnn .
bšd tdr'nn .
š'irh . lt'ikl 'ṣrm [.]
mnth . ltkl npr[m .]
(*KTU* 1.6.II.30-37)

She seized the son of 'Ēl, Mot:
With the sword she split him,
With the sieve she winnowed him,
With the fire she burnt him,
With the millstone she ground him,
In the field she did scatter him.
The birds indeed ate his flesh;
The fowls indeed devoured his parts.

While some details of the Ugaritic ritual remain obscure,[56] the cultic *Sitz im Leben* of the text can hardly be disputed. The passage reflects a cultic drama performed to celebrate the victory of life over death in the agricultural cycle of the year. In a later scene, Ba'l himself destroys his enemies in mythological combat.[57] Although Mot was supposedly already dismembered and crushed, he lamented that it was because of Ba'l that he was subjected to the process: he was burnt, ground, winnowed, and scattered in the sea.[58]

---

56. See de Moor, *The Seasonal Pattern*, 212-215; idem, *An Anthology of Religious Texts from Ugarit* (NISABA 16; Leiden: Brill, 1987) 89-90; Margalit, *A Matter of Life and Death*, 159-162.

57. *KTU* 1.6.V.10-19. See Chapter One.

58. Cf. the ritual enactment of Mot's demise in *KTU* 1.23.9-11, for which, see T. H. Gaster, "A Canaanite Ritual Drama: The Spring Festival at Ugarit," *JAOS* 66 (1946) 49-76.

A related ritual may be present in the golden calf episode in Exodus 32. There it is Moses who acted on behalf of YHWH: he became angry (ויחר־אף), took the calf that the Israelites had made and burnt (שׂרף) it with fire, ground (ויטחן) it to powder, winnowed (ויזר)[59] it over the water, and made the people drink it (vv 19–20).[60] Thus, the golden calf was ceremonially destroyed, just like the mythological enemies of ʻAnat and Baʻl.[61]

In light of this parallel, I am inclined to regard the reference to YHWH's anger (ויחר־אף יהוה) in 2 Sam 6:7 as authentic to the ritual.[62] The element of divine anger understandably belongs with the motif of the divine warrior's advance against the enemies. Thus one reads of YHWH's anger (חרה, אף, עברה) against River // Sea (Hab 3:8, cf. v 12), and his anger (אף) against the "helpers of Rahab" (Job 9:13). Nature rocked and quaked at YHWH's advance because of his anger (אף) and the rebuke of the warrior comes from the breath of his nostrils (אף).[63]

It is possible, then, that a mock battle took place at the

59. Hebrew *zry* corresponds to Ugaritic *dry*.

60. See S. E. Loewenstamm, "The Making and Destruction of the Golden Calf," *Bib* 48 (1967) 481–490.

61. The watery enemies of the divine warrior are, likewise, crushed and given as food for scavengers (Ps 74:13–14).

62. *Contra* J. B. Peckham, *The Composition of the Deuteronomistic History* (HSM 35; Atlanta: Scholars, 1985) 93 n. 183. I should add that apart from the aetiology in v 8 (ויקרא למקום ההוא פרץ עזה) there is no evidence of deuteronomistic editing in this passage (vv 6–11). The ark is called ארון האלהים (vv 6, 7) and ארון יהוה (vv 9, 10), not ארון הברית or ארון ברית יהוה/האלהים as Dtr would have preferred (see Chapter One n. 4), and the idea of the ark residing in the house of ʻObed-'Edom the Gittite, bringing blessings to that house, is surely not deuteronomistic.

63. Ps 18:8, 16 // 2 Sam 22:8, 16.

prepared threshing-floor (גרן נכון).[64] But if such a drama lies behind the present narrative, it has been substantially forgotten or suppressed. Instead, the text focuses on the transfer of the custody of the ark from the family of Abinadab. The passage is reminiscent of the incident at Beth-Shemesh, where the divine warrior, smote (ויך, 1 Sam 6:19) the citizens of the city because they had looked into the ark. The tragedy occurred because people had failed to respect the boundary separating the sacred from the profane. So the question is asked: "Who is able to stand before YHWH, this holy God? To whom shall he go (יעלה)--away from us?" (1 Sam 6:20).[65] The answer is implied in the transfer of the ark into the custody of the family of Abinadab: it is the family of Abinadab that can stand before YHWH.

But now in 2 Samuel 6, it is someone from the family of Abinadab who has violated the taboo, and YHWH smote him (ויכהו, v 7). It appears that this part of the ritual has been embellished by the pro-Davidic narrator to explain how the custody of the sacred ark was transferred from the Abinadab family in Qiryat-Ye'arim to the custody of the Davidides. The smiting of the citizens of Beth-Shemesh emphasized the ark's sanctity and power, and prompted the question about its legitimate custodian. So here the narrator entertains no question about the sacred nature of the ark. The propagandistic intent of the episode as it stands is made blatantly clear in David's question about the ark's custody: "How shall the ark come to me?" (2 Sam 6:10). It is no longer the legitimacy of Qiryat-Ye'arim that is at stake, but Jerusalem and the Davidides.

According to the narrator, because David "feared YHWH" (v 9), the ark was not immediately transferred to the city of

64. On the cultic use of the threshing-floors, see J. Gray, "The Goren at the City Gate," *PEQ* 85 (1953) 118-125.

65. Note in a processional context (probably of the ark) following allusions to cosmogony: "Who will ascend the mount of YHWH? // Who will go up into his holy place?" מי־יעלה בהר־יהוה // ומי־יקום במקום קדשו (Ps 24:3).

David (v 10). Instead, it was diverted to the house of a certain ‘Obed-’Edom the Gittite (v 11). Again, it is impossible to reconstruct the historical event here, or argue with confidence what the hiatus in the house of ‘Obed-’Edom might have been in the ritual.[66] We can hear only the voice of the narrator. And we are told only that the new custodian of the ark was a "Gittite," a native of Gath, whose name was עבד־אדם. The reader is surprised that the new custodian of the ark is a Gittite, perhaps even a Philistine, whose name probably meant "the Servant/Worshipper of (the god) ’Adm."[67]

This interlude seems ironic indeed. The situation at the end of the ark narrative in 1 Samuel seems to have been reversed: ‘Uzzah the scion of the consecrated family of Abinadab has been struck dead, while blessing has come to the Gittite, called "Servant of ’Adm." The smiting of ‘Uzzah and the blessing of ‘Obed-’Edom seem completely arbitrary to the reader. But that is precisely the point of the episode: the election of David and the Jebusite city is just so. YHWH had chosen the unexpected. It is perhaps also not coincidental that the ark’s ascent to Jerusalem mirrors the rise of David to some extent. Even as David sojourned briefly among the Philistines of Gath (1 Sam 21:10-15), so the ark was with ‘Obed-’Edom the Gittite for three months. Yet the presence of YHWH remained with the ark and continued to bring blessings to those who would care for it. According to the

---

66. Engnell's connection of אדום here with ’Udm in the KRT cycle (*KTU* 1.14.III.30-31, V.41-42) and a putative *hieros gamos* seems too far-fetched to be convincing. The reconstruction is predicated on a purely cultic-ritual interpretation of both 2 Samuel 6 and the KRT texts, as well as his dubious identifications of geographical and personal names. See his *Studies in Divine Kingship*, 163-166.

67. The theophoric element refers to an earth-deity known in Amorite onomastica (see Huffmon, *Amorite Personal Names*, 158-159) and is perhaps to be identified with *ỉtwm* the consort of Rešep mentioned in an Egyptian magical text (see Fulco, *The Canaanite God Rešep*, 67-68).

narrator, it was because of the blessings that David was determined to transfer it to the city which he had named for himself (vv 11-12).[68]

## D. THE MARCH OF THE DIVINE WARRIOR

The ark was carried into Jerusalem "with joy" (בשמחה, v 12). As the bearers of the ark marched (צעדו) every six "marchings" (צעדים), animal sacrifices were made. Miller and Roberts have called attention to parallels with Akkadian inscriptions regarding the return of divine images,[69] while McCarter finds analogy with inscriptions pertaining to the inauguration of a new city.[70] Not enough attention has been paid to the vocabulary of David's procession, however. In the first place, it should be noted that the marching of the ark (note צעדו, צעדים) follows the "smiting of Uzzah" (פרץ עזה)

68. OL and LXX$^{L}$ assume a plus: ויאמר דוד אשיב את הברכה אל־ביתי "and David said: "I will restore the blessing to my house." McCarter (*II Samuel*, 165-166) defends the longer reading as original, arguing that a scribe removed the less-than-benevolent motif to "protect David." I am inclined to agree with this and will only add that the movement from "the house of Abinadab" (v 3) to "the house of 'Obed-'Edom (vv 10-11) climaxes with "the house of David" (v 12).

69. *The Hand of the Lord*, 14-17. In particular, they point to a premature report of a procession to have been conducted by Esarhaddon (see R. Borger, *Die Inschriften Asarhaddons Königs von Assyrien* [AfO 9; Graz: Weidner, 1967] 88-89, §57, 18-20; cf. K. M. Streck, *Assurbanipal und die letzen assyrischen Könige bis zum Untergang Nineveh* [VAB 7/3; Leipzig: Hinrichs, 1916] 264, 7-11), noting that as in 2 Samuel 6, (1) military personnel were involved in the procession, (2) there was music and rejoicing, and (3) ritual sacrifices were made to the deity at regular intervals.

70. "The Ritual Dedication of the City of David in 2 Samuel 6," 273-278.

in the procession. This mirrors the sequence in the preceding chapter, where the "sound of YHWH's marching (קול צעדה) follows the "breaking of Waters" (פרץ מים). This would suggest that the procession was at least in part a dramatization or reenactment of YHWH's victorious march, following the victory over his enemies.

It is hardly accidental that the verb used of the procession here is צעדו; the root צעד is, after all, relatively uncommon in the Hebrew Bible. The verb is used in the most archaic texts in connection with the march of the divine warrior (Judg 5:4; Ps 68:8; Hab 3:12). Psalm 68, which certainly dates to the early monarchy, is especially relevant since it was probably connected with the procession of the ark.[71] As in 2 Samuel 6, the procession here is conducted "with joy" (בשמחה, v 4). Praise is urged for the deity, who is called רכב בערבות "the one who rides through the expanse," a name that recalls the epithet of the storm-god Ba'l/Hadd as *rkp 'rpt* "the Rider of the Clouds."[72] The approach of the deity is expressed thus:

אלהים בצאתך לפני עמך
בצעדך בישימון
ארץ רעשה אף שמים נטפו

---

71. So Fretheim ("The Cultic Use of the Ark of the Covenant in the Monarchial Period," 147-164), who calls the psalm an "Ark Liturgy," and H. Weil, ("Exégèse du Psaume 68," *RHR* 117 [1938] 75-89), who sees the psalm as a liturgy used in conjunction with the procession of the ark into the city of David. Note the similarity of v 1 to the Song of the Ark (Num 10:35).

72. In the light of the similarity of Ps 68:5 with Isa 62:10 and the motif of the desert march in the latter, I am not inclined simply to translate רכב בערבות as "Rider of Clouds," as is frequently done. Rather, my translation reflects what I believe to be a double reference intended by the poet (1) to the deity who marches through the vast expanse of the desert *and* (2) to the skies (cf. רכב בשמי שמי קדם in v 34 and Deut 33:26; Ps 18:11 // 2 Sam 22:11).

מפני אלהים זה סיני
מפני אלהים אלהי ישראל
גשם נדבות תניף אלהים
נחלתך ונלאה אתה כוננתה
(Ps 68:8-10)

God,[73] when you set forth before your people,
When you marched forth from the wilderness,[74]
The earth quaked, yea, the heavens dripped.[75]
Before God, the One from Sinai;
Before God, the God of Israel.
Copious rain you showered,[76] O God.
You established your conquered patrimony,[77]

---

73. This is one of the so-called Elohistic Psalms, so we should perhaps assume that the text originally had יהוה instead of אלהים throughout.

74. See Miller, *The Divine Warrior in Early Israel*, 233 n. 125.

75. For the meaning of this figure, see D. R. Hillers, "A Convention in Hebrew Literature: Reaction to Bad News," *ZAW* 77 (1965) 86-90. We should now add the suggestive phrases from the fragments of the plaster inscriptions of Deir ʻAllā, *tṭpn šr* "they dripped heavy rain" (cf. Arab. θ*arra*) and *tṭpn ṭl* "they dripped dew." See Hoftijzer and van der Kooij, *Aramaic Texts from Deir ʻAlla*, Combination II, ll. 34, 35 and pp. 251-252. On *nṭpw*, see W. F. Albright, "A Catalogue of Early Hebrew Lyric Poems (Psalms LXVII)," 20; Cross, *Canaanite Myth and Hebrew Epic*, 101.

76. For the meaning of *nwp*/*npp*, compare Arabic *nafnāfun* "drizzle." Cf. Prov 7:19, for which, see G. R. Driver, "Problems in 'Proverbs,'" *ZAW* 50 (1932) 142-143.

77. נלאה is certainly to be associated with the root *l'y*/*l'w* "to be strong, prevail, overpower" common in West Semitic PNs (cf. the Hebrew names לאה and לאיתיאל). See Huffmon, *Amorite Personal Names*, 224-225; Gröndahl, *Die Personennamen der Texte aus Ugarit*, 70, 154; Benz, *Personal Names in the Phoenician and Punic Inscriptions*, 336-337. So M. Dahood, "Hebrew-Ugaritic Lexicography IV," *Bib* 47 (1966) 408; *Psalms* II, 139-140. Most provocative in this

The remarkable similarities between this passage and Judg 5:4–5 are well known.[78] Both are parade examples of hymnic, perhaps liturgical, texts concerning the march of the divine warrior. In both passages, the march of the warrior causes nature to convulse.[79] This motif of nature's dance is also present in hymnic texts from Mesopotamia,[80] most of which appear to have been commissioned for the procession of divine images.[81] It is reasonable to assume, then, that the choice of the words צעדו and צעדים in the narrative indicates that the ritual procession of the divine emblem (the ark) was intended to be a dramatization of the march of the divine warrior.

The advance of the warrior is further suggested by the activities accompanying the procession of the ark in 2 Samuel 6. Two participles are employed to describe these activities:

---

connection is the pairing of *nḥlt* and *tl'iyt* (*KTU* 1.3.III.30–31). The latter occurs most frequently in the expression *ǵr tl'iyt* "mount of victory/conquest," a designation for Ṣaphon (*KTU* 1.10.III.28, 32; 1.101.3). I take נחלתך ונלאה to be in hendiadys.

78. See E. Lipiński, "Juges 5.4–5 et Psaume 68.8–11," *Bib* 48 (1967) 185–206; A. Globe, "The Text and Literary Structure of Judges 5,4–5," *Bib* 55 (1974) 173–176.

79. See S. E. Loewenstamm, "The Trembling of Nature During the Theophany," in *Comparative Studies in Biblical and Ancient Oriental Literatures* (AOAT 204; Neukirchen-Vluyn: Neukirchener, 1980) 173–189.

80. See Lipiński, "Juges 5:4–5 et Psaume 68:8–11," 186–187; Mann, *Divine Presence and Guidance*, 30–49, 184–185. Cf. F. Stummer, *Sumerisch-akkadische Parallelen zum Aufbau alttestamentlicher Psalmen* (Paderborn: Schöningh, 1922) 40–46; W. F. Albright, "The Song of Deborah in the Light of Archaeology," *BASOR* 62 (1936) 26–27.

81. See W. W. Hallo, "The Cultic Setting of Sumerian Poetry," in *Actes de la XVII^e Rencontre assyrologique internationale* (Études recuéilles par André Finet; Ham-sur-Heure: Comité belge de recherches en Mésopotamie, 1970) 120–121.

מכרכר (vv 14, 16) and מפזז (v 16). The former occurs in the Hebrew Bible only in conjunction with this procession. It has traditionally been derived from *kwr* or *krr* because there are, supposedly, South Semitic cognates suggesting whirling, rotating, twisting, or like actions.[82] In recent years, however, commentators have pointed to the occurrence of the Ugaritic expression *ykrkr 'uṣb'th* (*KTU* 1.4.IV.29–30). Hence scholars frequently assert that מכרכר is "an activity of the finger."[83] But it is hardly certain that Ugaritic *ykrkr* refers to an activity of the finger in the pertinent text. Indeed, to judge by the chiasmus in the bicolon, *ykrkr* involves the toes rather than fingers:

p'nh lhdm yθpd
ykrkr 'uṣb'th
(*KTU* 1.4.IV.29–30)

I take the verb *ykrkr* to suggest an iterative action meaning "to prance, skip," or the like. Thus, the related Hebrew noun כר (ram) is named for the skipping, prancing movement of the animal.[84] Hebrew מכרכר, therefore, must refer to a skipping, prancing movement like that of a ram.

---

82. So J. Morgenstern, "The Etymological History of the Three Hebrew Synonymns for "to Dance,' ḤGG, ḤLL and KRR, and their Cultural Significance," *JAOS* 36 (1917) 321; M. I. Gruber, "Ten Dance-Derived Expressions in the Hebrew Bible," *Bib* 62 (1981) 338–339.

83. So Y. Avishur, "*KRKR* in Biblical Hebrew and Ugaritic," *VT* 26 (1976) 257–261; G. W. Ahlström, "*KRKR* and *ṮPD*," *VT* 28 (1978) 100–102. Following this line of argument, McCarter emends MT מכרכר בכל עז to מכרכר בכל<י> ע<ץ> "fingering--i.e., strumming on a sonorous instrument" (*II Samuel*, 163).

84. Cf. W. Eilers, "Zur Funktion von Nominalformen," *WO* 3 (1964–66) 132. כר may also refer to the battering ram which, of course, involves repeated action. One may also mention כרכרות "dromedaries," which may have been named for the prancing movement of the creature as well.

One may draw an analogy from the relation of the noun עוף "bird" with the participle מעופף "flying." Thus, עוף : מעופף :: כר : מכרכר. If מעופף refers to the action of a bird (flying), then מכרכר refers to the action of the ram (prancing).

This understanding of the verb fits with the occurrence of *ykrkr* in Ugaritic. Following the defeat of Ba'l's enemies, 'Athirat came to the abode of 'Ēl at the source of the double-deep.

hlm . 'il . kyphnh
yprq . lṣb . wyṣḥq
p'nh . lhdm . yθpd
wykrkr . 'uṣb'th

(*KTU* 1.4.IV.27-30)

Lo, 'Ēl saw her--
He eased[85] his frown and laughed,[86]

---

85. Literally "loosened" or "removed."

86. The widely accepted interpretation of *yprq lṣb* as opening of mouth is based on a convoluted argument proffered by E. Ullendorf, "Ugaritic Marginalia," *Or* 20 (1951) 271-272. Ullendorf begins with an Arabic cognate *liṣb* (supposedly "small ravine" > "narrowness" > "straits") which is compared with the Homeric idiom ἕρκος ὀδόντων "enclosure of the teeth." Accordingly, to part the "straits of the mouth" (i.e. the rows of teeth) is to laugh. New light is shed on the term in a recently published omen text (*KTU* 1.103.49), which contains a description of malformed fetus with "its eye in its *lṣb*" (*w'nh blṣbh*). The context suggests that *lṣb* means something like "front," perhaps "forehead." See A. Herdner, "Nouveaux textes alphabétiques de Ras Shamra XXIV$^{e}$ campagne, 1961," *Ugaritica* VII (MRS 18; Paris: Mission Archéologique de Ras Shamra, 1978) 44-60. Cf. also *KTU* 1.114.29 where something called *ḫš* is placed on 'Ēl's face/forehead (*lṣbh*) presumably to resuscitate him from his drunkenness. Arabic *laṣiba* "be tight" is used of a sword stuck in the scabbard, as well as a finger stuck in a ring. It is

On the footstool he did stomp his feet,[87]
And his toes he did tap (i. e. he pranced).

The response of 'Ēl to the coming of 'Athirat was no mere activity of fingers or toes. It was sufficiently animated, so to speak, that 'Ēl thought that he might have aroused the goddess:

hm . yd . 'il mlk yḫssk .
'ahbt . θr . t'rrk
(*KTU* 1.4.IV.38-39)

Does the virility[88] of 'Ēl the king excite you?
Does the love of the Bull arouse you?

---

frequently used of skin and flesh, and figuratively of miserly, niggardly, stingy persons (cf. the modern colloquialism "uptight"). See M. Ullmann, *Wörterbuch der klassischen arabischen Sprache* II/1 (Wiesbaden: Harrassowitz, 1972) 625-654. I take the expression *yprq lṣb*, literally "he loosened his face," to be an expression of joy. Cf. *KTU* 1.17.II.10; 1.6.III.16.

87. The root θ*pd* is usually connected with the noun *m*θ*pdm* (*KTU* 1.1.III.20; 1.3.IV.35; 1.2.III.3) and Hebrew משפתים (Gen 49:14; Judg 5:16; cf. שפתים, Ps 68:14). The Hebrew noun has been explained by O. Eissfeldt ("Gabelhürden im Ostjordanland," [1949] in *KS* III, 61-66; "Noch Einmal Gabelhürden im Ostjordanland," [1954] in *KS* III, 67-70) as part of the structure of a sheep-fold. Cf. Egyptian *sbty* "surrounding wall" (*Urk.* IV, 661, l. 5). The noun in Ugaritic is usually associated with Arabic θ*affada* "layers." The basic meaning of the verb is "to add on" or "to repeat." Hence the verb here meaning "stomp, tap." Cf. A. Caquot and M. Sznycer, *Textes Ougaritiques* I (Littératures anciennes du Proche-Orient 7; Paris: Cerf, 1974) 171 note y.

88. Given the parallelism of *yd* with *'ahbt* we must take the root to be *ydd* "to love" (cf. Hebrew *ydd*, Arabic *wdd*). But *yd 'il* is elsewhere used of 'Ēl's penis and sexual prowess (*KTU* 1.23.33-35), so we should assume *double entendre* here.

'Ēl's response was no twirling of fingers or wriggling of toes, as most translations suggest. Rather, it was a vigorous and passionate dance of joy. So, too, David pranced before YHWH "with all vigor" (בכל עז), as the ark was brought into the city in joyous procession (בשמחה).[89]

Another participle, מפזז, is employed to describe David's dance in v 16. The word is probably related to the verb יפזו in Gen 49:24 whose context (vv 22–26) is, unfortunately, obscure; the text appears to be hopelessly corrupt. The focus of the passage is on Joseph, who is likened to an animal, *bn prt* (v 22).[90] If the subject of the verb in v 24 is still Joseph, then we may conclude that the verb has to do with the movement of an animal--the *bn prt*, that is, a calf. The cognates of Hebrew *pzz* suggest the sudden and rapid movements like that of frightened or excited animals. In Arabic, *fazza* is used of gazelles, antelopes and horses--particularly of these animals running wild in the face of thunderstorms. There is also the noun, *'afzaz*, which refers to a spry young antelope. The verb in Syriac, likewise, denotes the agility and strength of animals. It is used of lambs and kids skipping and frisking about.[91] The word מפזז, therefore, probably describes a dance involving leaps and sudden dashes like animals. Thus, the participles describing David's dance, מכרכר and מפזז, both appear to be associated with animal movements.

Instead of MT מפזז ומכרכר, LXX$^B$ has ὀρχούμενον καὶ ἀνακρουόμενον, probably reflecting Hebrew מרקד ומכרכר. The participle מרקד also appears in 1 Chron 15:29, which has מרקד ומשחק. LXX$^B$ of 2 Sam 6:21 has David saying: καὶ

89. We should also note that in *KTU* 1.6.III, the good news of Ba'l's victory prompted 'Ēl to rejoice (*šmḫ*). He stomped his feet on the footstool, as the heavens rained oil and the wadis flowed with mead.

90. Cf. Ugaritic PN *prt*, *bn prt*. See Gröndahl, *Die Personnenamen der Texte aus Ugarit*, 175.

91. R. Payne Smith, *Thesaurus Syriacus* II (Oxford: Clarendon, 1901) 3078–3079.

παίξομαι καὶ ὀρχήσομαι ἐνώπιον κυρίου "I will revel and I will dance before YHWH" (presuming Hebrew ושחקתי ורקדתי לפני יהוה).[92]

In the light of our exegesis so far, it is especially provocative to find the verb רקד associated with the procession of the ark. The verb occurs frequently in the Hebrew Bible, precisely in connection with the convulsion of nature at the approach of the divine warrior, and the ancient hymnic texts likened this trembling of nature to the dance of animals. The liturgy of Psalm 114 is particularly instructive in this regard:

הים ראה וינס
הירדן יסב לאחור
ההרים רקדו כאילים
גבעות כבני־צאן
מה־לך הים כי תנוס
הירדן תסב לאחור
ההרים תרקדו כאילים
גבעות כבני־צאן
מלפני אדון חולי ארץ
מלפני אלוה יעקב
ההפכי הצור אגם־מים
חלמיש למעינו־מים
(Ps 114:3–7)

The Sea looked and fled;
The Jordan turned back.
The Mountains danced like rams,
The Hills like sheep.
What's with you, O Sea, that you flee?
O Jordan that you turn back?
O Mountains that you dance like rams?
O Hills like sheep?

92. See H. Orlinsky, "*Hā-rōqdîm* for *hā-rēqîm* in II Samuel 6:20," *JBL* 65 (1946) 25–35.

Writhe before the Lord, O Land!
Before the God of Jacob,
Who turned the rock into a pool of water,
The *ḥallāmîš*-rock into fountains of water.

The language of this psalm is clearly liturgical. Here the great salvific event at the sea and the crossing of the Jordan are symbolically re-presented, apparently in a cultic drama at the temple. Sea and River are depicted as the divine warrior's enemies who fled at his approach--even as YHWH's enemies fled when his presence was invoked before the ark (cf. Num 10:35; Ps 68:2). The presence of the holy warrior prompted the mountains and hills to dance like animals--a dance that may have been acted out.[93] As the divine warrior approached, nature danced in joy, in anticipation of the deity's fructification of creation.[94]

This motif of nature's convulsion before the divine warrior is found also in Psalm 29, which is generally regarded as an archaic hymn of the theophany of the storm-god:

קול יהוה שׁבר ארזים
ישׁבר יהוה < >[95] ארזי < >לבנון
< >ירק־ד־ם[96] כמו־עגל לבנון

93. Such cultic performances are widely attested in the ancient Near East. As evident from the Standard Babylonian explanatory texts, the role of the god was usually played by the king, while actors played the roles of the enemies or allies of the divine warrior. In one ritual combat, cult-dancers performed amid the din of clappers and hallooing. Some participants danced (*iraqqudū*), while the *kurgarru* chanted battle songs and singers responded with "cries of joy." See Livingstone, *Mystical and Mythological Explanatory Works*, 122-123.

94. See Propp, *Water in the Wilderness*, 23-25.

95. We should omit all prosaic elements like the *nota accusativi* and the definite article in this archaic text.

96. Assuming the enclitic *m*.

ושרין כמו בן־ראמ־ם
קול יהוה חצב להבת־אש
קול יהוה יחולל אילות[97]
קול יהוה יחיל מדבר
יחיל יהוה מדבר קדש
(Ps 29:5–7, 9a, 8)

The voice of YHWH breaks the cedars;
The voice of YHWH breaks the cedars of Lebanon.
    He makes Lebanon dance like a calf;
    Sirion like the calf of a wild-ox.
The voice of YHWH cuts down the Fiery Flame,[98]

---

97. V 9a is misplaced. I believe it belongs with v 7, which lacks a parallel line. It owes its present position to the confusion with the verb יחיל in v 8 (*bis*). The absence of internal matres in early Hebrew orthography would have made the verbs quite similar (יחלל/יחל). A scribe either misread the second verb or interpreted it as an alternate (reduplicated) formation of the same root חול/חיל. The latter would be odd, however, for the *pōlēl* would mean "to writhe, calve, birth" (cf. Isa 51:2; Ps 90:2; Job 1:39) not "to *cause* to writhe/calf/birth." In that case, one would expect the subject to be אילות, as it is in Job 39:1, but that is impossible in the context of Ps 29:9a. In support of my reconstruction, one notes that *ḥṣb* is paired with *ḥll* in Isa 51:9, where the arm of YHWH is called to put on *strength* (עז) and asked, "was it not you who cut down (מחצבת) Rahab? Was it not you who pierced (מחוללת) Tannin? Was it not you who dried up Sea and the waters of the great deep?" In Ps 89:11, the slaying of Rahab is חלל רהב (cf. מחצבת רהב in Isa 51:9), whereas חלל is used for the slaying of the "fleeing serpent" in Job 26:13. V 9b is much too short to stand by itself; it may be an explanatory gloss introduced to explain יחולל אילות, when אילות was interpreted as trees (i.e., *'êlôṯ*). In my reconstruction, the bicolon contains 9 syllables per line (4:4 in the Ley-Sievers system, with an a b c d // a b c′ d′ pattern), quite in agreement with this portion of the hymn.

98. For this interpretation, see C. Kloos, *Yhwh's Combat with the Sea* (Leiden: Brill, 1986) 59–60. Among the

The voice of YHWH pierces the Hinds.[99]
The voice of YHWH makes the desert writhe,[100]
YHWH causes the holy desert to writhe.[101]

Significantly, the dance of nature follows his victory over waters (cf. על־מים, על־מים רבים, v 3), and precedes the accession of YHWH in the sanctuary (vv 9c, 10) and the blessing of YHWH's people (v 11). Thus, we have the following order in the poem:

(1) Victory over the unruly waters, vv 3–4
(2) March of the divine warrior, vv 5–9a
(3) Accession of the deity, vv 9c–10
(4) Blessing of the people, v 11

---

assistants of Yamm/Nahar are "'Atik, the calf of 'Ēl," "Fire, the bitch of 'Ēl," "ðbb, the daughter of 'Ēl." Cf. also *KTU* 1.2.I.32, where Fire is Mot's lackey. See P. D. Miller, Jr., "Fire in the Mythology of Canaan and Israel," *CBQ* 27 (1965) 259; R. S. Hendel, "'The Flame of the Whirling Sword': A Note on Genesis 3:24," *JBL* 104 (1985) 671–674.

99. "Hinds" perhaps is a military designation (cf. אילי מואב in Exod 15:15) for the monsters that accompanied Yamm. Cf. P. D. Miller, Jr., "Animal Names as Designations in Ugaritic and Hebrew," *UF* 2 (1970) 177–186.

100. The language recalls the prowess of Ba'l as warrior, as in a letter of Abimilki of Tyre: *ša iddin rigmašu ina šamê kīma addi ù ta[r]gub gabbi māti ištu rigmīšu* "who gives his voice from heaven like Hadd, and at his voice all the land trembles" (*EA* 147.13–15). Cf. *LKA* 53.21: *[ša ina rigim] pīšu...iḫīlū ṣērū* [at the voice of whose] mouth...the steppes writhed." See E. Ebeling, *Die akkadische Gebetsserie Šu-ila "Handerhebung"* (VIO 20; Berlin: Akademie, 1953) 98. One notes that the verb for the trembling of the steppes is from middle weak *ḫâlu*, which is frequently used of kings in battle contexts (see *CAD* 8, 55). Cf. Hebrew *ḥwl* in the context of theophany in Ps 97:4; 77:17; 114:7; Hab 3:10. For other parallels, see J. L. Cunchillos, *Estudio del Salmo 29* (Valencia: Soler, 1976) 204–209.

101. Or "the desert of Qadesh." See O. Loretz, *Psalm 29* (UBL; Altenberge: CIS, 1984) 87–92.

The sequence is similar in the narrative account of David's procession, where we have victory over the "waters" (the encroaching enemies) at Ba'l Peraṣim (// the smiting of 'Uzzah), followed by the march of the divine warrior here. As we shall see, the accession of YHWH follows, and then the expected blessing of the people in a symbolic banquet. This sequence is surely no coincidence!

In view of the vocabulary of dance associated with the procession of the ark, I would venture to suggest that David and his retinue were participating in dances imitating animal movements.[102] Their purpose, to judge from the sequence of events in the procession, was to dramatize the dance of nature before the divine warrior. Thus, the refrain that they were prancing, leaping, and skipping "before YHWH" (לפני יהוה, vv 5, 14, 16) alludes not only to the actual dancing before the ark, but to the convulsion of nature *before the presence of* YHWH the warrior (cf. Pss 68:9; 97:5; 114:7, etc.).

The imitation of animal movements in cultic dancing is suggestive in light of the ubiquitous depiction of animals together with human participants in cultic vessels discovered throughout the ancient Near East. There is, moreover, evidence for cultic dancing in the glyptic art of the second millennium.[103] Several seal impressions from Syria–Palestine show cultic participants hand in hand, apparently in a circle dance.[104] One of these clearly shows horned quadrupeds and

102. On such dances in various cultures, see C. Sachs, *World History of Dance* (trans. B. Schönberg; New York: Norton, 1963) 79–85.

103. See C. Epstein, "Early Bronze Age Seal Impressions from the Golan," *IEJ* 22 (1972) 209–217; A. Ben-Tor, "Cult Scenes on Early Iron Age Seal Impressions from Palestine," *Levant* 9 (1977) 90–100.

104. See Ben-Tor, "Cult Scenes on Early Bronze Age Cylinder Sea Impressions from Palestine," figs. 13, 14, 16, 20, 25, 26; Epstein, "Early Bronze Age Seal Impressions from Golan," fig. 2:6, pl. 52.A; M. Prausnitz, "Note on a Cylinder Seal Impression," *'Atiqot* 1 (1955) 139, figs. 1, 2.

human beings dancing together.[105] An example from El-Karm has the upper bodies of two human figures, each with outstretched arms and horns growing out of his or her head, perhaps indicating that the dancers were wearing animal masks.[106] These examples suggest that human worshippers were playing the roles of animals in the cultic rituals.[107] A seal from Ur depicts nude dancers with animal masks performing before a sanctuary.[108] In this example, the dancer closest to the shrine has one leg lifted up, apparently leaping or prancing like an animal. This dancer appears with horns like those of goats, rams, or ibexes.

The nudity of some of these cultic dancers is most intriguing. We may conjecture that 'Ēl's animated dance before 'Athirat was in the nude as well, since the deity reckoned that he had sexually aroused his consort (*KTU* 1.4.IV.21-39). In terms reminiscent of this Ugaritic passage, David is said to have uncovered himself in his dance (2 Sam 6:20-22).[109] In 2 Sam 6:14, however, he is said to be prancing vigorously before YHWH, "girded in a linen ephod"--perhaps implying that was all he had on.

Finally, from recent excavations at Tel Dan comes a marvelous clay plaque depicting a dancer in a vigorous dance, with a lute in hand and one leg lifted up.[110] The dancer

---

105. Epstein, "Seal Impressions from Golan," 214; O. E. Ravn, *A Catalogue of Oriental Cylinder Seals and Seal Impressions in the Danish National Museum* (Copenhagen: National Museum of Denmark, 1960) no. 121.

106. Cf. Ben-Tor, "Cult Scenes on Early Bronze Age Cylinder Seal Impressions from Palestine," 96 and fig. 21.

107. Ibid., 96-100.

108. L. Legrain, *Ur Excavations* III (Oxford: Oxford University, 1936) pl. 19, no. 374. Another example (pl. 17.328) shows a nude dancer, but no sanctuary is depicted.

109. See below.

110. See A. Biran, The Dancer from Dan, the Empty Tomb and the Altar Room," *IEJ* 36 (1986) 168-187, pl. 19.A, fig. 2.1. A fragment of a plaque showing only one leg, presumably of a dancer, has also been found (fig. 2.2).

appears to be wearing a mask.[111] Interestingly, the excavator associates this plaque with the dance of David.[112]

In the light of such evidence, I would venture to suggest that David and his followers were performing cultic dances that imitated animal movements. David was prancing (מכרכר), frisking about (מפזז) and skipping (מרקד) like animals to dramatize the dance of nature before the divine warrior--as the warrior returns from battle to claim his kingship on the newly won territory.

## E. THE ACCESSION

According to the narrator, "David and all the house of Israel were bringing up the ark of YHWH with shouting (תרועה) and with the sound of the Shophar" (v 15). The end of the "bringing up" (מעלים) is not specified. We assume from the context that the implicit destination is the city of David, that is, Jerusalem. But perhaps more than a geographical destination is at issue here.

The "shouting" (תרועה) is associated mostly with battles (Num 10:5-6; Jer 4:19; 49:2; Amos 1:14; 2:2; Zeph 1:16; Job 39:25; 2 Chron 13:12), including those that explicitly involve the presence of the ark (Josh 6:5, 20; 1 Sam 4:5-6).[113] It is apparently a victory shout connected also with the

---

111. Another example of a mask has been uncovered at Dan. See A. Biran, "Tel Dan, 1981," *IEJ* 32 (1982) 138-139, pl. 16 B. For other examples elsewhere in the ancient Near East, see A. Parrot, "De la Méditerranée à l'Iran: masques énigmatiques," *Ugaritica* VI (MRS 17; Paris: Mission Archéologique de Ras Shamra, 1969) 409-418; E. Stern, "Phoenician Masks and Pendants," *PEQ* 108 (1976) 110-118. Farther afield, evidence of cultic animal masks are found in Charsada. See R. D. Barnett, "Homme masqué ou dieux-ibex?" *Syria* 43 (1966) 259-276, pls. 19.2, 20.2, 3.

112. Biran, "The Dancer from Dan," 170-171.

113. See Humbert, *La 'Terou'a'*, 7-9.

inauguration of sanctuaries (Ezr 3:11–13) and the coronation of kings (Num 23:21).

Thus, in the context of a procession celebrating the kingship of YHWH and his victory over the unruly sea monsters, the תרועה is mentioned:

אשר<ו>[114] העם יודעי < > יהוה[115]
באור פניך יהלכון
בשמך יגילון כל היום
ובצדקתך ירמו [תרועה][116]
כי תפארת עז[נ]ו[117] אתה
וברצנך תרים קרננו
כי ליהוה מגננו
ולקדוש ישראל מלכנו
(Ps 89:16–19)

The people who know YHWH march;
In the effulgence of your presence they proceed.
At your name they rejoice all day long;

---

114. MT has אשרי but I prefer to follow R. Clifford ("Psalm 89: A Lament Over the Davidic Ruler's Continued Failure," *HTR* 73 [1980] 43) in reading אשרו (from PS *'θr "to march, proceed"), assuming the common graphic confusion of *wāw* and *yōḏ*. The parallelism of *'šr* and *hlk* is attested also in Mal 3:14–15; Job 31:7. In Ugaritic, we find the pair *'aθr* // *hlk* in *KTU* 1.14.II.30–42 in the context of a military advance.

115. I follow the reconstruction of W. L. Moran in his "Review of G. W. Ahlström's, *Psalm 89: Eine Liturgie aus dem Ritual des leidenden Königs*," *Bib* 42 (1961) 238–239.

116. Ibid. Read יָרִמוּ תְּרוּעָה in accordance with the idioms להרים קול בתרועה (Ezek 21:27), בתרועה בשמחה להרים קול (Ezr 3:12) and in light of the parallelism of גיל and רוע (Zech 9:9).

117. Emending MT עזמו with Cross (*Canaanite Myth and Hebrew Epic*, 161 n. 71), who notes that *mēm* and *nūn* were easily confused in the seventh and sixth centuries B.C.E. and that the shift from third person to first person between v 17 and v 18 probably accounts for the error in MT.

At your name they rejoice all day long;
And at your victory[118] they raise a shout,
Surely you are the glory of our strength;[119]
By your favor is our horn exalted.
Yea, YHWH is indeed[120] our Benefactor,[121]
Indeed, the Holy One of Israel is our King.

In this poem, the תרועה is at once associated with the victory of the divine warrior over the watery monsters and the enthronement of the warrior as king. The unruly sea is kept in control, the monster Rahab is destroyed, and the enemies are scattered (vv 10–11). The procession celebrates the kingship of the deity. The political dimension of the procession is evident in the verses that follow: the exaltation of YHWH mirrors that of the Davidic king. Indeed the king is depicted in terms blatantly reminiscent of the divine warrior: his hand will be set against Sea and his right hand against River (v 26); he will be made the pre-eminent one, "the *'elyôn* of all the kings of the earth" (v 28).

In Psalm 98, all the nations of the earth are called to "shout (הריעו) to YHWH" in his victory (v 4), join in the celebration with lyres, trumpets, "the sound of the Shophar," and "shout to the King, YHWH" (vv 5–6). Even the unruly waters now join in the celebration of YHWH's accession as king of the universe (7–8).

---

118. Cf. צדקות יהוה in Judg 5:11.

119. It is tempting to see an allusion to the ark here, since תפארת and עז are used of the ark (cf. esp. Ps 78:60–61, where they occur together). See Davies, "The Ark in the Psalms," 51–53.

120. Assuming emphatic *lāmed* with Dahood, *Psalms* II, 315.

121. For this divine epithet, see M. Dahood, "Ugaritic Lexicography," in *Mélanges E. Tisserant* I (Studi e Testi 231; Vatican City: Pontifical Biblical Institute, 1964) 94; *Psalms* I, 16–17; M. O'Connor, "Yahweh the Donor," *Aula Orientalis* 6 (1988) 47–60.

The same themes of victory and kingship are found in Psalm 47, which, most scholars, following Mowinckel,[122] associate with the procession of the ark and the enthronement of YHWH. Even H.-J. Kraus, who is generally skeptical about the existence of an enthronement festival in Israel, concedes that vv 5 and 8 at least "permit us to think of the course of a cultic enthronement."[123] The psalm is, in any case, taken as a liturgy connected with the procession of the ark and the notion of YHWH's kingship. It is with good reason that this text is taken as a reflex of the procession of the ark in 2 Samuel 6: the vocabulary in v 6 especially suggests it. Thus, in the liturgy the deity is said to ascend (עלה) with the shout (בתרועה) and with the sound of the Shophar (בקול שׁופר), even as the ark was "brought up" (מעלים) "with the shout and with the sound of the Shophar" (בתרועה ובקול שׁופר) by the cultic participants in 2 Samuel 6:

2 Sam 6:15   מעלים את־ארון יהוה   בתרועה   ובקול שׁופר
Ps 47:6      עלה   אלהים בתרועה יהוה בקול שׁופר

To be sure, the ark is not explicitly mentioned in the liturgy (Psalm 47), but such is the nature of poetic and liturgical texts. Akkadian references to the procession of divine images are regularly couched in theological terms; the statues are simply referred to as gods and goddesses, or the deities are mentioned by name.[124] Thus, in the narrative

---

122. *Psalmenstudien* II, 3-4.

123. *Psalmen* I (BKAT 15/1; 5th ed; Neukirchen-Vluyn: Neukirchener, 1978) 503. ET: *Psalms 1-59* (Minneapolis: Augsburg, 1988) 467.

124. See, for example, the usage of *ilu* (*CAD* 7, 102-103), *iltu* (ibid., 90), and *ištaru* (ibid., 274). In the Ugaritic texts, too, the divine names are mentioned instead of explicit reference to the images. Cf. *KTU* 1.91.10, 11, 14; 1.43.1-2. See J. M. Tarragon, *Le culte à Ugarit d'après les textes de la pratiques en cunéiformes alphabétiques* (CahRB 19; Paris: Gabalda, 1980) 98-126.

account (2 Samuel 6), the causative of *'ly* is used because the deity is represented by the ark. But in the liturgy (Psalm 47) it is God who "ascends."

כל־העמים תקעו־כף
הריעו לאלהים בקול רנה
כי־יהוה עליון נורא
מלך גדול על־כל־הארץ
ידבר עמים תחתינו
ולאמים תחת רגלינו
יבחר לו < > נחלתו[125]
< > גאון יעקב < > אהב[126]
עלה אלהים בתרועה
יהוה בקול שופר
(Ps 47:2–6)

Clap your hands, all peoples,
Shout to God with the sound of jubilation!
For YHWH is the awesome 'Elyôn,[127]
The great king over all the earth.
He has subdued peoples under us,
And nations under our feet.
He has chosen his patrimony for himself,

---

125. MT has יבחר־לנו את־נחלתנו. LXX and Peshiṭta support the emendation of the suffixes to third person. The 1 cp reading is influenced by the suffixes in the preceding line. Roberts ("The Religio-Political Setting of Psalm 47," 130) argues that *bḥr l + direct object* is "not a good Hebrew construction" (but see Josh 24:15, 22; 2 Sam 24:12; Job 34:4; Ps 135:4, etc.). He posits that the original text had יבחר אתנו לנחלתו which became garbled through a process that cannot be recovered. I prefer, however, to omit את as a prose particle that would not have been present in the early monarchy when, according to Roberts, this text was composed.

126. Omit את and אשר as prose particles.

127. See Roberts, "The Religio-Political Setting of Psalm 47," 130.

The pride of Jacob whom he loves.
God has ascended with the shout;
YHWH with the sound of the Shophar.

The nations are asked to celebrate the accession of YHWH to the position of the 'Elyôn.[128] תקע and רוע are both used in conjunction with the ritual procession of the ark.[129] The former is found in the context of coronation of kings.[130] The latter is used in the proclamation of kings, and should be associated with the "shout of the king" (תרועת מלך) in Num 23:21.[131] The liturgy thus celebrates the rise of YHWH to the supreme position in the divine council. Hence we find the summons to the nations, indeed, the gods of the nations, to join in praise of YHWH as king.[132] The enthronement of YHWH is explicitly stated in v 9:

מלך אלהים על־גוים
אלהים ישב על־כסא קדשו

God has become king over the nations;
God has sat down on his holy throne.

---

128. Dahood (*Psalms* I, 283–284) posits that העמים ( < *'*mm* II) refers to the gods of the nations, and he takes the לאלהים as vocative. Yet, he admits that the construction *hry' l-DN* occurs elsewhere (Pss 66:1; 81:2; 95:1–2; 98:4; 100:1) with the *lāmed* as a preposition. See, further, the critique of Dahood in P. D. Miller, "Vocative Lamed in the Psalter: A Reconsideration," *UF* 11 (1979) 632–633.

129. Note especially the concentration of both terms in Joshua 6 and Numbers 10.

130. 1 Kgs 1:34; 2 Kgs 9: 13; 11:14 // 2 Chron 23:13. See E. Lipiński, *La royauté de Yahwé dans la poèsie et le culte de l'ancien Israël* (Brussels: Paleis der academiën, 1965) 352–355.

131. Cf. 1 Sam 10:24; 1 Kgs 1:39; Pss 89:16; 98:4–6.

132. See esp. vv 7, 10. Cf. Pss 29:1–2; 97:7; 148:2; Deut 32:43 (*per* LXX and 4QDt).

The political significance of the liturgy is further indicated by the allusions to the victory over the nations and YHWH's own patrimony (נחלה), the "pride of Jacob" (גאון יעקב).[133] This liturgical text celebrates the ascension of the deity to a higher place, not just geographically, but in mythologico-political sense as well: the victorious warrior was "going up" to his conquered mountain as king. In this connection, Lipiński has called attention to the following Ugaritic passage of Ba'l's enthronement, where the roots *'ly* and *yθb* both occur:[134]

y'l . b'l . ǵ[r . tl'iyt]
bn . dgn . bš[d . nḥlth][135]
b'l . yθb . lks['i . mlkh]
bn . dgn . lkḥ[θ . drkth]
(cf. *KTU* 1.10.III.11–14)

Ba'l went up to the mo[unt of victory;]
The Son of Dagan to his fi[eld of patrimony.]
Ba'l sat enthroned on [his] thro[ne of kingship;]
The son of Dagan on his se[at of dominion.]

Linking this Ugaritic text with Psalm 47, Lipiński notes the royal connotation of the verb *'ly* in West Semitic.[136] The ascent of Ba'l to his mount of victory is tantamount to his

---

133. I take גאון יעקב to refer to Jerusalem, even as גאון כשׂדים in Isa 13:19 refers to Babylon. Cf. O. Eissfeldt, "Jahwes Königsprädizierung als Verklärung national-politischer Ansprüche Israels," (1972) in *KS* V, 219.

134. E. Lipiński, "Yāhweh mâlāk," *Bib* 44 (1963) 443–444; *La royauté de Yahwé*, 396–397.

135. Cf. שׂדה נחלת ישׂראל in Judg 20:6. The meaning of *šd nḥlt* would be the same as *'arṣ nḥlt* (*KTU* 1.4.VIII.13–14; 1.3.VI.16), as the frequent parallelism of *šd* and *'arṣ* suggests (*KTU* 1.3.III.13–14, V.16–17; 1.5.VI.6–7, 27–28; 1.6.III.16–17).

136. "Yāhweh Mâlāk," 445–446; *La royauté de Yahwé*, 396–397.

claim of kingship. This is borne out in another text, a hymn celebrating Ba'l's enthronement:[137]

b'l . yθb . kθbt . ǵr .
hd . r['y] kmdb .
btk . ǵrh . 'il . ṣpn .
bt[k] ǵr . tliyt .
šb't . brqm . [yr][138]
θmnt . 'iṣr . r't
'ṣ . brq y[mn][139]

(*KTU* 1.101.1-4)

Ba'l sits enthroned,
like a throne is the mountain.[140]
Hadd the She[pherd], like Flood.
In the midst of his mountain, divine Ṣaphon[141]

---

137. See L. R. Fisher and F. B. Knutson, "An Enthronement Ritual at Ugarit," *JNES* 28 (1969) 157-167.

138. Reconstructed after Cross, *Canaanite Myth and Hebrew Epic*, 148 n. 5

139. Ibid.

140. Recently Kloos (*Yhwh's Combat with the Sea*, 48) denied the royal connotation of *θbt* here, prefering to interpret the line as a reference to the deity's "sitting" like the mountain and flood. Apart from the dubious imagery, it must be noted that *θbt* always has royal connotations in Ugaritic (see *KTU* 1.14.I.23; 1.3.VI.15; 1.4.VIII.13; 1.5.II.16; 1.5.III.3; 1.6.VI.28) and there are no infinitives of like pattern in the language (so one finds *nš'i* instead of *š'it* and *ntn* instead of *tt*). Cf. also Hebrew שבת in 1 Kgs 8:13 (// בית זבל); Exod 15:17, Ps 68:17, and so forth.

141. The parallelism of *'il ṣpn* with *tl'iyt* suggests that the former is not a divine name here. See M. Pope, "Marginalia to M. Dahood's Ugaritic-Hebrew Philology," *JBL* 85 (1966) 461-462. Ṣaphon is identified with Ḫazzi, a mountain deity in Hittite mythology (*Ugar*. V, 44). See A. Goetze, "The City Khalbi and the Khabiru People," *BASOR* 79 (1940) 32-34.

In the mids[t of] his mount of victory.
Seven [he casts] his lightning bolts.
Eight arsenals of thunder.
A lightning tree he [wields].

The portrayal of Ba'l in this text is quite close to the mythological depiction of his triumphal entry into his new abode. In the myth he wields a "cedar tree" in his right hand as he enters to take his throne (*KTU* 1.4.VII.41-42). This portrayal in both myth and liturgy is in harmony with representations of Ba'l in iconography. Typically, he is depicted in a standing position, with a thunderbolt in one hand and a lightning tree in the other.[142] Statues of a divine warrior in a similar combat posture are widely attested in the Levant.[143] Indeed, a remarkable remnant of such a statue has recently been discovered in the tenth century stratum (XIV) of the City of David.[144] It is the right hand of a bronze statuette, with a perforation through the hand where a weapon or scepter once had been.[145]

On a limestone stela discovered near the temple of Ba'l at Ugarit[146] the god is seen with two horns on his head.[147]

142. See A. Caquot and M. Sznycer, *Ugaritic Religion* (Iconography of Religions 15/8; Leiden: Brill, 1980) pls. VIII.c; IX.a, b, c, d; X.

143. See O. Negbi, *Canaanite Gods in Metal* (Tel Aviv University Institute of Archaeology 5; Tel Aviv: Peli, 1976) 29-41, 46-47. Negbi compares this "male warrior in smiting pose" with the iconography of Ba'l.

144. See Y. Shiloh, *Excavations at the City of David* I (Qedem 19; Jerusalem: Institute of Archaeology, 1984) 17, 60, pl. 29.3, fig. 24.

145. The fist is approximately 4 cm long, which means that the statuette must have been about 38 cm high, thus about twice the average size of such figures.

146. C. F. A. Schaeffer, "Les fouilles de Minet el-Beida et de Ras Shamra, Quatrième Campagne (Printemps 1932)," *Syria* 14 (1933) 123.

147. Cf. ll. 6-7 of this text (*KTU* 1.101).

The deity is in his typical combative pose. Below the deity are wavy lines, no doubt representing the unruly waters over which he had triumphed.

One must again consider Psalm 29, which climaxes with the enthronement of the divine warrior:

יהוה למבול ישב
< > ישב יהוה מלך לעולם
(Ps 29:10)

YHWH sits enthroned on Flood;[148]
YHWH sits enthroned, an eternal king.

Here the enthronement of the deity is the result of his victory over the unruly waters. This corresponds in ritual to the placing of the divine emblem on a dais symbolizing the cosmic mountain over the chaotic waters. In Mesopotamia, the dais represented the watery monster, Tiamat. This is evident in a text describing the temples of Babylon which says concerning the dais: *tiāmat šubat ᵈBēl ša ᵈBēl ina muḫḫi ašbu* "Tiamat is the seat of Bēl, on which Bēl is seated."[149] Livingstone also cites a text which supports such a view of the ritual: *[aššš]um bēl ša ina akīt ina qabal tâmtim ašbu* "Because of Bēl, who sits in the middle of Tiamat in the *akītu*."[150] This is certainly the ritual-mythological background of YHWH's enthronement in Psalm 29.

But recently C. Kloos has denied that the enthronement over Flood has anything to do with the conflict myths.[151] Kloos argues that מבול in Ps 29:10 can only refer to the

148. For the idiom *yšb l*, see M. Tsevat, *A Study of the Language of the Biblical Psalms* (SBLMS 9; Philadelphia: Society of Biblical Literature, 1955) 15, 50; idem, "Alalakhiana," *HUCA* 29 (1958) 131–133.

149. *PSBA* 22, l. 14.

150. *AfO* 17.315; 19.118 *apud* Livingstone, *Mystical and Mythological Explanatory Works*, 156.

151. *Yhwh's Combat with the Sea*, 62–69.

"cosmic waters" (that is, מבול = תהום = Tiamat), asserting that the concept here resembles "Mesopotamic Tiamat, not Ugaritic Yam."[152] Whereas in Ugaritic myth and ritual the ultimate victory of Ba'l was represented as his enthronement over Yamm, Kloos denies that the same notion is present in Psalm 29, which she believes is closer to the imagery of Tiamat (i.e., cosmic waters). But since the dais (*šubtu*!) in the inner sanctum of the temple apparently represented Tiamat in Akkadian rituals, I do not find the distinction between "Mesopotamic Tiamat" and Ugaritic Yamm convincing. Moreover, I should note that in the god-lists from Ugarit we find the equation ᵈ*Tâmtu* (Tiamat) = *Ym*, thus indicating that the distinction was not made between the two deities in ancient Canaan.[153] Against Kloos, therefore, I must insist that the enthronement of the deity cannot be separated from the conflict myth; there is no clear distinction between the enthronement over the watery chaos monsters and the cosmic waters.

The contention of Kloos is that this portion of the hymn has to do with fertility, and so מבול contains "an implicit reference to rain."[154] Hence, against most scholars, she defends the integrity of v 11, which invokes the blessing (יברך) of strength (עז) and peace (שלום) from YHWH, arguing that these requests are not necessarily tied to history and not necessarily an Israelite innovation.[155] She cites, *inter alia*, (1) *KTU* 1.5.VI.23-25 (= 1.6.VI.6-7), where the blessings on the "the multitude" are in doubt because of Ba'l's demise, and (2) two letters (*KTU* 2.44.5-6; 5.9.I.2-4) which contain a greeting formula wishing peace (*šlm*) and strength (*'z*) for the

152. Ibid., 67.

153. J. Nougayrol, "RS 20.24 (Pantheon d'Ugarit)," *Ugaritica* V (MRS 16; Paris: Imprimerie Nationale, 1968) 45; cf. *PRU* IV, 85.

154. *Yhwh's Combat with the Sea*, 90.

155. Ibid., 90-91.

recipients.[156] Although the evidence does not allow the limitation of the blessings to fertility, as Kloos would have it, I find the arguments for the integrity of v 11 quite persuasive. I should only add that the element of blessing is symbolized in myth and ritual by the banquet in the name of the victorious deity.[157]

The sequence of events in Psalm 29 mirrors the drama in 2 Samuel 5–6. The two texts, one prosaic–narrative and the other poetic–liturgical, are surprisingly similar in structure:

| | 2 Samuel 5–6 | Psalm 29 |
|---|---|---|
| Victory over Waters | 5:20–25 | vv 3–5 |
| Dance of Nature | 6:12–14, 16 | vv 6–9b |
| Accession | 6:15–17 | vv 9c–10 |
| Blessing | 6:18–19 | v 11 |

The sequence in 2 Samuel 6 is, however, interrupted by the reference to Michal in v 16. Her presence poses a *crux interpretum*, and so the verse is usually excised and, together with vv 20–23, regarded as secondary. Michal is frequently associated with the motif of the *femme fatale* who peers through the window, a motif thought to be present in Judg 5:28; 2 Kgs 9:30; Prov 7:6 (LXX), Cant. 2:9, and in ivory carvings throughout the Levant.[158] She looked out of the window (נשקפה בעד החלון) and, seeing David's revelry, she despised him.

The episode is, indeed, out of place in the cultic drama; the scene probably does not belong to the ritual. Yet, there is

---

156. But see other examples in A. L. Kristensen, "Ugaritic Epistolary Formulas: A Comparative Study of Ugaritic Epistolary Formulas in the Context of the Contemporary Akkadian Formulas in the Letters from Ugarit and Amarna," *UF* 9 (1977) 150–153, 157.

157. See my discussion below.

158. On this motif, see S. Abramsky, "The Woman Who Looked Out the Window," *Beth Mikra* 25 (1980) 114–124.

a connection with the divine warrior motif that must be considered, a deliberate connection that the narrator makes. The language of Michal's looking through the window echoes the longing of Sisera's mother in the Song of Deborah:

בעד החלון נשקפה
ותיבב אם סיסרא בעד האשנב
(Judg 5:28)

She looked through the window,
The mother of Sisera gazed through the lattice.

In this ancient poem, Sisera's mother is juxtaposed and starkly contrasted with the blessed Jael, between whose feet Sisera ignominiously fell. Here the woman who peered through the window is aligned with the enemy of the divine warrior and with the cursed people who did not come to the warrior's help. The wisest of her maids answered her wrongly, but she herself knew the answer to the question that she asked, namely, why the troops of her people had not returned. She knew that the people of YHWH were dividing (יחלקו) the spoils of war at the expense of her own people.

Michal, who is explicitly called "the daughter of Saul," is brought up by the narrator for propagandistic reasons--to signal the end of Saulide aspirations to the throne.[159] The pro-Davidic narrator could not resist an anti-Saulide polemic in reporting the events, but the theme of the polemic is in keeping with the theme of the divine warrior's march--at least in one tradition. Through the window Michal peered and perceived the victory of YHWH's army, now led by David, and so she despised him (ותבז לו). She is, thus, portrayed as an enemy of YHWH's anointed. Like the mother of Sisera, she peered through the window only to perceive the demise of her own family. Sisera's mother was bereaved; at the expense of

159. Cf. Smelik, "De intocht van de Ark in Jerusalem," 32-34.

her house the people of YHWH distributed (יחלקו) the spoils of war (Judg 5:30). The ancient poem concludes that the enemies of the holy warrior would perish, while the friends would rise in might like the sun (Judg 5:31). The narrator of 2 Samuel 6, then, was perhaps trying to associate Michal with the divine warrior's enemies who perished. David, on the other hand, was aligned with the allies of the divine warrior. Thus the word used in v 19 for David's action is, similar to the Song of Deborah, ויחלק. The closing verse of 2 Samuel 6, therefore, pronounces Michal's tragedy: "Michal the daughter of Saul had no children until the day of her death" (v 23).

## F. THE BANQUET

David's party brought the ark and installed it "in its place" (במקומו) in the tent-shrine that David had prepared for it (v 17). The king offered sacrifices: "burnt-offerings before YHWH" (עלות לפני יהוה) and שלמים. The sacrifice was not, however, a private exercise of piety, but a public demonstration of authority.[160] The mention of the שלמים should already clue one to the political significance of the sacrifice. The word is probably to be related to Akkadian *šulmānu*, a type of offering mentioned frequently in the Amarna letters in diplomatic protocol.[161] Thus, B. Levine has argued that the *šulmānu* was a tribute brought by the vanquished and the subordinate to the king at the *Königsritual*.[162]

The political function of the *šulmānu*-offerings in the myth of the divine warrior is probably best illustrated in

160. On the politics of sacrifice, see G. A. Anderson, *Sacrifices and Offerings in Ancient Israel* (HSM 41; Atlanta: Scholars, 1987).

161. Ibid., 44–49.

162. *In the Presence of the Lord* (SJLA 5; Leiden: Brill, 1974) 17–18.

Enuma Elish.[163] In that myth, Marduk defeated Tiamat, the primordial deep. He captured her, killed her, and stood upon her carcass: the divine warrior stood in triumph over the watery deep. When the other gods saw his victory "they rejoiced and were glad," and they brought him gifts and *šulmānu* (l. 134). Thus, the *šulmānu*-offering here is a tribute of the gods in the divine council to the ruling god of a city who, by virtue of his victory over his enemies, has ascended to the position of the supreme deity.

It is hardly surprising, therefore, that the offering of *šĕlāmîm* in the Hebrew Bible is frequently fraught with political overtones.[164] At the anointing of Saul, the people offered *šĕlāmîm* before YHWH and "rejoiced greatly" (1 Sam 11:14–15). Following the account of the dream that legitimated Solomon's accession (1 Kgs 3:1–15),[165] one reads that the king "offered burnt offerings and *šĕlāmîm* and made a banquet for all his servants" (1 Kgs 3:15). The celebration of the inauguration of the Solomonic temple, likewise, included the offering of the *šĕlāmîm* (1 Kgs 8:63-64) and a great communal feast that went on for seven days, after which the people were sent home "joyful and glad of heart for all the goodness that YHWH had done for David his servant and for Israel his people" (1 Kgs 8:66).

So, according to the report of the ark procession in 2 Samuel 6, following the ascent to Jerusalem (the conquered mount), David blessed the people in the name of YHWH Ṣĕḇā'ôṯ, that is, on behalf of the divine warrior, and he distributed to each person חלת לחם אחת ואשפר אחד ואשישה אחד "a ring-bread, a date-cake, and a raisin cake" (v

163. *EE* IV.93–134.

164. See Levine, *In the Presence of the Lord*, 3–52 and the literature cited therein, and recently, Anderson, *Sacrifices and Offerings in Ancient Israel*, 49–51.

165. For the propagandistic intent of the dream narrative, see C. L. Seow, "The Syro-Palestinian Context of Solomon's Dream," *HTR* 77 (1984) 141–152.

19).[166] This was evidently a symbolic banquet, a ritual celebrating the accession of the divine warrior. It represented the sort of banquet that Ba'l held after his victory over his enemies and the completion of his temple.[167] To this feast Ba'l invited the seventy sons of 'Athirat, that is, all the deities of the divine council (*KTU* 1.4.VI.40–59). The banquet was a public demonstration of Ba'l's beneficence which he exercised as victor. As is evident from *KTU* 1.91, the banquet was tantamount to a claim of authority; it was a celebration of Ba'l's rise to the position of king. Typically in the Ugaritic texts, it is 'Ēl, the chief god of the pantheon, who presides over the divine banquet in his palace (*KTU* 1.2.I.20–22; 1.114; 1.108; etc.). But here, following Ba'l's victory, we find the young god hosting the banquet himself. He assumed the role that was traditionally ascribed to 'Ēl. Later in the same tablet, Ba'l sits enthroned (*yθb*) and gloats:

'ḥdy . dymlk . 'l . 'ilm .
lymr'u[168] 'ilm . wnšm .
dyšb['] . hmlt . 'arṣ .
(*KTU* 1.4.VII.49–52)

I alone am the one who rules over the gods,
Who fattens gods and humans,
Who satisfies the multitudes of the earth.

---

166. L. Koehler, "Äschpar Dattelkuchen," *TLZ* 4 (1948) 397–398; idem, "Loch- und Ringbrot," *TLZ* 4 (1948) 154–155. J. Morgenstern ("A Chapter in the History of the High-Priesthood," *AJSL* 55 [1938] 7, 10) posits that the אשישה was connected with the New Year festival. Cf. R. Patai, "Hebrew Installation Rites," *HUCA* 20 (1947) 202.

167. Note, in Hosea 3, the association of the אשישה with Canaanite fertility cults, perhaps with the worship of Ba'l.

168. Perhaps we should read *<d>ymr'u*, assuming that the three bottom wedges have been omitted inadvertantly.

Similar themes are found in Enuma Elish, where Marduk celebrates his victory over Tiamat and the establishing of his new abode with a great banquet (*EE* VI.69–94). Before the gods of the divine assembly, Babylon was proclaimed the favorite dwelling place of Marduk. There, in Babylon, the deities took their seats, and the stations in the heavens were fixed. When the great gods had assembled, they extolled the destiny of Marduk, and they bowed down before him. They acknowledged his kingship over all the gods of heaven and the netherworld. Since the myths in Mesopotamia were acted out in state-sponsored rituals, one may assume that this divine banquet was represented in the great communal meals that the king hosted, thus manifesting the beneficence that his reign brought.[169]

Here again, parallels can be drawn with Gudea's procession of the divine statue into Lagash.[170] Ningirsu the warrior was brought into the newly constructed temple, accompanied by a battle shout (cf. the תרועה in Israelite rituals), and there was great rejoicing in the land. Gudea slaughtered animals and brought libations for the gods, so that "the Anunnaki of Lagash feasted with the lord Ningirsu in that place."[171] Again, the banquet of the gods was played out in the feasting that the state sponsored, a feasting which lasted seven days (cf. 1 Kgs 8:65), during which period there was peace in the land and no distinction between slaves and nobles.[172] Ningirsu the holy warrior was exalted above the other gods, and that exaltation was mirrored on earth by the rise of Gudea, who became the "Shepherd of Ningirsu." Such were the politics of ritual!

So it was that David presided at the ritual banquet in the name of the victorious warrior, distributing food to all the

---

169. See Livingstone, *Mystical and Mythological Explanatory Works*, 136–170.

170. Gudea Cylinder B. See von Soden, *Sumerische und akkadische Hymnen und Gebete*, 166ff.

171. Gudea Cylinder B.V.18.

172. Gudea Cylinder B.XVII.18–XVIII.8.

multitudes. Through him the blessings of YHWH were transmitted to all the people, and that beneficence of the holy warrior-king was dramatically demonstrated in the cultic banquet. Clearly, the accession of the deity brought blessings to YHWH's people. So Psalm 29 appropriately concludes with the invocation of blessing: יהוה יברך את־עמו בשלום "May YHWH bless his people with peace!" According to the narrative of 2 Samuel 6, the blessings of the triumphant warrior were mediated through David in this ritual banquet: ויברך את־העם בשם יהוה צבאות "he (David) blessed the people in the name of YHWH Ṣĕḇā'ôṯ" (2 Sam 6:18).

Psalm 132, which is connected with David and the ritual procession of the ark, alludes to the banquet where YHWH satisfied the multitudes, even as Ba'l, according to the Ugaritic myth about his rise to power, satisfied the multitudes:

זאת־מנוחתי עדי־עד
פה־אשב כי אותיה
צידה ברך אברך
אביוניה אשביע לחם
(Ps 132:14–15)

This is my resting place forever and ever.
Here will I sit enthroned for I desired it.
I will indeed bless her with provision.
I will satisfy her needy with bread.

Given the highly symbolic event that the induction of the ark was, it is not surprising that in the exilic period the messianic banquet came to be associated with the name of David (Isa 55:1–5). According to Deutero-Isaiah's re-presentation of the divine warrior myth, the decisive victory of YHWH in a new battle would lead to a new procession to Zion and a new banquet on that holy abode of

YHWH.[173] The eternal covenant would be made universal in the name of David, who would be made "a witness (עד) to all peoples, a leader (נגיד) and commander (מצוה) of the peoples" (Isa 55:5).

## G. POSTSCRIPT

The Michal episode in vv 20–23 has always been an enigma to scholars, who have generally regarded it as secondary.[174] My own analysis of the text would tend to confirm the opinion that the passage does not properly belong with the preceding unit. The report of the cultic procession and installation of a divine emblem appropriately concludes with the celebration of the victory in a ritual banquet. The mythic pattern is complete with the celebration of the divine banquet.

2 Sam 6:22–23 appears to be a variant account of the cultic drama led by David. Its presence here is perhaps prompted by the narrator's reference to Michal in v 16. Nevertheless, it must be admitted that a later redactor apparently saw fit to include it just at this point, linking it at once to the cultic dramatization of the divine warrior's victory celebration and the attempt to build a temple for YHWH (2 Samuel 7). It is not amiss, therefore, to briefly consider the place of this unit in the politics of David's revelry, if only as a postscript to our study of David's procession of the ark.

The meaning of the passage is unclear. The reason for Michal's objection to David's public performance is not

173. L. R. Fisher ("From Chaos to Cosmos," *Encounter* 26 [1965] 191–194) discerns a movement through Isaiah 51–55 of what he calls "the Ba'l creation form", a movement "through conflict, kingship, new creation (and its vocation), temple building, and banquet."

174. So Rost (*The Succession to the Throne of David*, 86–90), who takes it as the first episode of the Succession Narrative, and most commentators following him.

explicitly stated, nor is the nature of David's humiliation described. Sexual jealousy is apparently not the issue but rather politics, for the passage affirms the election of David and emphasizes the demise of the house of Saul.

A commonly accepted interpretation, following the reconstruction of royal investitures in Mesopotamia and Egypt, is that a coronation drama is involved here. Others speak of a *hieros gamos*, where the king and his consort play the parts of the god and his consort respectively in a fertility ritual of some sort.[175] Accordingly, the point of the episode is the scorning of Michal, who was refused her rightful role in the sacred marriage. Still others view the text as an honest assessment and subtle criticism of David's womanizing tendencies.[176] It has not been noticed, however, that three of the verbal roots, *gly*, *kbd*, and *śḥq* ( = *ṣḥq)*, and a biform of *qll* are, in fact, found in close proximity in the Ugaritic passage of 'Athirat's pilgrimage to the abode of 'Ēl at the source of the double-deep:

tgly . ðd . 'il
wtb'u qrš . mlk . 'ab . šnm
lp'n . 'il . thbr .
wtql tšthwy . wtkbdh
hlm . 'il . kyphnh
wprq . lṣb . wyṣḥq
(*KTU* 1.4.IV.23-28)

She uncovered the tent of 'Ēl,
and entered the pavilion of the king,
the father of years.
At the feet of 'Ēl she bowed and fell;

175. Notably, J. R. Porter, "The Interpretation of 2 Samuel VI and Psalm CXXXII," *JTS* 5 (1954) 161-173.

176. F. Crüseman, "Zwei alttestamentliche Witze. I Sam 21:11-15 und II Sam 6:16, 20-23 als Beispiel einer biblischen Gattung," *ZAW* 92 (1980) 223-227.

She worshipped and honored him.
Lo! 'Ēl saw her indeed--
He eased his frown and revelled.

What precisely happened in this scene is unclear. 'Ēl responded to 'Athirat's approach with excitement, performing an animated dance which he thought might have aroused his consort. Nevertheless, the issue of the encounter is not in doubt. 'Athirat complained that Ba'l, though triumphant, did not yet have a temple, a permanent home like the other gods. Instead, Ba'l continued to seek shelter in the dwellings of others. And so 'Ēl responded by giving permission for the construction of Ba'l's temple: "Let a house be built for Ba'l!"[177]

In another episode, 'Anat, the consort of Ba'l, likewise complained that victorious Ba'l had no temple. She, too, came to petition 'Ēl on Ba'l's behalf, uncovering (*gly*) the tent of 'Ēl and entering the domicile as 'Athirat did.[178] She declared:

mlkn . 'al'iyn . b'l
θpṭn 'in . d'lnh .
(*KTU* 1.3.V.32-33)

Mighty Ba'l is our king,
Our judge, over whom there is no one.

Yet, there was no house for Ba'l like the gods, no permanent dwelling befitting a deity of his stature. So Qudš-wa-'Amrur is ordered to go before Kothar-wa-Ḫasis, to request the craftsman to build the house for Ba'l:

lp'n . kθ<r> . hbr . wql
tštḥwy . wkbd . hwt .
(*KTU* 1.3.VI.18-20)

177. *KTU* 1.4.IV.62.
178. *KTU* 1.3.V.15.

Bow down at the feet of Kothar and fall,
Prostrate and honor him.

In yet another text, Kothar-wa-Ḫasis himself uncovered (*gly*) and entered (*bw'*) the tent of 'Ēl, and did obeisance (*wql [. y]štḥw[y .] ykb[dnh.]*) before 'Ēl, performing the same ritual that others had performed in anticipation of the construction of a temple, though his concern here was with a temple for Yamm/Nahar.[179]

It is more than a little curious, then, that Michal accused David of being "uncovered" (*gly*) and, perhaps sarcastically, of being "honored" (*kbd*). And David took it as a matter of pride that he "revelled" (*śḥq*), "fell" (*nqlty*), and was "honored" (*kbd*). Even though it is impossible to reconstruct the details of the ritual, and to know how this passage relates to the preceding narrative about the procession, one may conjecture that David's action might have been conceived as related to the attempt to build a temple/palace for YHWH following the deity's victory and accession in his newly conquered domain. The situation is reminiscent of Ba'l's plight immediately after his victory over his enemies: the triumphant divine warrior did not yet have a house, that is, a permanent dwelling befitting a god of his stature. The connection with the ritual evidenced in Ugaritic mythology is even stronger when one considers that in a liturgical reference to the procession of the ark, the call is "Let us come (נבואה) to his tabernacle // Let us bow down (נשתחוה) at his (YHWH's) footstool."[180] The account in vv 20-23, then, is of a ritual that is properly the prelude to the construction of the temple, which David proposes to do in the next chapter (2 Samuel 7).

---

179. *KTU* 1.2.III.5-6.
180. Ps 132:7.

## H. SUMMARY OF RESULTS

Scholars have long recognized that 2 Samuel 6 contains material for the legitimation of the Davidic dynasty.[181] The foregoing investigation of the chapter has confirmed that conclusion. 2 Samuel indeed compares David favorably with Saul and asserts the end of Saulide political claims in no uncertain terms. But the chapter also marks the end of the claims of the house of Abinadab, the custody of the ark being passed from that family to the house of David. The reference to the ark's brief sojourn in the care of the Gittite, moreover, may be a subtle legitimation of David, who also sought refuge in Gath prior to his rise to power. The pro-Davidic propaganda woven through the chapter would indicate an early date for the bulk of the narrative, a date in the early monarchy, when there were questions about the legitimacy of David either as the leader of all the tribes, or as the custodian of the cultic emblem of the Shilonite confederacy.

But the chapter does not only provide evidence of legitimation in a political document, namely, the History of David's Rise. It also tells of David's demonstration of his authority in a public ritual. In this regard, McCarter is surely correct to reject the purely liturgical reading of this text.[182] He argues persuasively that David's procession is no mere reflex of a ritual in the post-Davidic monarchy, as some scholars have proposed. Rather, 2 Samuel 6 has to do with the inauguration of the new city and is, thus, comparable with similar religio-political rituals performed elsewhere in the ancient Near East. But one may go beyond McCarter to show that the ritual over which David presided was located in a mythic pattern, namely, that of the divine warrior's rise to supremacy. Despite minor reworkings, 2 Samuel still reflects

---

181. Cf. A. Weiser, "Die Legitimation des Königs David," *VT* 16 (1966) 325-354.

182. "The Ritual Dedication of the City of David," 273-278.

the sequence of the ritual that David sponsored to dramatize the accession of the divine warrior; the mythic pattern that the ritual followed is still discernible in the narrative.

McCarter has insisted that the passage on the victory over the Philistines (2 Sam 5:17–25) serves as an introduction to the account of the procession.[183] Indeed, the passage provides the necessary framework for understanding the ritual. Here, for the first time in the Hebrew Bible, the defeat of Israel's enemies is likened to the defeat of the unruly waters. Seeds were sown here that would appear full-blown later in the Zion tradition as the *Völkerkampf* motif in which YHWH is portrayed as fighting for Israel against the unruly nations who surrounded Zion, even as the unruly waters constantly threatened to inundate the earth. The successes of Israel in their battles with the Philistines on the eve of their entry into Jerusalem provided the inspiration for the theology of Zion's inviolability: YHWH would always defeat the chaotic nations, as surely as he defeated the chaotic waters! The passage on the battle with the Philistines tips the reader off that the procession should be interpreted in the light of the victory of the divine warrior over his enemies.

The induction of the ark is presented as a celebration of victory. The terms of revelry (*śḥq* = *ṣḥq*) and joy (*śmḥh*) are, in Canaanite mythology, associated with the celebration of victory in divine battle as well as the establishing of a new abode for the victorious deity. They are also used in like manner later in the Zion tradition.

The episode on the smiting of 'Uzzah serves now to legitimate the transfer of the ark from the custody of the house of Abinadab to the house of David. But the vocabulary of the smiting of 'Uzzah, inasmuch as it echoes the breaking of the enemies at Ba'l Peraṣim, suggests that there is more behind the propaganda of the pro-Davidic narrator. The episode may, in fact, contain an allusion to a ritual smiting of the enemies at a threshing-floor that had been prepared for

183. *II Samuel*, 143.

the cultic drama. In Mesopotamia, such sham battles were conducted in the religio-political dramas sponsored by the state. As the Standard Babylonian explanatory texts make plain, such rituals dramatized the victory of the patron deities of the state over its enemies in cosmogonic combat.

Following the smiting of ʻUzzah, the ark was carried in procession into Jerusalem. The terms צעדו and צעדים recall the approach of the divine warrior in some archaic hymnic texts, and, as in the report of YHWH's victory over the Philistines in the preceding chapter (vv 21-25), the marching followed the divine warrior's smiting. Moreover, the dances that accompanied that march--described by the participles מכרכר "prancing," מפזז "leaping," and מרקד "skipping"--may indicate the convulsion of nature, which is said to dance like animals in the face of the divine warrior's march. I posit, therefore, that the cultic participants may have been dramatizing the divine warrior's homeward march, with animated dancing that simulated the dance of nature accompanying that march.

The purpose of the whole procession was to dramatize the accession of YHWH as king. So the text speaks of David and his retinue "causing the ark of YHWH to ascend with the shout and the sound of the Shophar" (מעלים את־הארון יהוה בתרועה ובקול שופר). The ascent of the ark signified the rise of YHWH to a higher place, namely as the supreme deity, a king among the gods. It is not simply a higher geographical destination of which the text speaks, but an exalted position for the victorious deity. Hence, at the climax of the celebration was a ritual banquet over which David presided in the name of YHWH Ṣĕḇāʼôṯ. This corresponds to the victory banquet which the victorious warrior hosts.

From beginning to end, the ritual dramatized the accession of the deity as victorious king, according to the ancient Near Eastern myth of the divine warrior. In ancient Canaan this myth was typically told of Baʻl, who overcame his enemies Yamm/Nahar/Mot to become king of all. To judge from Israel's earliest hymnic texts, the myth was known to and adapted by the tribes of Israel in their cultus by the end of the Late Bronze age. Perhaps YHWH had even come to be identified with Ba'l among certain Israelite tribes of the hill country, as is evident from the sudden increase in the number of cities with Ba'l names, precisely coinciding with the increase of Israelite settlements there in that period,[184] and the appearance of a number of Israelite personal names with Ba'l as theophoric element.[185] Certainly, the myth was known already at Qiryat-Ye'arim, which was also called Qiryat-Ba'l "City of Ba'l," Ba'lah, or Mount Ba'l.

By the end of the eleventh century, the myth of Ba'l had been adapted for the *hieros logos* of the ark-sanctuary at Qiryat-Ye'arim (Qiryat-Ba'l) to explain the temporary demise of the ark and to give assurance to the devotees of YHWH that the deity had, despite his apparent defeat, in fact triumphed over his enemies. YHWH at Qiryat-Ye'arim was not a deity firmly enthroned as king, but a feisty warrior god seeking to defeat his enemies and claim dominion.

With the political and military successes of David, however, the myth of the triumphant divine warrior was given substance. The Philistines, who had long been a menace to Israel, had been soundly defeated. The stage was set for the exaltation of the deity to the supreme position of the Most High god--hence the religio-political drama of the divine warrior's rise to power. The procession was YHWH's "rite of passage," as Flanagan puts it, through victory in combat, the

---

184. A. F. Rainey, "The Toponymics of Eretz Israel," *BASOR* 231 (1978) 1-17; B. Mazar, "The Early Israelite Settlement in the Hill Country," *BASOR* 241 (1981) 75-85; B. Rosen, "Early Israelite Cultic Centres in the Hill Country," *VT* 38 (1988) 114-116.

185. One of David's children was named *Ba'ălîyāda'* (1 Chron 14:7; although in 2 Sam 5:16 he appears as *'Ĕlîyāda'*) and another is called *Yāp̄î*ª', a name expressing confidence in the deity as divine warrior. See Miller, *The Divine Warrior in Early Israel*, 76-78. Cf. Amorite personal names *Ya-a-pa-aḫ-*ᵈ*IM*, *Ya-pi-iḫ-*ᵈ*IM*, *Ba-li-a-pu-uḫ*.

triumphant return with the accompanying dance of nature, accession, and the manifestation of his beneficence to all his people. In the new political arena of the Davidic monarchy, the kingship of Israel's god could be affirmed again, as it was at Shiloh. Hence the name of the ark at Shiloh is invoked once more: "the ark of YHWH Ṣĕḇā'ôṯ who sits enthroned on the cherubim." A new synthesis of mythological traditions--of 'Ēl and Ba'l--is now possible in the Israelite cultus.

## CHAPTER THREE

# ARK PROCESSION AND DAVIDIC POLITICS

Psalm 132 has the distinction of being the only text in the Psalter that mentions the ark explicitly (v 8),[1] and it does so in a liturgical fashion, invoking the advance of YHWH in a manner reminiscent of the ancient Song of the Ark (Num 10:35). Moreover, the invocation follows an allusion to a ritual act apparently led by David in שׂדי יער (v 6), which is commonly assumed to be a poetic name for Qiryat-Ye'arim. Hence, most scholars see the psalm as reflecting, at least in part or in some earlier form, a ritual procession of the ark.

Any discussion of the cultic background of this psalm must begin with the contribution of Sigmund Mowinckel. It was he who most vigorously defended the association of this text with the procession of the ark. He argued that Psalm 132 was an ancient royal liturgy connected with the annual enthronement of YHWH during the autumn New Year festival and, thus, is to be associated with other "enthronement texts" of the Psalter.[2] In fact, Mowinckel contended that this psalm was part of *the* text for the annually performed drama of YHWH's enthronement in Jerusalem.[3] His general hypothesis has found wide, if qualified, acceptance. Notably, in his dissertation on the cultic procession of the ark, Fretheim identifies the psalm as an "ark liturgy" composed in its entirety for this ritual in the period of the monarchy.[4]

Other commentators, however, are not so sanguine about the *Sitz im Leben* of the psalm, as Mowinckel presented it.

---

1. But for possible allusions to the ark, see Davies, "The Ark in the Psalms," 51–61.

2. *Psalmenstudien* II, 93, 178; *Psalms in Israel's Worship* I, 114–115, 129, 174–177.

3. *The Psalms in Israel's Worship* I, 175.

4. "The Cultic Use of the Ark of the Covenant in the Monarchial Period," 128–147.

Kraus, in particular, goes to great lengths to dispute Mowinckel's association of the procession of the ark with the enthronement of the deity.[5] He prefers, rather, to speak of a Royal Zion Festival celebrating the twin election of David and Zion. But Kraus does not deny that the procession of the ark lies in the background of Psalm 132, only that it was connected with the enthronement ritual. Indeed, he believes that the Zion Festival was based originally on David's transfer of the ark and Nathan's Oracle, and that the ritual procession during the festival was intended to legitimate the Davidic dynasty and Jerusalem.[6]

Despite variations in the details, most interpreters concede that there is an allusion to the procession of the ark in Psalm 132. Yet, it must be admitted that there is no unanimity on this matter. A. Weiser, for instance, insists that there is no possibility of an allusion to the procession in the psalm since the ark, according to his interpretation of v 7, is already in the temple.[7] The assumption of an annual procession of the ark in Psalm 132 has also been most vigorously challenged by D. R. Hillers, who cuts to the core of the matter by denying that v 8 is a summons for the ark to march *to* the "resting place".[8] Hillers maintains that the verse has nothing to do with the procession of the ark. Rather, he believes that it is simply a prayer for YHWH to intervene on

---

5. *Königsherrschaft*, 27–99; *Psalmen* II, 1057–1061; *Worship*, 183–188.

6. Kraus, *Psalmen* II, 1057–1064. Cf. also, Porter ("The Interpretation of 2 Samuel vii and Psalm cxxxii," 161–173), who depends on both Mowinckel and and Kraus.

7. *The Psalms* (OTL; trans. H. Hartwell; Philadelphia: Westminster, 1962) 781. Weiser contends that v 8 is simply an appeal for the deity to appear in cultic theophany "above the wings of the cherubim upon the ark," but he ignores the explicit reference to YHWH's coming with the ark in the parallel line.

8. "Ritual Procession of the Ark and Ps 132," *CBQ* 30 (1968) 48–55.

behalf of the king and, as such, is comparable with the general use in the Psalter of the imperative קום addressed to the deity.[9]

Closely related to the question of the procession is the date of the psalm, with scholarly opinion ranging from the Davidic period,[10] to the Maccabbean.[11] Arguing for a tenth century provenance, Dahood and Cross have identified what they regard as archaisms, including the use of שׁנת[12] instead of שׁנה (v 4), the relative particle זו (v 12), the plural משׁכנות used in a singular sense (vv 5, 7), the verb ישׁב for divine dwelling (vv 12, 14), and the idiom ישׁב ל instead of normal ישׁב על (v 12).[13] Yet, it must be admitted that the psalm is not uniformly archaic. Unless significant emendations are attempted, the presence of the *nota accusativi* in v 1 and

---

9. Ibid., 51.

10. So, for example, H. Gunkel, *Die Psalmen* (HKAT 1/2; Göttingen: Vandenhoeck & Ruprecht, 1926) 568; Dahood, *Psalms* III, 241; Cross, *Canaanite Myth and Hebrew Epic*, 94-97. Cf. B. Halpern, *The Constitution of the Monarchy* (HSM 25; Chico, California: Scholars, 1981) 17-19.

11. So F. Hitzig (*Die Psalmen* [Heidelberg: Winter, 1835] 200-201) cites Simon Maccabeus' discovery of Mount Zion in 1 Macc 13:51, and W. F. Cobb (*The Book of Psalms* [London: Methuen, 1905] 381) claims that the ruler in the psalm is Simon. This extremely late dating is rare, however. More common is the placing of the psalm generally in the post-exilic period. So esp. R. J. Tournay, *Voir et entendre Dieu avec les Psaumes* (CahRB 24; Paris: Gabalda, 1988) 163-165; H. Kruse, "Psalm CXXXII and the Royal Zion Festival," *VT* 33 (1983) 279. See the survey of scholarship in C. B. McCarthy, "Psalm 132: A Methodological Analysis," Unpublished Ph.D. Dissertation (Marquette University, 1968) 37-49 and the brief but excellent overview in L. C. Allen, *Psalms 101-150* (WBC 21; Waco, Texas: Word, 1983) 204-209.

12. Hardly to be pointed שֵׁנַת, as Kruse ("Psalm CXXXII and the Royal Zion Festival," 281 n. 13) implies. The inf. cs. of ישׁן is יְשֹׁן (Qoh 5:11).

13. Dahood, *Psalms* III, 242; Cross, *Canaanite Myth and Hebrew Epic*, 97 n. 24.

the relative particle אשר in v 2 would make such an early date unlikely.[14] In the latter instance, Cross simply reconstructs דוד in place of אשר on stylistic grounds.[15] He also reads אלמדם<ו> *metri causa*, restoring the more archaic *-mo* for the 3 mp suffix instead of *-m* (אלמדם, v 12).[16]

As it stands, the poem may be divided into two halves of ten lines each (Part A: vv 1-10; Part B: vv 11-18).[17] The first half concerns the fulfillment of David's oath to YHWH; the second half concerns YHWH's oath to David. In vocabulary and themes, the two halves mirror one another, indicating an intricate structure that must have been the work of a skillful composer.[18]

Despite the argumentation of a few scholars, the psalm presupposes the monarchy, and there is nothing that compels a late date. The association of YHWH with the designation ארון עזך "your mighty ark" (v 8), especially with the imperative קומה יהוה, would tend to indicate an early date, when the ark was still used as a war palladium or, in any case, when it was still closely connected with YHWH as the divine warrior.[19] This text and the quotation of it in Chronicles (2 Chron 6:41) both place the event in the early monarchy. The focus on the election of Zion as YHWH's royal dwelling (vv 13, 14) accords with the tenor of Zion

---

14. Robertson (*Linguistic Evidence*, 63, 143) finds the occurrence of the relative אשר together with זו in Psalm 132 evidence of "archaizing."

15. *Canaanite Myth and Hebrew Epic*, 244.

16. Ibid., 283 n. 61; cf. Robertson, *Linguistic Evidence*, 65-66.

17. On the structure of the psalm, see T. E. Fretheim, "Psalm 132: A Form-Critical Study," *JBL* 86 (1967) 289-300; E. F. Huwiler, "Patterns and Problems in Psalm 132," in *The Listening Heart* (Fs. R. E. Murphy; ed. K. G. Hoglund et. al.; Sheffield: JSOT, 1987) 199-212.

18. So Fretheim, "Psalm 132," 299.

19. Cf. Num 10:35-36 (J); 14:42-44 (J); 1 Sam 4:3ff; cf. Pss 24:7-10; 78:60-61.

theology and not at all with exilic or post-exilic tendencies. The strong emphasis on the continuity of the Davidic line (vv 11-12, 17), moreover, suggests a time when the Davidic kings were still ruling.[20] On the other hand, the plea to the deity to "remember for David's sake" (v 1) and not reject the anointed (v 10), the polemic against unnamed enemies of the king, together with the assurance of a diadem (נזר) on the head of the anointed (vv 17-18), and the insistence on Zion as the place that the deity had chosen (vv 14-16) may indicate some measure of insecurity on the part of the Davidides, thus making a Davidic or Solomonic date less than satisfactory.

The period immediately following the death of Solomon and the division of the Davidic empire would fit the mood of the poem. I am inclined to think that this was a royal psalm composed in the aftermath of the split to legitimate the Davidic court and its capital, Jerusalem. So it appeals to the deity to "remember" David and his pious acts (v 1), and not to "turn away the face" of the anointed (v 10). The apologist for the Davidic dynasty turned to archaic material to support his arguments, citing portions of an ancient liturgical text, or perhaps several liturgical texts, associated with the procession of the ark into Jerusalem under David.[21] He recalls the old

20. So R. Kittel, *Die Psalmen* (KAT; Leipzig: Scholl, 1929) 404-405.

21. Already in 1959, O. Eissfeldt ("Psalm 132," [1959] *KS* III, 483) argued that vv 6-9 should be isolated as a quote from an older source. But others have discerned archaic sources beyond these verses. So, O. Loretz (*Die Psalmen* II [Neukirchen-Vluyn: Kevelaer-Neukirchener, 1979] 292) regards vv 2-5, 11, 14-18 as coming from an older source, and K. Seybold (*Wallfahrtspsalmen* [BTS 3; Neukirchen: 1978] 43 and "Der Redaktion der Wallfahrtspsalmen," *ZAW* 71 [1979] 256) holds that vv 3-9 and 14-18 are archaic. I am inclined to think that vv 3-5, 6-9, 11b-15 are liturgical materials from the Davidic period. One should note also the attempt of C. B. Houk ("Psalm 132, Literary Integrity, and Syllable-Word Structures," *JSOT* 6 [1978] 41-46) to identify older portions of the poem on the basis of the syllable counts.

divine epithet, אביר יעקב "the Bull of Jacob," which had probably been associated with the ark at the central sanctuary of Shiloh (vv 2, 5), and speaks of David's initiative in finding a "place" for YHWH (v 5), thus subtly implicating the Saulides for neglecting the cult. It is implied that the ark had become neglected and forgotten precisely in the territory of the *northern* tribes, in Ephrathah (i.e., Ephraim, or the vicinity of Qiryat-Ye'arim) // the Highland of Ya'ar[22]--so much so that a search had to be launched to find it (v 6). So the Israelites had come together to the abode of the deity to invite the deity to the new resting-place (vv 7-8). The poem reminds YHWH of the irrevocable oath sworn to David of an enduring dynasty (v 11). But the over-confidence of the Solomonic reign has been tempered somewhat, it seems, as the conditional element of the covenant is reiterated (v 12). Moreover, the theme of David's election is supported by the emphasis on Zion as YHWH's abode of choice (v 13). It appears that, for this psalmist, the election of David and election of Zion went hand in hand. Accordingly, it is in Zion ("here") that the deity had chosen to be enthroned--not at any competing site (v 14). It is in Zion where YHWH has decided to dwell, and bless his people and provide victuals for the multitudes (v 15). It is in this chosen abode ("there") that YHWH would "cause the horn to sprout" and prepare the "lamp" for his anointed (17). The apology ends with an allusion to the failure of the "enemies" of the Davidic king who will be clothed with shame, while the anointed scion of David will bear the sign of the consecrated king (v 18).[23]

---

22. For this translation, see below.

23. Tadmor's comment regarding apologetic works in Mesopotamia is apt: "[T]hey were composed not so much to reflect apologetically upon the past but rather to serve certain imminent political aims in the present or some particular design for the future." See H. Tadmor, "Autobiographical Apology in the Royal Assyrian Literature," in *History, Historiography and Interpretation* (ed. H. Tadmor and M. Weinfeld; Jerusalem/Leiden: Magnes/Brill, 1983) 37.

On him will be the diadem (נזר), which was the very symbol of kingship that Saul wore until he died (2 Sam 2:10) and which later Davidides passed on as a token of their consecration (cf. 2 Kgs 11:12).

## A. DAVID'S OATH TO YHWH

The psalm opens with a prayer to YHWH, followed by what appears to be the basis of the appeal:

זכור־יהוה לדוד
את כל־ענותו[24]
אשר נשבע ליהוה
נדר לאביר יעקב
אם־אבא באהל ביתי
אם־אעלה על־ערש יצועי
אם־אתן שנת לעיני
לעפעפי תנומה
עד־אמצא מקום ליהוה
משכנות לאביר יעקב
(Ps 132:1–2)

Remember, O YHWH, for David's sake,
all his humility.[25]
How he swore to YHWH,
Vowed to the Bull of Jacob.

---

24. A word is usually restored here *metri causa*. But, lacking textual evidence and a convincing proposal that would explain the loss of the word, I have resisted any reconstruction.

25. Reading עֲנָוָתוֹ (cf. LXX, Vulg., Syr.) instead of the Dp inf. עֻנּוֹתוֹ (MT) which is unattested elsewhere. This reading was profferred by F. Perles, *Analekten zur Textkritik des Alten Testaments* (Munich: Ackermann, 1895) 65 and defended by A. R. Johnson, *Sacral Kingship in Israel* (2d ed.; Cardiff: University of Wales, 1967) 20; Hillers ("Ritual Procession of the Ark and Ps 132," 53) and others.

"I will not enter the shelter of my home;
Nor climb upon the comfort of my bed.
I will not grant sleep to my eyes,
Nor slumber to my eyes,
Until I find a place for YHWH,
A tabernacle for the Bull of Jacob."

YHWH is asked to remember לדוד. Here David is neither the subject, as Dahood would have it;[26] nor, strictly, is it the direct object of the imperative.[27] Rather, the deity is asked to remember *for David's sake.*

Hillers[28] and W. Schottroff[29] have called attention to West Semitic dedicatory inscriptions wherein the deities are asked to remember the pious deeds of the devotee. From Larnax Lapethos, for instance, comes an inscription on a votive image set up in the temple of Melqart by a certain Yatonba'l as a memorial (*skr*) for his name, dedicated for his own life, his descendants, and especially his legitimate scion (*lṣmḥ ṣdq*).[30] The deity is asked in the inscription to remember Yatonba'l's pious deeds and bestow favor on him and his descendants (l. 15).[31] Accordingly, Hillers cite biblical texts where the idiom זכר ל appears in reference to the pious initiatives of individuals (Neh 5:19; 13:14, 22, 29, 31; 2 Chron 6:42), and posits that Psalm 132 may have descended from one of the "epigraphic" psalms, that is, those that may have

26. Dahood (*Psalms* III, 242) assumes the vocative-*lāmed*, but see the critique of Miller in "Vocative Lamed in the Psalter," 617–637.

27. So *KJV*, *JB*.

28. "Ritual Dedication of the Ark and Ps 132," 53.

29. *'Gedenken' im alten Orient und im Alten Testament* (WMANT 15; Neukirchen-Vluyn: Neukirchener, 1964) 225.

30. *KAI* 43, esp. ll. 3, 11.

31. The text reads: *wyskrn mlkrt* "May Melqart remember me!"

originally been displayed on stelae.[32] Hillers' biblical examples are, however, all derived from the post-exilic period, whereas such "epigraphic psalms" would presumably be much earlier. It should further be noted that none of the inscriptions cited actually involves the idiom *zkr l*; in each case, the devotee named is the *direct object* of the remembering, *not* indicated by the preposition *l*. The parallels that Hillers cite are at best imprecise.

Against those who seek to locate the idiom in a judicial context,[33] W. Schottroff has emphasized the importance of the covenant as background for understanding the use of זכר in the Hebrew Bible.[34] This is certainly an important observation for Psalm 132, given its interest in the covenant (v 12).[35] Specifically in regard to the idiom זכר ל, one notes that it occurs frequently in petitions to the deity to avert disasters, the basis for the plea being God's covenant with individuals in generations gone by.[36] Thus, in the face of divine wrath and impending rejection for the construction of the golden calf, Moses prayed: זכר לאברהם ליצחק ולישראל עבדיך אשר נשבעת להם בך "Remember *for the sake of* Abraham, Isaac and Israel, your servants to whom you swore by yourself!" (Exod 32:13; cf. Deut 9:27).[37] The thrice repeated preposition

32. "Ritual Procession of the Ark and Ps 132," 53–55, citing H. L. Ginsberg, "Psalms and Inscriptions of Petition and Acknowledgement," in *Louis Ginzberg Jubilee* I (New York: American Academy for Jewish Research, 1945) 159–171.

33. So H. J. Boecker, *Redeformen des Rechtslebens im Alten Testaments* (WMANT 14; Neukirchen-Vluyn: Neukirchener, 1964), esp. 106–111.

34. *'Gedenken' im alten Orient und im Alten Testament*, 202–211.

35. See H. Gese, "Der Davidsbund und die Zionserwählung," *ZTK* 61 (1964) 14.

36. Cf. Pss 25:7; 106:45; 136:23; Exod 32:13; Lev 26:45; Deut 9:27.

37. Exodus 32 is, of course, commonly recognized as related to Jeroboam's making of the golden calves (1 Kgs 12:25–33). For the priority of Exodus 32 over the

ל in this verse indicates not the object of the remembering, but the *basis* of the appeal. The prayer is not made for those named as "servants" of YHWH (cf. עבדך in Ps 132:10) to whom the deity had vowed, but for a generation of their descendants who faced the prospect of divine rejection. The petition is based on the covenant relationship that existed because of God's vows to those named by the preposition ל. The focus was on the crisis at hand and those who were facing the threat of YHWH's rejection, but the basis of the appeal was the covenant that YHWH had established in the past with the individuals indicated by the preposition ל. It is probable, then, that one should understand the idiom זכר ל in Psalm 132 as a prayer not of and for David himself, but for descendants of David in a crisis. The appeal is for YHWH to remember the covenant with David. The covenant connection in the use of the idiom זכר ל is further evident in a post-exilic psalm which acknowledges that YHWH "remembered for their sake his covenant" (ויזכר להם בריתו, Ps 106:45). The prayer in Psalm 132, then, may indicate a political crisis in which the Davidides appeared in danger of losing divine support. Hence the psalm pleads with YHWH to remember "for David's sake," reminding the deity of the covenant relationship with David.

The structure of the psalm confirms this interpretation. The insecurity of the Davidic king, indicated by the petition for YHWH to remember the David in v 1, is reiterated in v 10, thus forming an *inclusio* for the first half of the poem (Part A: vv 1–10). At the beginning and the end of Part A, the deity is asked to remember *for the sake of David* (ל in v 1 // בעבור in v 10). If I am correct in my contention that the basis for the petition indicated by the idiom זכר ל in v 1 is the covenant (specifically the covenant with David), then the second half of the psalm (Part B: vv 11–18) mirrors the

---

deuteronomistic version in 1 Kings 12, see B. S. Childs, *The Book of Exodus* (OTL; Westminster: Philadelphia, 1974) 559–562.

first in its resolution: that YHWH will indeed keep the covenant with David. The irrevocable oath (covenant) of YHWH is stated in v 11, the beginning of Part B, and the poem concludes with the assurance of security for the Davidic king (vv 17–18).[38] The concluding assurance in vv 17–18, then, answers the petition at the beginning of the psalm.

The object of YHWH's remembering is, according to v 1,[39] David's "humility." Hillers rightly calls attention to the stela erected by Zakkur,[40] the king of Hamath, which Zakkur erected in honor of his patron deity Iluwer.[41] The inscription begins with an introduction of the king as a "humble man" (*'š 'nh*) whose kingship the gods supported (*KAI* 202.1–2). The inscription goes on to list the military accomplishments of Zakkur (which he attributes to divine help), his building projects (including fortresses and temples), and especially the

38. See C. Brekelmans, "Psalm 132: Unity and Structure," *Bijdragen* 44 (1983) 262.

39. Assuming the correctness of the Masoretic pointing. The *nota accusativi* is unlikely in archaic poetry. Not impossibly, we may restore the waw--conjunctive with LXX and assume defective orthography for *'wt* "sign" (cf. Gen 1:14; Exod 3:12; 4:8, 17, 30; 7:3; 8:19; 10:1, 2, 12:13; Num 2:2; 14:22; Deut 4:34; 7:19; 11:3; 29:2; 34:11; 1 Sam 10:7, 9; Isa 44:25; Jer 32:20; Pss 74:4; 78:43; 105:27; Job 21:29; Neh 9:10), which would have easily led to the misinterpretation of the word as the marker of direct object. The allusion here would then be to David's act as a token of good faith (cf. אות אמת in Josh 2:12). But this is perhaps too daring a reading. Hence, I would retain the *nota accusativi* and note the attestation of it already at Kuntillet 'Ajrud (see Z. Meshel and C. Meyers, "The Name of God in the Wilderness of Zin," *BA* 39 [1976] 10, fig. 4) and in the Moabite Stone (*KAI* 181.5, 6, 7, 9, 10, 11, 12, 13, 14, 30) of the ninth century--not long after the composition of this psalm.

40. Hillers has "Zakir" but we compare PN *zkwr*, attested in the Elephantine papyri. See Cowley, *Aramaic Papyri of the Fifth Century B. C.*, 10.3; 22.3, 98, 107, etc.

41. "The Ritual Procession of the Ark and Ps 132," 53. See *KAI* 202.

building of the temple of Iluwer and the erection of this stela. The reference to his own "humility" at the outset of the inscription is part of the royal propaganda, for "humility" is in fact a mark of legitimate leadership in the eyes of the gods and the populace, and virtually synonymous with piety.[42] In like manner, the kings of Mesopotamia frequently called themselves humble, even as they boasted of their achievements.[43] In short, the mention of David's humility at the beginning of the psalm is propagandistic. It is directed at the deity as well as the audience or readers and serves to introduce the accomplishments of David to be mentioned in the verses that follow.

The basis of the petition is the vow which David had fulfilled--that he would grant himself no rest or sleep until a "place" would be found for the deity. To document this claim, the apologist quotes from an old liturgy that was probably composed for the procession of the ark during the reign of David (vv 3-5, 6-9), using the divine epithet "Bull of Jacob" (אביר יעקב) to establish the link (vv 2, 5).

Scholars sometimes speak of a "ritual search" for the ark--corresponding to the search for the lost, imprisoned or dead gods in the Babylonian *akītu* festivals[44]--leading to its discovery and reinstatement in the sanctuary.[45] This view is highly conjectural, however. It also assumes that Psalm 132 is a liturgical text used for an annual procession of the ark similar to the Babylonian rituals of divine enthronement. The text only states that a search was launched for the ark. The allusion here is not to a putative annual ritual, but to David's

42. Cf. Num 12:3; Zech 9:9.

43. See, for example, Borger, *Die Inschriften Asarhaddons*, 12, Episode 1, line 17. For other examples, see *CAD* 1/II, 455-456.

44. For the general conceptual background, see H. Frankfort, *Kingship and the Gods* (Chicago: University of Chicago, 1978) 321-325.

45. Mowinckel, *Psalms in Israel's Worship* I, 176; cf. J. H. Eaton, *Psalms* (London: Methuen, 1967) 291-292.

transfer of the ark from Qiryat-Ye'arim to Jerusalem. It was in that ritual that David prepared a *place* (מקום) for the ark in Jerusalem (2 Sam 6:17), and here in the old liturgy, David promises to find and establish a *place* (מקום) for the deity (v 5). The king's pious commitment, according to our poem, was indicated by his willingness to suspend rest and sleep until the expressed task was accomplished.

B. G. Ockinga recently observed that the content of David's oath (vv 3-5) is reminiscent of certain Egyptian royal inscriptions from the reigns of Amenhotep III and Sethos I.[46] In particular, he noted the occurrence of two themes in the Egyptian texts: (1) the king's vigilance, indicated by the sleepless nights he suffers, and (2) the search for something that will benefit the god. The parallels are suggestive, but it is probably premature to conclude, as Ockinga did, that "the psalmist has skillfully adapted the Egyptian phraseology."[47] As Ockinga himself recognized, there may be similar idioms from Mesopotamia as well.[48]

The cylinders of Gudea may be cited as providing an early Mesopotamian analogue for David's commitment.[49] In a dream, the *ensi* of Lagash received instructions to build a sanctuary for Ningirsu (Cylinder A, I.17-21). During the construction of the temple, he was vigilant: "he did not sleep at night, nor slumbered during the day."[50] Piously he followed through on his commitment till the temple was completed.

---

46. "An Example of Egyptian Royal Phraseology in Psalm 132," *BN* 11 (1980) 38-42.

47. Ibid., 40.

48. Ockinga mentions Akkadian *dalāpu* "to be awake, to be sleepless, to work ceaselessly, to continue (work) into the night," but mentions no possible parallels.

49. On the complex issue of Gudea's date, see P. Steinkeller, "The Date of Gudea and His Dynasty," *JCS* 40 (1988) 47-53.

50. Cylinder A, XVII.8-9. See the translation of Falkenstein and von Soden in *Sumerische und akkadische Hymnen und Gebete*, 153.

Then, he ushered in the statue of Ningirsu "the warrior" (*UR.SAG*)[51] in a procession during the New Year.[52]

Another important parallel is found in a fragment of a bilingual composition commemorating the return of the divine statue of Marduk to Babylon, probably in the reign of Nebuchadnezzar I (1124–1103 B. C. E.):

> [ù.gul] gá.gá še.še.ga lú.igi.du(8).a.bi sag.uš ab.ta.bu.bu.lu en.e šà.ba.a.ni na.me mu.un.bu.i šà.ne.ša(4) nam.mi.in.gub
> [mut]-nen-nu-ú mu-un-dag-ri šá ana(DIŠ) ta-mar-ti-šú kak-da-a pu-tuq-qu-ma a-di ú-šam-ṣu-šú ma-la lib-bu-uš la ik-la-a un-nin-ni
> [en.]e i.bí bar.ra alam sukud.da.a.ni u(4).šú.uš.e múš.nu.túm.ma su.gurum.ma su.mu nu.kud.da úr.ra.a.ni ge(6).dùg.ga.bi nu.til.la.e.da.ni ù.sá.na.nam
> [a]-di at-tap-la-su la-an-šu e-la-a u(4)-mi-šam la na-par-ka-a ṣur-ri qid-da-a-ti ina(AŠ) zu-um-ri-ya la ip-par-su-ú-ma ina(AŠ) ut-lu mu-ši ṭa-a-bu la ú-qat-ta-a šit-ti
>
> (IV *R* 20, 5-9; *AJSL* 35, 139)

> The pious one, the obedient one, who constantly waited for his appearance, did not cease praying until he had satisfied all his heart's desire. Until I had seen his exalted form, everyday my heart did not leave; bowing did not leave my body. Moreover, in the pleasant lap of the night I did not complete my sleep.

This is one of the texts that Miller and Roberts urged as parallels for 2 Samuel 6 which, they argue, is an account of

---

51. This is a standard epithet for Ningirsu. See K. Tallqvist, *Akkadische Götterepitheta* (StudOr 7; Helsinki: Academic Bookshop, 1938) 162–164, 404–405.

52. Cylinder B, III.5–7; IV.23–V.2.

the return of the ark corresponding to the return of divine statues in Mesopotamia.[53] According to this bilingual inscription, it was through the pious persistence of the king that Marduk returned to Babylon, taking "a road of joy" to the holy city (ll. 9–11). The people marvelled as they witnessed the procession, and the deity entered the city, taking his place in his "abode of rest" (*šubat neḫti*, ll. 17–18). Thereupon, the heavens and the earth, as well as the mountains and the sea offered their abundance, even as the nations brought their tribute to the deity who is here called "the one without equal" (*la maḫra*) and "lord of lords" (*bēl bēlī*, ll. 21–22).[54]

This fragment appears to have been the continuation of another text which W. G. Lambert edited, although there is a break between the two.[55] The entire text was written apparently for the legitimation of Nebuchadnezzar I, highlighting his pious deeds over against the failures of his predecessor. In the previous regime, the divine images had been captured, the shrines had been destroyed, and the land acted as if there were no gods.[56] But now, under the new king, Marduk was persuaded to return to his city of choice from which he would rule.

In a fragmentary hymn, again concerning the return of the divine statue,[57] the efforts of the king are said to have

---

53. See *The Hand of the Lord*, 13–14, and 79–82 (Appendix, Text 3).

54. For the significance of such language, see M. Weinfeld, "Zion and Jerusalem as Religious and Political Capital: Ideology and Utopia," in *The Poet and The Historian* (HSS 26; ed. R. E. Friedman; Chico, California: Scholars, 1983) 94–95.

55. "Enmeduranki and Related Matters," *JCS* 21 (1967) 126–138, Text 1.

56. See ll. 15–24 of the inscription in Lambert.

57. *DT* 71; *BA* V, 386ff. See M. Weippert, "'Heiliger Krieg' in Israel und Assyrien," *ZAW* 84 (1972) 482; Miller and Roberts, *The Hand of the Lord*, 14 and Appendix, Text. 4.

prompted the return.[58] There appears also to be a polemic against the preceding king, who was accused of neglecting the cult: "he trusted in his own strength," "he did not remember your divinity," and he did not keep his oath.[59]

Such polemics are, of course, part and parcel of political propaganda throughout the ancient Near East. The royal inscriptions of Mesopotamia in particular are replete with such enumerations of the failures and incompetence of the preceding regimes.[60] Especially prominent in this regard is the motif of the neglect of the cult and the consequent abandonment of the city by the patron deities. The inscriptions usually blame the preceding regimes for the capture of the statues (which is equated with the departure of the gods), and allowing the sanctuaries to fall into disrepair. In these inscriptions, the failures of previous kings are juxtaposed with the accomplishments of the current ruler, whose piety and ardor supposedly made possible the return of the gods. Typically, the kings who commissioned the inscriptions boasted of their own sponsorship of the cult, their refurbishing of the sanctuaries, and their restoring of the cult to prominence, particularly by ushering in the recaptured or newly refurbished cult statues to their place in the city.

A good example of this motif of the king as "the restorer of the forgotten cult" (*mušaklil paraṣ mašûti*) is in a foundation stela for Sennacherib's *akītu* house, which was built apparently as part of the king's systematic program to substitute his patron god Aššur for Marduk of Babylon as the high god in the land. In this inscription, Sennacherib (704-681 B. C. E.) portrayed himself as the pious restorer of the neglected cult:

58. *DT* 71, obv. 10-13.

59. *DT* 71, rev. 12, 13, 21.

60. A. K. Grayson, "Assyrian Royal Inscriptions: Literary Characteristics," in *Assyrian Royal Inscriptions* (Orientis Antiqui Collectio 17; ed. F. M. Fales; Rome: Instituto per l'Oriente, 1981) 44.

e-piš ṣa-lam $^{d}$Aššur(AN.ŠAR) u ilāni(DINGIR.MEŠ) rabûti(GAL.MEŠ) mu-šak-lil pa-ra-aṣ E-šár-ra ma-šú-u-ti ina bi-ri ina qi-bit $^{d}$Šamaš(UTU) u $^{d}$Adad(IM) mu-šar-bu-u šu-luḫ-ḫi-šu-un mu-tir $^{d}$ Lamassu(LAMMA) E-šár-ra ba-aš-ti a-na aš-ri-šu ša pa-liḫ ilāni(DINGIR.MEŠ) ša šamê(AN-e) u ilāni(DINGIR.MEŠ) $^{māt}$Aššur$^{ki}$ ra-biš mu-du-u mu-ul-li ilāni(DINGIR.MEŠ) rabûti(GAL.MEŠ) ina šub-ti-šu-nu

(*KAH* II, 122, ll. 3-8)[61]

Maker of the image of Aššur and the great gods; restorer of the forgotten cults of Ešarra, who through the oracle (and) through the command of Šamaš and Adad multiplies their rituals; who returns the awesome *lamassu*-spirit of Ešarra to its place; who fears the great gods of heaven and knows well the gods of Assyria, who elevates the great gods in their dwellings.

According to the inscription, Sennacherib commissioned the making of the images of Aššur and the other deities and caused the gods to dwell in their "restful abodes" (*šubāssun nēḫti*, l. 23), and he celebrated the "feast of the banquet of the king of the gods, Aššur" (*isinni qirīti ša šar ilāni $^{d}$Aššur*, l. 25).[62] The nature of the ritual return of the statues is clarified by another inscription describing a scene on the gate of the *akītu*-house: there was an image of Aššur advancing to battle "into the midst of Tiamat" (*ana libbi tiāmat*) riding a

61. Cf. D. D. Luckenbill, *The Annals of Sennacherib* (OIP 2; Chicago: University of Chicago, 1924) 135.

62. Sennacherib's boast of sweeping cultic reform apparently has some basis in history, for the structures of the temple of Aššur were radically altered in his reign. See G. van Driel, *The Cult of Aššur* (Studia Semitica Neerlandica; Assen: van Gorcum, 1969) 21-31.

storm chariot with his entourage.[63] The entire ritual celebrated the return of Aššur from battle to claim his kingship. It apparently dramatized the battle between Aššur and Tiamat and culminated in the enthronement of Aššur, the patron god of Sennacherib, on the dais of the inner sanctum, symbolizing that deity's reign over Tiamat.[64]

In like manner, Esarhaddon (680–669 B. C. E.) took pride in being a restorer of the neglected cult. He claimed to have refurbished the cult statues and restored them to their sanctuaries.[65] It was he, Esarhaddon insisted, who returned the captured images and caused them to dwell in the "restful abodes" (*šubtu nēḫtu*).[66] In anticipation of the ritual return of the newly refurbished statues, he even issued a report of how he led the gods in joyous procession from Aššur back to Babylon,[67] thus reversing what Sennacherib had done.

In a later period, Nabonidus (555–539 B. C. E.) charged that Sennacherib had caused the neglect of the cult at Babylon, since the latter brought the images in procession

63. Luckenbill, *The Annals of Sennacherib*, 139–149. The propagandistic intent of the entire scene, perhaps the procession itself, is evident at the end of the inscription, when the image of Aššur is identified with the image of Sennacherib, and it is asserted that he, Sennacherib, was "the conquerer in Aššur's chariot." See also A. L. Oppenheim, *Ancient Mesopotamia* (Chicago/London: University of Chicago, 1964) 264–265.

64 See W. G. Lambert, "The Great Battle of the Mesopotamian Religious Year: The Conflict in the Akītu House," *Iraq* 25 (1963) 189–190.

65. Borger, *Die Inschriften Asarhaddons*, 15–18, § 11, Episodes 10–15.

66. Ibid., 46, § 27, Episode 3, 24; cf. also 95, § 61 rev. 39.

67. Ibid., 88–89, § 57 18–20. Esarhaddon in fact died before he could lead the procession, and it was Asshurbanipal who sponsored it. See Streck, *Assurbanipal*, 264, ll. 7–11. Cf. Miller and Roberts, *The Hand of the Lord*, 15–17.

from Babylon to Aššur.[68] Nabonidus claimed that he himself had made possible the return of the gods and the restoration of the forgotten cult at Babylon. In a separate inscription, we find the mother of Nabonidus praying to the gods to help her son fulfill his obligations as commander-in-chief and restorer of the neglected cult (*paraṣ mašûti*).[69] In a dream, Sin responded to her request, promising that Nabonidus would restore the sanctuary and lead the gods in procession into it (Col. ii, 6-11). It is in this light that one should view the reference to David's piety in Psalm 132. He is seen as the pious restorer of the neglected cult of which the ark was the indispensible emblem.

It is significant that the deity is twice (vv 2, 5) called "the Bull of Jacob" (אביר יעקב). To judge by its mention in Jacob's blessing of Joseph in Gen 49:24, the epithet was used of 'Ēl in the Shiloh cultus, where the ark was the chief symbol of YHWH as warrior and king.[70] But the "Bull of Jacob," according to our text, did not have a proper "place" until David's initiative, which led to the resting-place in Jerusalem. If my dating of this psalm is correct, the use of the bull-epithet is hardly coincidental: it is a subtle polemic against any attempt to establish a competing shrine with bull iconography in the north. It is, at the same time, an affirmation of the ark as the symbol of and Jerusalem as the appropriate "place" for the "Bull of Jacob."

The composer quotes an archaic liturgical text used in connection with the procession of the ark. That ancient ritual apparently demonstrated the faithfulness of David over against his predecessor, Saul. By all accounts, the latter was unable to take custody of the ark, or uninterested in doing

---

68. See Langdon, *Die neubabylonischen Königsinschriften* 270ff.

69. C. J. Gadd, "The Harran Inscription of Nabonidus," *AnSt* 8 (1958) 35-92; see l. 15.

70. Schreiner, *Sion-Jerusalem*, 177 n. 17; Fretheim, "Psalm 132," 291.

so.[71] The ark fell into oblivion and Israel mourned as the ark was left in Qiryat-Ye'arim (1 Sam 7:2). According to the Chronicler, it was David who initiated the restoration of the ark, saying: "Let us bring back the ark of our God to us, for we did not seek it in the days of Saul" (1 Chron 13:3). Here David's pious initiative is contrasted with Saul's negligence in a manner reminiscent of Akkadian royal literature.

The distinct impression in Psalm 132 is that the ark had fallen into oblivion, indeed, to the extent that a search had to be launched to rediscover it:

הנה שמענוה באפרתה[72]
מצאנוה בשדי יער
נבואה למשכנותיו
נשתחוה להדם רגליו
(Ps 132:6–7)

Lo! We heard of it in Ephrathah;
We found it in the Highland of Ya'ar.[73]
Let us come to his tent-dwelling,
Let us bow down to his footstool.

71. Ishida, *The Royal Dynasties in Ancient Israel*, 140–142) speculates that Saul's power base was located in Benjamin and his estrangement from Samuel and the priests of Nob was synonymous with a break with the Shilonite confederacy whose symbol of unity was the ark.

72. The 3 fs suff. in שמענוה and מצאנוה refers to the ark which is feminine in 1 Sam 4:17; 2 Chron 8:11. The feminine plural form (*'rwnt*) is attested in West Semitic inscriptions (see *DISO*, 25), and Akk. *arānu* is feminine (see *CAD* I/2, 231; *AHW* I, 65.

73. For שדי, see W. H. Propp, "On Hebrew *śāde(h)*, 'Highland,'" *VT* 37 (1987) 230–234. Josh 15:10 refers to הר יערים in the vicinity of Ba'lah (i.e., Qiryat-Ye'arim). Cf. also הר הבעלה in Josh 15:11. I take שדי יער "the Highland of Yaar" to be a poetic name for הר יערים "the Mount of Ye'arim." See S. Talmon, "הַר *har;* גִּבְעָה *gibh'āh*," *TDOT* III, 431. Cf. also גבעת קרית <י>ערים (Josh 18:28, LXX).

Scholars are sometimes troubled by the pronominal reference to the ark in v 6, since the ark is not explicitly named earlier.[74] But if these verses are extracted from an older liturgical text, it is certainly understandable that the "it" may refer to the ark after all. Eissfeldt has argued that vv 6-8 are artificially linked to the preceding unit of thought, noting that מצאנוה (v 6), משכנותיו (v 7), קומה (v 8) echo אמצא, משכנות, and מקום in v 5.[75] This may be correct, inasmuch as vv 3-5 and 6-9 may have come from different parts of an ancient ark liturgy. On the other hand, such repetitions and shifts in persons would not be out of character with liturgical material, so that vv 3-5 and 6-9 may belong to a common liturgy after all.

There is some question about the identification of Ephrathah in v 6, but three views are prevalent.[76] The first holds that it refers to Ephrathah of Judah, that is, the vicinity of Bethlehem.[77] Accordingly, it was in Ephrathah-Bethlehem, David's home district, whence they first learned of the ark's whereabouts and proceeded to find it.[78] But others argue that the name refers to Ephraim, noting that the gentilic אפרתי in 1 Sam 1:1 refers to an Ephraimite (cf. Judg 12:5, where אפרתי clearly means "Ephraimite") with connections to the

---

74. So M. Buttenweiser (*The Psalms*, [Chicago: University of Chicago, 1938] 378) would excise it from the text.

75. "Psalm 132," 483.

76. One may also mention the view that אפרתה is not a GN, but an appellative meaning "Fruitland," which is further interpreted as a cryptic allusion to the residence of the Messiah and of YHWH, namely, Jerusalem. See, Kruse, "Psalm CXXXII and the Royal Zion Festival," 294; McCarthy, "Psalm 132," 149-151. But since Ephrathah is a known GN in the Hebrew Bible, any allegorical interpretation ought to be considered only as a last resort.

77. Cf. Mic 5:1; Ruth 4:11; 1 Chron 4:4. So, for example, Kraus, *Worship*, 178; *Psalmen* II, 1063. Cf. Fretheim, "Psalm 132," 297.

78. So, for instance, Kraus, *Psalmen* II, 1063.

cult at Shiloh.[79] On the other hand, the parallelism with Highland of Ya'ar (= Qiryat-Ye'arim) would suggest Ephrathah of Benjamin, that is, the district in which Qiryat-Ye'arim was located.[80] The second name in v 6 is less disputed. Most scholars identify it as a poetic alternative of Qiryat-Ye'arim, also called "Mount Ye'arim" (Josh 15:10).[81] Since the ark was located at Qiryat-Ye'arim and not at Shiloh when it was brought to Jerusalem, the last interpretation is to be preferred.

By quoting the old liturgy, then, the apologist cites a historical datum,[82] namely, the transfer of the ark from the obscure sanctuary in Qiryat-Ye'arim to the city of David. The "we" of vv 6-7 would, of course, in the old liturgy have referred to the cultic participants; but here it is intended by the composer to include all who worshipped the "Bull of

---

79. Schreiner, *Sion-Jerusalem*, 48-49; Weiser, *Psalms*, 780.

80. According to 1 Chron 2:19, 50, Hur, the first-born of Ephrathah, was the grandfather of Qiryat-Ye'arim and Salma, the father of Bethlehem. This view was defended by F. Delitzsch, *Biblical Commentary on the Psalms* III (trans. F. Bolton; Edinburgh: T. & T. Clark, 1883) 309-310. Cf. Eissfeldt, "Psalm 132," 482; Cross, *Canaanite Myth and Hebrew Epic*, 94-95, n. 16; E. Vogt, "Benjamin geboren 'eine Meile' von Ephrata," *Bib* 56 (1975) 30-36.

81. Johnson (*Sacral Kingship in Ancient Israel*, 21) emends יַעַר to יָעִר, urging association with Elhanan ben-Ya'ir (2 Sam 21:19) as the original name of David and arguing that Ephrathah and שדי יער both refer to Bethlehem. But this view has not found wide acceptance. For other views, see A. Robinson, "Do Ephrathah and Jaar Really Appear in Psalm 136, 6?" *ZAW* 86 (1974) 220-222. Robinson denies that either GN is present in the text, preferring to emend the text at several points.

82. One may note in passing that Akkadian propagandistic inscriptions regularly contain verbatim quotes from ancient materials. See Grayson, "Assyrian Royal Inscriptions," 42.

Jacob." The apologist appeals to the historic procession of the ark from Ephrathah // Qiryat-Ye'arim in order to legitimate the location of the emblem the "Bull of Jacob" (the ark) in the south, thus attempting to forestall any transfer of allegiance to the newly established bull-shrines at Dan and Bethel.

The discovery of the forgotten ark-sanctuary is followed by a call to approach the deity's tent-dwelling and to bow down to his footstool. The mention of the tabernacle (משׁכנות) and the footstool (הדם רגליו) in v 7 recalls the abode of 'Ēl, for the Canaanite high-god is portrayed in West Semitic mythological texts and iconography as a tent-dweller and he is the only deity depicted on a throne with a footstool. This ties in neatly with the references to the deity as "the Bull of Jacob," which was probably used as an epithet of the deity as 'Ēl already at Shiloh.

Commentators sometimes suppose that a contradiction exists between v 7 and v 8, believing that the former presupposes the ark (assuming that the footstool is a reference to the ark),[83] whereas the latter calls for the deity to go to the sanctuary with the ark.[84] But this line of argument assumes (1) that the allusion to the ark as footstool presupposes the Jerusalem temple, and (2) that v 7 was a call to worship at the ark-sanctuary. The first assumption may be dismissed as fallacious, since the ark was already associated

83. This is possible, but by no means certain. The word הדם occurs just 6 times in the Hebrew Bible; only in the post-exilic text, 1 Chron 28:2, does it unequivocally refer to the ark. In Isa 66:1, it is the earth that is the footstool. In Ps 99:5, the footstool may refer to the temple. The occurrence of the word in Lam 2:1 is ambiguous; it may refer to the ark, the temple, or Zion. The occurrence of הדם in Ps 110:1 is not pertinent to the discussion here. One may further note that the expression מקם כפות רגלי "the place of the sole of my feet" refers to the temple, as does the phrase מקום רגלי "the place of my feet" in Isa 60:13 (// מקם מקדשׁי "place of my sanctuary"). Cf. H.-J. Fabry, "הֲדֹם *hᵃdhōm*," *TDOT* III, 332–334.

84. So Weiser, *Psalms*, 781.

with the kingship of YHWH at Shiloh. The footstool is not tied to the presence of the Jerusalem temple; indeed, the footstool probably refers not to the ark *per se*, but simply to the presence of YHWH as a divine king like 'Ēl in the Canaanite pantheon.

As for the second assumption, it must be observed that v 7 cannot be regarded simply as a call to worship at the ark-sanctuary. The vocables in the verse recall a ritual known in the Ugaritic texts, performed when visitors came to 'Ēl's tabernacle at the "Source of the Double Deep," that is, 'Ēl's mountain abode. Thus, 'Athirat entered (*tb'u*) the tent of 'Ēl and bowed down (*tšt ḥwy*), as 'Ēl "the Bull" (*θr*) sat on his throne, with his feet on his footstool (*hdm*).[85] 'Athirat approached the old deity on Ba'l's behalf to petition that a temple be established for Ba'l, for the young god did not yet have a permanent home like the other gods. In another instance, the craftsman of the gods, Kothar-wa-Ḫasis, entered (*yb'u*) the tent of 'Ēl and bowed down (*yštḥwy*) at the feet of 'Ēl "the Bull," although the footstool is not mentioned in this instance (*KTU* 1.1.III.22-26; 2.III.5-6). Here again, the issue is permission for the construction of a house for Ba'l. Both these texts are pertinent to our exegesis, inasmuch as they are concerned with the establishing of a place for a deity on the rise, a god who did not yet have a permanent home. In another text, the goddess 'Anat entered (*tb'u*) the abode of 'Ēl and bowed down (*tštḥwy*) before him to announce the demise of Ba'l and to seek a substitute to sit on the throne (*KTU* 1.6.I.32-43). The same ritual is performed by 'Anat at the tent-dwelling of 'Ēl when she came to seek restitution for Aqhat's rejection of her sexual overtures (*KTU* 1.17.VI.47-51). It appears, then, that the tent of 'Ēl was the place where divine decisions were made and wrongs rectified. The persons who *entered* the tent-dwelling of 'Ēl and *bowed down* at his feet/footstool were always seeking a decision on a matter at hand: sanction to build a temple for a deity, a divine king to

85. *KTU* 1.4.IV.20-30.

sit on the throne, or the rectification of a wrong. The ritual in the Ugaritic texts was never an end in itself.[86] So, too, in Ps 132:7 the coming (*bw'*) to the tent-dwelling of the deity and bowing down (*ḥwy*) are part of a mission, namely, to establish a proper place for YHWH. Hence one finds the invocation in v 8:

קומה יהוה למנחתך [87]
אתה וארון עזך

Come, YHWH, to your resting place,
You and your mighty ark!

Against the tide of an emerging scholarly consensus, Hillers denies that v 8 contains an allusion to the procession of the ark.[88] He argues, instead, that the preposition ל in this verse should be translated "from," in accordance with its usage in Ugaritic. He maintains that the imperative קומה here, as elsewhere in the Psalter, is merely a call for divine help. Even in the Song of the Ark (Num 10:35), the imperative קומה has to do with the departure of the divine warrior for combat, not with the return of the deity, Hillers argues.[89]

---

86. In Ugaritic literature, the root *ḥwy* is always used of messengers with a mission to complete, never simply of worship. See S. A. Meier, *The Messenger in the Ancient Semitic World* (HSM 45; Atlanta: Scholars, 1988) 154.

87. Cross (*Canaanite Myth and Hebrew Epic*, 94 n. 14) reads לנוחתך, citing 2 Chron 6:41 and arguing that MT מנוחתך is *lectio facilior* which anticipates מנוחתי in v 14. But the parallel in Chronicles reads not נוחתך, as one might expect, but נוחך, which may be a secondary derivation from the influence of בנחה in Num 10:36. So Allen, *Psalms 101–150*, 203; W. Rudolph, *Chronikbücher* (HAT 1/21; Tübingen: Mohr, 1955) 215.

88. "The Ritual Procession of the Ark and Ps 132," 49–50.

89. Ibid., 50.

Against Hillers, however, I should point out that מנוחה in the Hebrew Bible is never a locale from which one departs; it is always a destination or a goal (Num 10:33; Ruth 1:9; Deut 12:9; Pss 23:2; 132:14), a promise (1 Kgs 8:56; 1 Chron 28:2; Deut 12:9; 2 Sam 14:17; Isa 32:18; Ps 95:11), or the result of successful battles, namely, rest from war (1 Kgs 8:56; 1 Chron 22:8).[90] Moreover, the preposition ל occurs twice in the verse immediately preceding. In both instances the separative meaning is impossible: "Let us come *to* his tent-dwelling; let us bow down *at* his footstool" (v 7). Such a radical shift in the meaning of the preposition as Hillers has proposed would be most surprising when the preposition recurs in such proximity. One does not expect the same preposition to indicate destination in v 7 only to have it indicate the opposite direction in the next line. One should rather expect למנוחתך in v 8 to mean "to your rest," even as למשכנותיך in v 7 means "to your tent-dwelling." Furthermore, besides v 8, the preposition ל occurs 18 times in this psalm (vv 1, 2 [2x], 4, [2x], 5 [2x], 7 [2x], 11 [3x], 12 [2x], 13 [2x], 17 [2x]), but never indicating separation. Movement "away from" is conveyed by the preposition מ(ן) in this psalm, as in ממנה "from it" (v 11) and מפרי בטנך "from the fruit of your womb" (v 11). This is not to say that both prepositions cannot occur in a given language; but an isolated attestation of a putative separative ל in a text where the preposition recurs and the separative preposition מ(ן) occurs would be most odd indeed. It seems preferable to me to take קומה here not literally as an imperative of קום "to arise," but as an interjection. So we compare: קום־נא שבה ואכלה "Come on! Sit down and eat!" (Gen 27:19), קום עשה לנו אלהים "Come on! Make us a god!" (Exod 32:1), קום בלק ושמע "Come on,

90. In the Ahiram sarcophagus, *nḥt* parallels *ḥṭr mšpṭh* "the sceptre of his rule" and *ks' mlkh* "the throne of his kingship" (*KAI* 1.2). In the inscription of Azitawadda from Karatepe, *nḥt* is the consequence of benevolent rule for the gods and citizens alike (*KAI* 26.A.I.18; II.8, 13). Cf. also Sefîre (*KAI* 223.B.4).

Balaq! Listen!" (Num 23:18), קומה ונעלה "Come! Let us go up!" (Judg 18:9), קומה ונשובה "Come! Let us return!" (Jer 46:16). If קומה is not taken literally, there is nothing "incongruous" about the call to YHWH here to the resting-place.[91] We ought not translate the line "Arise, YHWH to your rest!" but "Come, YHWH! To your rest!"[92] The call is addressed to YHWH, but in the parallel line it is clarified: "you and your mighty ark." The procession of the ark is surely the historical referent in this invocation. The Chronicler, therefore, appropriately cites this text in conjunction with the induction of the ark into the temple:

ועתה קומה יהוה אלהים לנוחך
אתה וארון עזך
( 2 Chron 6:41)

Come, YHWH, O God, to your rest!
You and your mighty ark!

Despite the argumentations of Hillers, I believe there is no doubt that for the Chronicler, the call is for the deity to approach the "rest" rather than to depart from it.[93] The Chronicler quotes the ancient ark liturgy as the climax of

---

91. Hillers, "Ritual Procession of the Ark and Ps 132," 50.

92. Arguing that strophic structure in Psalm 132 is indicated by grammatical structure, Huwiler ("Patterns and Problems in Psalm 132," 201–205) sees v 8 as parallel to v 1. Hence she interprets the *lāmed* in v 8 in the same way as v 1, thus translating למנוחתך as "for the sake of your resting place." But she extrapolates from the specific idiom זכר ל to give the preposition ל a dubious meaning in v 8. Moreover, the same preposition occurs at the beginning of what she assumes is the beginning of the third strophe (v 11, לדוד). By her arguments for v 8, one should translate לדוד in v 11 as "for the sake of David," but she does not translate so.

93. Hillers, "Ritual Procesion of the Ark and Ps 132," 51–52.

Solomon's dedicatory prayer. Accordingly, when the invocation was uttered, fire descended from heaven and consumed the offerings, and the glory of YHWH filled the temple and the people sang: "Yea, he is good; Yea, his faithfulness is forever" (2 Chron 7:1–3).[94]

To judge from the Mesopotamian parallels, the invitation to the "resting-place" was probably uttered in conjunction with the placing of the ark in its new sanctuary--its "place" (מקום), according to the account in 2 Samuel 6. The act of placing the cult symbol in the capital was the climax of the ritual, symbolizing the victory of the divine king and the end of strife in the land.

In this connection, Cross has already urged comparison of the "resting place" with Ugaritic *nḫt*.[95] He cites Kirta's taking of his royal seat:

yθb . krt . l'dh
yθb . lks'i mlk
lnḫt . lkḥθ . drkt

(*KTU* 1.16.VI.22–24)

Kirta sat enthroned on his dais;
he sat enthroned on his royal throne,
on the comfort of his seat of dominion.

Here, as elsewhere in Ugaritic literature, *nḫt* is used of the throne of divine kings. It is used of the throne of 'Ēl in

94. One is reminded here of an Akkadian ritual text concerning the placing of the divine statue on the dais in the inner sanctum of the temple: "Then you shall lead the god in procession, you shall cause him to enter. You shall recite the incantation 'My King, in the goodness of your heart' up to the cella (and) place the god on his dais." See *BM* 45749, ll. 60–61, published in S. Smith, "The Babylonian Ritual for the Consecration and Induction of a Divine Statue," *JRAS* 57 (1925) 37–60, pls. ii–iv.

95. See n. 87 above.

the palace where he hosts other deities (*KTU* 1.22.I.18). It is probably also used of Ba'l's throne, where he sits enthroned after his defeat of his enemies (*KTU* 1.6.VI.34).[96] In all instances, *nḫt* is a desired place of rest for the divine king.[97]

In Akkadian royal literature, the kings frequently boasted that they installed the gods in their "restful abodes" (*šubat nēḫti*). Thus, in the previously cited foundation inscription from Sennacherib's *akītu*-house (*KAH* II, 122), the king claimed to have restored the neglected cult: he commissioned new images of the gods to be made, and caused them to dwell in their restful abode (*šubassunu nēḫti*). In this instance, the placing of the statue of Aššur in the sanctuary symbolized at once the rest of the god from his battle with Tiamat and his enthronement over her--represented by the statue of the god on the dais in the cella.[98]

This understanding of the deity's "restful abode" finds support in a cultic-mythical text concerning the exaltation of Nabû, where the king is said to have brought the deity (that is, the cult statue of Nabû) into the sanctuary and "caused him to dwell in the restful abode" (*šubat nēḫti ušēšibšu*).[99] The event is interpreted as the enthronement of the deity over Sea: *ana maštakīšu ṣīru eli tiāmat gallat[i] ukīn šēpuš[šu]* "he established his feet on his lofty abode, upon Tiamat, the rolling Sea."[100] Once again, we note the royal connotation of the restful abode. That rest is a destination or goal to be attained, not a point of departure.

Thus, also, in a fragment of a psalm addressed to Bēl and Bēlit, one reads:

---

96. The reconstruction of *nḫt* here, which is widely accepted, is based on *KTU* 1.3.IV.3. Cf. also *KTU* 1.1.IV.24.

97. Note the royal connotation of מנוחה in Isa 11:10; 1 Chron 22:9.

98. Cf. Luckenbill, *The Annals of Sennacherib*, 135-136.

99. E. Ebeling, *Parfümrezepte und kultische Texte aus Assur* (Rome: Pontifical Biblical Institute, 1950), pl. 26, l. 8.

100. Ibid., pl. 26, l. 13.

[ki.tuš.ne.ḫa.za] dúr.gar.ra.zu.dè
[šubat ne]-eḫ-ti-ka ina a-ša-bi-ki
en ḫun.gá ḫu.mu.ra.ab-bé
[ṣi]-i-ru nu-uḫ liq-bi-ki
(*K*. 5098, rev. 4-7)[101]

When you sit at your restful abode,
O exalted (lord), let him say to you: "Rest!"

The evidence supports the traditional interpretation of Psalm 132 as indicating a procession of the ark to its "place" in Jerusalem. My contention is not that the entire psalm was used in conjunction with the procession of the ark,[102] nor even that there was an annual reenactment of that historic procession. Rather, I believe that the psalm contains an old liturgy used with the procession of the ark under David. Specifically, the parallels from the Akkadian royal inscriptions pertaining to the return of the cult statues would tend to confirm the connection of the liturgy with the *return* of the ark to prominence--after a period of oblivion in the days of Saul. Hence, Psalm 132 fits very well with the procession of the ark in 2 Samuel 6, which suggests that the induction of the ark into the city of David was a dramatization of the divine warrior's triumphant return from battle to claim his rightful kingship in his newly won mount.

Cross is correct, therefore, to relate the core of this text with Psalm 24, which, he convincingly argues, is a liturgy associated with the procession of the ark as the emblem of the divine warrior.[103] He compares the entrance liturgy and

---

101. Cf. *BA* 10/1, 83, No. 9, rev. 4-7; *KAR* 106, 5ff; IV *R* 9 rev. 25ff. This fragment supplements IV *R* 27, no. 2 (*K*. 4898).

102. As Fretheim ("Psalm 132," 289-300) argues.

103. *Canaanite Myth and Hebrew Epic*, 91-105.

the summons for the gates to lift their heads (Ps 24:7–10),[104] with the challenge of Ba'l to the gods of the divine council who had dropped their heads to their knees in fear of Yamm: *š'u 'ilm r'aštkm* "Lift up, O gods, your heads!" (*KTU* 1.2.I.27).

The gods in this Ugaritic text are asked to lift up their heads, that is, to take heart,[105] because they could count on Ba'l to defeat Yamm. Ba'l dared to proclaim his victory over Yamm even before the battle had begun. The imagery in Psalm 24, Cross argues, is "one of full personification of the circle of gate towers which like a council of elders sat waiting for the return of the army and its Great Warrior gone

---

104. For a survey of various views regarding the imagery, see A. Cooper, "Ps 24:7–10: Mythology and Exegesis," *JBL* 102 (1983) 37–60. Cooper argues that this text is a fragment of a "descent myth," but gives no other examples of this myth in the Hebrew Bible, nor explains how the descent myth was assimilated into Israel's liturgical traditions (see the superscription in LXX, and the use of the psalm according to Jewish traditions). He contends that פתחי עולם refers to the gates of the netherworld and that מלך עולם is an epithet of Osiris, citing West Semitic *bt 'lm* "grave." But *bt 'lm* never means anything more than grave, or the house of *eternal* rest (cf. the Ahiram sarcophagus, *KAI* 1.1), not the netherworld. Cooper also compares the call for the gates to lift up their heads with Egyptian *f3y ḥr.ṯn* "lift up your faces" (see A. de Buck, *The Egyptian Coffin Texts* [OIP 67; Chicago: University of Chicago, 1951] Spell # 312), but the imperative in the Egyptian text is addressed to the gatekeepers, not the gates.

105. The idiom "to lift up (one's) head" occurs in *KTU* 1.16.III.12 where it conveys the hope of farmers expecting rain. In biblical Hebrew, it is associated with freedom and hope (Gen 40:13, 19; 2 Kgs 25:27 // Jer 52:31; cf. Ps 83:3) or, with the negative particle, for entrapment (Judg 8:28; Zech 2:4; Job 10:15). See M. I. Gruber, *Aspects of Non-Verbal Communication in the Ancient Near East* II (Studia Pohl 12; Rome: Pontifical Biblical Institute, 1980) 598–614; M. Dahood, "Ugaritic Studies and the Bible," *Greg* 43 (1962) 77–78.

to battle."[106] So in Psalm 24, YHWH the warrior "strong and mighty" (עזוז וגבור; cf. ארון עזך in Ps 132:8) enters as the triumphant "King of Glory." The procession is appropriately described as an ascent to the mountain of YHWH (v 3)[107] and the cultically purified participants are called "seekers of the face of [the God] of Jacob" (Ps 24:6).[108] In Ps 132:9, the participants in the procession are simply described as priests clothed in righteousness and "pious ones" who jubilate.[109]

The strophe ends with a supplication on behalf of the Davidic king:

בעבור דוד עבדך
אל־תשב פני משיחך
(Ps 132:10)

For the sake of David your servant,
Do not turn away the face of your anointed.

Advocates of a preexilic date have generally not reckoned with the insecurity of the royal figure in this psalm. As I have already intimated, the idiom זכר ל in v 1 indicates that a crisis was at hand. The psalmist appeals to the deity to remember "for David's sake"--that is, to consider the present generation on account of the covenant with David. Now at the end of the first half of the psalm, the composer returns to the

106. *Canaanite Myth and Hebrew Epic*, 98.

107. Note that in v 3 both *qwm* and *'ly* are used and the sanctuary is called a *mqwm*.

108. MT has מבקשי פניך יעקב, which makes no sense. Hence, most commentators follow LXX and Syr. to omit the 2 ms suff. and restore אלהי. But the addition of the suffix is difficult to explain. I am inclined to read simply: מבקשי פניך <אלהי> יעקב "those who seek your presence, O God of Jacob!"

109. For the meaning of חסידיך, see K. D. Sakenfeld, *The Meaning of Hesed in the Hebrew Bible* (HSM 17; Missoula, Montana: Scholars, 1978) 244.

person of David: בעבור דוד עבדך "for the sake of David, your servant" (v 10). In the golden calf episode, Moses petitioned the deity to "remember for the sake of Abraham, Isaac, and Israel your servants to whom you swore" (Exod 32:13), that their descendants might be preserved.[110] So in Psalm 132, YHWH is asked to remember for the sake of David "your servant" (vv 1, 10) and not to repulse the descendant of David--as if there was a real danger of YHWH doing so.[111] This apparent crisis of confidence may be connected with the split of the monarchy, and the accompanying danger of defection to the northern sanctuaries which Jeroboam had set up. So v 10 concludes Part A of the poem.

But v 10 also provides a transition to the next strophe, since the use of the root שׁוב in אל תשׁב anticipates the promise from which YHWH will not turn (ישׁוב, v 11).[112] This verse summarizes the concern in the first ten lines of the psalm: that YHWH should remember "for David's sake" and not reject his anointed. The historic relation between YHWH and David is fleshed out in this first part of the psalm (vv 1-10), with the emphasis falling on the piety of David as dramatized in the procession of the ark. The second half of the psalm will return to the issue implicitly broached in v 1, namely, the covenant faithfulness of YHWH to David, only it will emphasize *YHWH's* keeping of his covenant promise.

---

110. Cf. also the expression בעבור אברהם עבדי "for the sake of Abraham my servant" in the Yahwistic narrative on the renewal of the Abrahamic promise (Gen 26:24). See I. Riesener, *Der Stamm* עבד *im Alten Testament* (BZAW 149; Berlin: de Gruyter) 164.

111. For the meaning of the idiom השׁיב פנים, see 1 Kgs 2:16-20, 2 Kgs 18:24 // Isa 36:9; Ezek 14:6.

112. So Fretheim, "Psalm 132," 292, 294.

B. YHWH'S OATH TO DAVID

The second half of the psalm (Part B) begins with an oath by YHWH to David, thus corresponding to the oath that David swore to YHWH (Part A):

נשבע־יהוה לדוד
אמת לא־ישוב ממנה
מפרי בטנך [אשיב][113]
אשית לכסא־לך
אם־ישמרו בניך בריתי
ועדותי זו אלמדם
גם־בניהם עדי־עד
ישבו לכסא לך
(Ps 132:11-12)

YHWH swore to David,
A surety from which he will not turn back:
"Your offspring [I will cause to be enthroned];
I will place (them) on your throne.
If your sons keep my covenant,
And my stipulation[114] which I teach them.

113. The line is too short as it stands in MT. Most commentators restore a word *metri causa*. I assume that אושיב was lost by homoiarkton (cf. the following word, אשית), perhaps when it was written defectively, אשיב (cf. 1 Sam 12:8; 30:21; Job 36:7; Ezr 10:2, 10, 17, 18; Neh 13:23, 27).

114. On the basis of the parallelism, we should assume the vocalization *'ēdûtî* "my stipulation," for which meaning, see D. R. Hillers, *Covenant* (Baltimore: Johns Hopkins University, 1969) 158-166; Cross, *Canaanite Myth and Hebrew Epic*, 165-273; T. Veijola, "Zu Ableitung und Bedeutung von *hē'îd* I in hebraischen: Ein Beitrag zur Bundesterminologie," *UF* 8 (1976) 347-349; M. Parnas, "*'Ēdût, 'Ēdôt, 'Ēdwôt* in the Bible, Against the Background of the Ancient Near Eastern Documents," *Shnaton* 1 (1975) 235-246; B. Volkwein, "Masoretisches *'ēdūt, 'ēdwōt, 'ēdōt*--'Zeugnis' oder 'Bundesbestimmungen'?" *BZ* 13 (1969) 18-40.

Their children also, forever,
Shall sit upon your throne."

The composer again turns to ancient liturgical material. The shift from the third person reference to the deity in v 11a to the first person in v 11b indicates that a quote is being introduced. This finds some confirmation in the archaisms of vv 11b-12: the expressions אשית לכסא לך (v 11) and ישבו לכסא לך (v 12) are archaic,[115] as is the relative particle זו.[116] The apologist quotes from the ancient promise in order to establish the reliability of YHWH's word. As indicated already in Part A of the poem, it is the covenant with David that is at issue here.[117] YHWH's vow is called a "surety" (אמת) which, of course, recalls Nathan's Oracle (2 Samuel 7) and, specifically, David's response to it: "You are God, your words are אמת!" (2 Sam 7:28). In 2 Samuel 6-7, that oath follows David's procession of the ark into Jerusalem. YHWH promised David an enduring dynasty (בית), when David offered to build YHWH a permanent "house" (בית): David's kingdom will be "sure" and his throne will last forever (2 Sam 7:16). So here, too, the promise of an eternal dynasty follows the allusion to the procession of the ark into the city and the establishment of YHWH's "place."[118]

---

115. See p. 127 n. 148, above. In non-early Hebrew, the preposition על would have been used instead of ל. So in 11QPs[a] one finds אשית על כסא (v 11) and יעלו לכסא (v 12), both of which are attempts at "standardizing" the Hebrew.

116. See Robertson, *Linguistic Evidence*, 63.

117. See Gese, "Der Davidsbund und die Zionserwählung," 14; Kraus, *Psalmen* II, 1064.

118. The relation of Psalm 132 and 2 Samuel 6-7 has, of course, been noticed before. So, recently, E.-J. Waschke ("Das Verhältnis alttestamentlicher Überlieferungen im Schnittpunkt der Dynastiezusage und die Dynastiezusage im Spiegel alttestamentlicher Überlieferungen," *ZAW* 99 [1987] 157-179, esp. 170-171), who traces the development of Davidic hope from its genesis in the Davidic period.

The irrevocable nature of YHWH's oath to David is reiterated elsewhere in the Hebrew Bible, notably in the so-called "last words of David" (2 Sam 23:1–7) and in the following portion of an old liturgy:

אחת נשבעתי בקדשי
אם־לדוד אכזב
זרעו לעולם יהיה
וכסאו כשמש נגדי
(Ps 89:36–37)[119]

Once I swore by my holiness;
I will not be false to David.[120]
His seed will exist forever;
And his throne like the sun before me.

This fragment is part of a larger liturgical unit (Ps 89:20–38), which appropriately also follows a procession celebrating the deity's victory in cosmogonic combat and the subsequent enthronement of the deity as universal king.[121] The propagandistic intent of the liturgy is made plain by the comparison of David with Saul, who was supposedly overlooked in David's favor,[122] and by the language of David's exaltation:

ואמונתי וחסדי עמו
ובשמי תרום קרנו
ושמתי בים ידו

119. On the relation of this poem with the Nathan Oracle in 2 Sam 7:1–17 and 1 Chron 17:1–15, see Ishida, *The Royal Dynasties in Ancient Israel*, 81–99 and the literature cited therein.

120. For Akkadian parallels to this idiom, see Ishida, *The Royal Dynasties in Ancient Israel*, 92.

121. Cf. G. Ahlström, *Psalm 89* (Lund: Gleerup, 1959) 98–131.

122. Cf. v 20 and Psalm 151 in LXX and 11QPs[a].

ובנהרות ימינו
הוא יקראני אבי אתה
אלי וצור ישועתי
אף־אני בכור אתנהו
עליון למלכי־ארץ
לעולם אשמור־לו חסדי
ובריתי נאמנת לו
ושמתי לעד זרעו
וכסאו כימי שמים
(Ps 89:25–30)

My fidelity and faithfulness are with him;
And by my name shall his horn be exalted.
I will set his hand against Sea,
And his right hand against River.
He shall proclaim to me: "You are my father,
My god and the rock of my salvation!"
Yea, I will appoint him first-born,
'Elyôn over the kings of the earth.
Forever I will keep my loyalty for his sake,
And my sure covenant for him.
I will establish his seed forever,
And his throne will be like the days of heaven.

The exaltation of the deity over the forces of chaos is reflected in David's exaltation over his enemies--"his horn shall be exalted" (cf. Ps 132:17). In a daring use of myth, the poet compares the king to the divine warrior: the king will also set his hand over the unruly waters, Sea and River, and become the *'elyôn* over the kings of the earth. Moreover, the Davidic throne is guaranteed by divine promise to last forever; it is founded upon the irrevocable oath of YHWH to David.

But as Psalm 132:12 makes plain, the promise made to David is not without stipulations. The successors to the Davidic throne are to abide by the dictates of the covenant. This element of conditionality in the irrevocable promise is troublesome to many.[123] Some perceive a blatant contradiction between the irrevocable promise of v 11 and the conditional corollary in v 12.[124] This is, of course, based on the long-held assumption of two distinct traditions, the Sinaitic covenant being conditional, and the Davidic covenant being unconditional. But as J. D. Levenson has observed, the two traditions are not mutually exclusive.[125] There is no evidence at all that the Davidic covenant, in fact, replaced the Sinaitic; rather, "within the national covenant lies another, restricted to one family, the royal house of David."[126] Conditionality is not necessarily incompatible with the idea of an enduring dynasty. The irrevocable promise of an everlasting dynasty did not exempt the Davidic kings from the Sinaitic law. As B. Halpern puts it, "the contract of Ps 132:11-12 might be said to be conditional, but given the fulfillment of the conditions, eternal."[127]

So in Ps 132:12, the eternal promise has a conditional element lodged between two affirmations of the promise of an enduring dynasty; the condition is embedded in the eternal promise. But this conditionality is not a deuteronomistic

---

123. Indeed, L. Perlitt (*Bundestheologie im Alten Testament* [WMANT 36; Neukirchen-Vluyn: Neukirchen, 1969] 51-52) insists that the very notion of a covenant with YHWH was the invention of the Deuteronomic school. But see the critique of D. J. McCarthy, "*b*$^{e}$*rît* in Old Testament History and Theology," *Bib* 53 (1972) 110-121.

124. Thus Mettinger, *King and Messiah*, 256.

125. See J. D. Levenson, "The Davidic Covenant and Its Modern Interpreters," *CBQ* 40 (1978) 210-215; idem, *Sinai and Zion* (New Voices in Biblical Studies; Minneapolis: Winston, 1985) 99-101. The priestly "eternal" covenant for instance, is "conditional" inasmuch as it entailed the keeping of the covenant (Gen 17:7).

126. *Sinai and Zion*, 99.

127. Cf. Halpern, *The Constitution of the Monarchy*, 36. Halpern invokes the case of the Elides, who were given an eternal promise which was, nevertheless, revoked when they sinned (1 Sam 2:30).

innovation, as is often suggested,[128] nor is it a synthesis of the two covenant traditions late in the monarchical period.[129] Rather, it was already present in the traditions of the league with which the ark was associated, traditions patterned after the itinerant 'Ēl who dwelled in a tent.[130]

That element of conditionality in the enduring promise was apparently reiterated and emphasized after the division of the kingdoms.[131] In a long recitation of history (Psalm 78) that was intended to legitimate the southern sanctuary and the Davidic dynasty, one reads of the unfaithfulness of the Ephraimites: לא שמרו ברית אלהים "they did not keep the covenant of God" (v 10), and ולא נאמנו בריתו "they were not faithful to his covenant" (v 37). In this anti-northern polemic, which dates from the divided monarchy before the fall of Samaria in 722 B. C. E.,[132] God had "established an עדות in Jacob, and placed a תורה in Israel" (v 5),[133] but the Ephraimites had disobeyed the covenant and they did not

128. So T. Veijola, *Verheissung in der Krise* (Annales Academiæ Scientiarum Fennicæ, Sarja-Ser. B 220; Helsinki: Suomalainen Tiedeakateneia, 1982) 161-162; A. Caquot, "La prophétie de Nathan et ses échos lyriques," *Congress Volume Bonn 1962* (VTSup 9; Leiden: Brill, 1963) 221-224; Mettinger, *King and Messiah*, 256 n. 12.

129. So Ollenburger, *Zion, the City of the Great King*, 61.

130. That is to say, the conditionality of the covenant was symbolized by the mobility of the tent-shrine. So Cross, *Canaanite Myth and Hebrew Epic*, 233.

131. Cf. Weinfeld ("The Covenant of Grant," 196) who argues for the origin of the conditional element after the political separation of Israel and Judah, an element which was subsequently developed and given full expression by the deuteronomists.

132. See the discussion of J. Day, "Pre-Deuteronomic Allusions to the Covenant in Hosea and Psalm LXXVIII," *VT* 36 (1986) 8-12 and the literature cited there.

133. Note תורה // ברית in Ps 78:10 and עדות // ברית in Ps 132:12.

keep his stipulations (ועדותיו לא שמרו, v 56). Hence the northern sanctuary at Shiloh was destroyed and the ark was captured (vv 58–66), and YHWH chose David and Zion instead (vv 67–72).

The reference to the covenant in Psalm 132, therefore, is in keeping with the pro-Davidic propaganda. But here the apologist does not go beyond the monarchical period to speak of the giving of the covenant first to the north, as is done in the recitation of Psalm 78. Rather, the poet begins with David's receiving of the promise of an enduring dynasty, a promise that is eternally valid, provided that his successors will keep the covenant (v 12). Without referring to the early history of the covenant, the apologist simply identifies the Davidides as the recipients of the covenant which the south has inherited. It is suggestive, therefore, that one finds עדות associated with the נזר "diadem" (cf. v 18) in a southern coronation ritual in 2 Kgs 11:12.[134] The עדות was a sign of YHWH's enduring, albeit conditional, promise to David.

Along with the theme of the irrevocable promise to David is the election of Zion as YHWH's special abode:

כי־בחר יהוה בציון
אוה למושב לו
זאת־מנוחתי עדי־עד
פה־אשב כי אותיה
(Ps 132:13–14)

---

134. See Mettinger, *King and Messiah*, 286–289 and the literature cited therein. Urging comparison with the Egyptian enthronement rites, G. von Rad ("The Royal Ritual in Judah," in *The Problem of the Hexateuch and Other Essays* [trans. E. W. Trueman Dicken; London: SCM, 1966] 225–231) compared the עדות with the royal protocol that legitimated the Egyptian kings. Although the evidence is scant, there is reason to believe that the עדות was a tangible token of the covenant. See Johnson, *Sacral Kingship in Ancient Israel*, 23–25; Volkwein, "Masoretisches *'ēdūt, 'ēdwōt, 'ēdōt*," 31.

For YHWH has chosen Zion;
He has desired it as his abode.
This is my resting-place forever and ever;
Here I will sit enthroned, for I have desired it.

Here, again, we must reject any suggestion that the election of Zion is a deuteronomistic invention.[135] The tradition is much older than the deuteronomic school.[136] We find it already in Psalm 78, which remembers the rejection of Shiloh (not Samaria, as the pro-Judean psalmist would surely have insisted if the destruction of that city had already taken place) for the failure of the northern tribes to keep the covenant (עדות // ברית) that the deity had established, and which climaxed in the divine election of Zion:

וימאס באהל יוסף
ובשבט אפרים לא בחר
ויבחר את־שבט יהודה
את הר־ציון אשר אהב
ויבן כמו־רמים מקדשו
כארץ יסדה לעולם
(Ps 78:67-69)

He rejected the tent of Joseph,
And the tribe of Ephraim he did not choose.
But he did choose the tribe of Judah,
Mount Zion which he loved.[137]
He built his sanctuary like the heavens,
like the netherworld he founded it forever.[138]

---

135. So W. H. Schmidt, "Kritik am Königtum," in *Probleme biblische Theologie* (Fs. G. von Rad; ed. H. W. Wolff; Munich: Kaiser, 1971) 446 n. 17; Veijola, *Verheissung in der Krise*, 161.

136. See Weinfeld, "Zion and Jerusalem as Religious and Political Capital," 82-93.

137. Cf. Ps 87:2.

138. See Chapter One, n. 80.

The motif of Zion's election is also evident in a text from the early monarchy wherein the ascent of the deity from Mount Sinai to Mount Zion is said to have been viewed with envy by the more rugged mountains:

הר־אלהים הר־בשן
הר גבננים הר־בשן
למה תרצדון
הרים גבננים
< >הר[139] חמד אלהים לשבתו
אף יהוה ישכן לנצח
<ב>רכב[140] אלהים רבתים
אלפי שנ<ני ישר>א<ל[141]
ארני ב<א>[142] מסיני בקדש
עלית למרום שבית שבי

(Ps 68:16–19a)

Mighty mountain, mount Bashan,
Rugged mountain,[143] mount Bashan,
Why do you look enviously[144]
O rugged mountains?
The mountain which God desired for his dwelling,
Surely YHWH shall dwell (there) forever.
With the chariotry of God, two myriads,
Thousands of the archers of Israel,
Adonay comes from Sinai in holiness.

---

139. Omit the definite article as dittography. It is neither required nor expected in archaic poetry.

140. I assume ב was lost by haplography, owing to the graphic likeness of *bêt* and *rēš* in the palaeo-Hebrew scripts.

141. Partly following Albright, "Notes on Psalm 68 and 134," 2–4; "Early Hebrew Lyric Poems," 25. See also Chapter One, n. 164.

142. MT has בם סיני, but see Deut 33:2.

143. That is, with many humps or ridges.

144. Cf. Sir. 14:22.

You have ascended to the height;
You have captured captives.[145]

The allusion to the accompanying military retinue recalls the incipit of the liturgy used with the ark's return from holy war (Num 10:36). Earlier in the psalm (v 2), we find a call--again echoing the ancient Song of the Ark (Num 10:35)--for the divine warrior to go forth into battle. Now, following the victory of the deity (vv 12-15), the procession marches to the new abode of God, Zion.[146] The neighboring rugged mountains look with envy as the choice of Zion is made plain in the procession:[147] Zion is the mount of YHWH's desire, the abode of choice. It would become the deity's dwelling forever. The divine warrior is said to have ascended to the "height" (*mrwm*), a term reminiscent of Ba'l's abode in "the heights of Ṣpn" (*mrym ṣpn*).[148]

The motif of Zion's election appears to be ancient, going back to the procession of the ark under David.[149] The processional entry of the ark, representing YHWH and his entourage, signified the final decision of the deity to reside in the newly won mount, Zion. So Psalm 47, which celebrates the

145. The mention of captives is reminiscent of holy warfare. Cf. 1QM xii.9: קומה גבור שבה שביכה "Come, O Warrior, take your captives captive!"

146. Not surprisingly, therefore, S. Mowinckel (*Der achtundsechzigste Psalm* [Avhandlinger utgitt av Det Norske Videnskaps-Akademi i Oslo, II; Hist.-Filos. Klasse 1; Oslo: Dybwad, 1953] esp. 10-11, 56-59) argued for the liturgical use of this psalm in the annual enthronement festival. Cf. also the important study of J. Gray, "A Cantata of the Autumn Festival: Psalm LXVIII," *JSS* 22 (1977) 2-26.

147. For the conceptual background, see Clifford, *The Cosmic Mountain*, 137 n. 54; E. D. van Buren, "Mountain Gods," *Or* 12 (1943) 79-80.

148. *KTU* 1.4.IV.19; V.23; 1.3.IV.1, 38; etc.

149. Schreiner (*Sion-Jerusalem*, 51) correctly points out that the significance of the ark procession led by David is encapsulated in Ps 132:13.

accession of YHWH and the election of Zion, states that YHWH has chosen (בחר) the patrimony for himself, namely, "the pride of Jacob (Jerusalem) which he loves" (Ps 47:5).

Roberts has observed that the tradition of Zion's election must have become quite firmly established by the end of Solomon's reign, for Jeroboam I apparently could not establish a competing sanctuary in the north without paying a heavy political price.[150] Whereas the election of David may have been easily disputed in the north, the tradition of Zion as YHWH's abode was more firmly lodged. Even in northern circles, the priority of Jerusalem was taken for granted.[151] Hence, one finds the coupling of David and Zion in Psalm 132--as if the apologist wanted to tie the two traditions inextricably together.[152]

The language of YHWH's dwelling in Zion points to a date some time during the monarchy and renders problematic any suggestion of deuteronomistic influences. Zion is called the deity's מושב ("residence"), a term that does not appear anywhere in deuteronomistic writings of the abode of God. The word is employed in an old tradition of the abode of 'Ēl, put in the mouth of the arrogant prince of Tyre by Ezekiel: "I am 'Ēl, at the residence (מושב) of God do I sit enthroned (ישבתי), in the midst of seas" (Ezek 28:3).[153] Ezekiel's polemic was against the arrogant prince who dared to compare himself to the Canaanite high god, claiming to be "wise like 'Ēl," although he was only a human (Ezek 28:2, 6).[154] Significantly,

---

150. Cf. 1 Kgs 14:1-18. Roberts, "The Davidic Origin of the Zion Tradition," 343.

151. Ibid.

152. Cf. Weinfeld, "Zion and Jerusalem as Religious and Political Capital," 90.

153. See Pope, *El in the Ugaritic Texts*, 98-99; W. Zimmerli, *Ezekiel* II (Hermeneia; trans. J. D. Martin; Fortress: Philadelphia, 1983) 78; Clifford, *The Cosmic Mountain*, 169-170.

154. Cf. the wisdom of 'Ēl in Ugaritic literature, *KTU* 1.3.V.30; 4.IV.41; 4.V.3; 16.IV.2.

the abode of 'Ēl is further specified in vv 13–14 of the same chapter in Ezekiel as the paradisaic garden of 'Ēl, which is equated with the holy mountain (הַר קֹדֶשׁ) of God. This divine residence is certainly to be connected with Ugaritic *mθb 'il* "dwelling of 'Ēl" (*KTU* 1.3.V.39; 1.4.I.13; 4.IV.52), as Clifford has noted.[155] In every occurrence of *mθb 'il* in Ugaritic, contrast is made between 'Ēl, who had a permanent home, and Ba'l, who did not. The mention of YHWH's מושב, therefore, probably indicates the fulfillment of David's desire to find YHWH a place. The entry of the ark into the city signified the establishing of a place for YHWH, for the deity had chosen Mount Zion above all other mountains as the divine מושב--even as 'Ēl dwelled as the high god in his mountain abode.

In our psalm, Zion becomes YHWH's residence by choice: פה אשב כי אותיה "Here will I sit enthroned, for I desired it" (v 14). The language is patently undeuteronomistic. The deuteronomist(s) would not have used the verb ישב of YHWH's dwelling on earth; for them, the deity resided (ישב) in heaven, whereas the hypostatic name of the deity is made to tabernacle in the earthly sanctuary (לשכן שמו שם).[156] The verb has a royal connotation which does not fit the image of the deity in deuteronomistic theology. The root ישב is found already in pre-deuteronomistic traditions, indeed, in archaic contexts of YHWH's enthronement as victorious king.[157] This is, of course, the image of the deity associated with the ark at Shiloh, where YHWH was identified with 'Ēl, the high god in the Canaanite pantheon and the divine king *par excellence*--so the appropriateness of the reference the deity's מושב. The enthronement of God is also implied in the procession of the

---

155. *The Cosmic Mountain*, 169 n. 90.

156. See esp. 1 Kgs 8:14–66. For scholarly discussion on the issue, see S. D. McBride, "The Deuteronomic Name Theology," Unpublished Ph.D. dissertation (Harvard, 1969), esp. 204–210; Mettinger, *The Dethronement of Sabaoth*, 38–79; Clements, *God and Temple* 92 n. 2.

157. Exod 15:17; Ps 68:17; 1 Kgs 8:12.

ark in 2 Samuel 6, which is concerned with the accession of the deity and the claiming of his newly won mount, although it must be admitted that the verb ישׁב does not occur in that account. The root does occur, however, in Solomon's induction of the ark at the inauguration of the temple. A poetic fragment from the lost Book of Yashar is quoted in conjunction with this procession:[158]

בנה בניתי בית זבל לך
מכון לשבתך עולמים
(1 Kgs 8:13)

I have indeed built a royal house for you,
A dais for your eternal dwelling.

The royal imagery of YHWH in Psalm 132, then, is not deuteronomistic. Moreover, Mount Zion is regarded as YHWH's eternal מנוחה in the psalm (v 14). This, too, is a pre-deuteronomistic notion. For the deuteronomist(s) the מנוחה is something that the king gives to the subjects.[159] In fact, the word is never associated with the deity in the deuteronomistic writings. By contrast, מנוחה in v 14 is the abode of the deity and appears to have royal connotations, corresponding to the royal rest (comfort) in West Semitic and Akkadian inscriptions.[160] The mention of YHWH's מנוחה in the psalm suggests the enthronement of YHWH, as dramatized in the procession of the ark.

In the previously cited bilingual inscription from the reign of Nebuchadnezzar I, one reads that the pious

158. Cf. LXX, for which see J. Gray, *I & II Kings* (OTL; Philadelphia: Westminster, 1976) 211–212; O. Loretz, "Der Torso eines kanaanäische-israelitischen Tempelweihespruche in 1 Kg 8, 12–13," *UF* 6 (1974) 478–480.

159. Deut 12:9; 1 Kgs 8:56; 2 Sam 14:17.

160. Cf. M. Metzger, "Himmlische und irdische Wohnstatt Jahwes," *UF* 2 (1970) 139–158, esp. 157; Kraus, *Königsherrschaft*, 51–54.

commitment of the king to the restoration of the statues, dramatized by the king's sacrifice of sleep, prompted the return of Marduk to his city:

> [š]à.bi túm.ma a.ra uru.gibil mu.un.gin.a.ni šà.bi.ta
> níg.ḫul nim.ma$^{ki}$.ke(4) kaskal a.li.ri ḫar.ra.an
> asilal ḫé.en.da še.še.ga šà.šu.an.na.ta mu.un.dib
> šá ub-la lìb-ba-šú a-lak Babili(URU.GIBIL$^{ki}$)
> i-ku-šam-ma iš-tu qí-rib lem-né-ti e-lam-ti
> ḫar-ra-an šu-lu-lu! ú-ru-uḫ ri-šá-a-ti
> ṭu!-da-at taš-me-e ù ma-ga-ri iṣ-ba-ta ana(DIŠ)
> qí-rib Babili(ŠU.AN.NA$^{ki}$)
>
> (IV *R* 20, 12-14)
>
> That which his (Marduk's) heart desired--to go to Babylon--he achieved, and from the midst of wicked Elam he took a road of praising, a path of joy, a way of favor and acceptance to the midst of Babylon.

The triumphant procession of the cult statues into the city apparently signified divine favor for the city. In the language of political propaganda, it was the deity's desire to enter or reenter the city and to reside in it.

The motif of the election of the city is evident in the mythological texts, as well. Thus, following Marduk's victory in cosmogonic battle, the sanctuary was erected as a restful dwelling where the gods were to repose forever (*E E* VI.52-54).[161] The gods assumed their assigned stations, a banquet was conducted, and Babylon was said to be constructed by Marduk's desire (*EE* VI.57). When the gods of the Annunaki sat down to dine at the banquet, they

---

161. For the place of Enuma Elish in cultic drama, see T. Jacobsen, "Religious Drama in Ancient Mesopotamia," in *Unity and Diversity* (JHNES; ed. H. Goedicke and J. J. M. Roberts; Baltimore: Johns Hopkins University, 1975) 65-97.

proclaimed Babylon the favorite city of the gods: "Here is Babylon, your favorite dwelling place" (*annam bābili šubat narmekun*).[162] In the Eridu Creation account one reads:

> [ka.dingir.ra].ki ba.ru e.sag.il.la šu.ul
> bābilu(KA.DINGIR.RA)$^{ki}$ e-pu-[uš] E-sag-ila šuk-lul
> [dingir a.]nun.na.ke(x) e.ne uru.bi ba.an.dù
> ilāni(DINGIR.MEŠ) a-nun-na-ki mit-ḫa-riš e-pu-uš
> [uru] kù.ga ki.tuš šà.dùg.ga.ke(x) e.ne mu.maḫ.a mi.ni.in.sa(4)
> ālu(URU) el-lu šu-bat ṭu-ub lib-bi-šu-nu ṣi-ri-iš im-bu-u
>
> (*CT* 13, pl. 36, ll. 14-16)

> Babylon was made, Esagila was completed;
> The gods, the Anunnaki, he (Marduk) created altogether.
> The holy city, the dwelling of their hearts' delight, they majestically called it.

It is likely that the creation myths were recited during the procession of divine statues in Mesopotamia. The processional entry of the statues into the city signified the election of the city by the victorious god to be the eternal abode from which the universe would be governed.

In light of this probable background of the procession of the ark, it is significant to find an allusion in Ps 132:15 to the deity's beneficence exercised in his chosen city. YHWH promises to bless the city with provisions, and its poor will be satiated with food. The mention of YHWH's blessings and the provision of victuals is certainly congruous with the procession of the ark. As we have seen in Chapter 2 of this study, David's induction of the ark culminated in a symbolic banquet, a ritual enactment of the divine banquet that the victorious gods held. Even as a feast followed the victory of Marduk in the Akkadian creation myth, and a banquet

162. *EE* VI.70-72.

followed the victory of Ba'l in the Ugaritic myth, so YHWH's victory over his enemies was followed by a demonstration of his beneficence for his subjects. The provision of food for the multitudes is tantamount to the exercise of kingship. Thus in Ugaritic mythology, Ba'l's triumphal entry into his new abode culminates in his enthronement (*KTU* 1.4.VIII). He sits enthroned (*yθb*, *KTU* 1.4.VIII.42) in his palace on his newly won mount, gloating over his enemies whom he had defeated, and declaring his supremacy over the gods of the divine council: it is he alone who is king over the gods, who fattens gods and humans alike, "who satiates the multitudes of the earth" (*dyšb['] hmlt 'arṣ*).[163] The victory of Ba'l and his consequent enthronement resulted in the satiation of the multitudes. Conversely, the defeat of Ba'l at the hands of his enemies raised the specter of destitution for the multitudes (cf. *KTU* 1.5.VI.24-25; 6.I.7). The beneficence of Ba'l was the mark of his sovereignty over the universe.

So, too, the mention of YHWH's blessing and provision of food for the poor is not out of place in an account of the ritual procession of the ark. The reference to the deity's blessing is no incidental allusion to the acts of charity carried out at the temple, as is sometimes supposed.[164] Rather, as in 2 Samuel 6 and Psalm 29, the manifestation of the deity's blessings was an integral part, if not the climax, of the whole cultic drama. The provision of food in Ps 132:15 corresponds to the symbolic meal that David sponsored in conjunction with the induction of the ark into Jerusalem (2 Sam 6:19).

Throughout the ancient Near East, the procession of divine images into a city was a public and highly symbolic ritual which was a royal prerogative to conduct. It dramatized the deity's acceptance of the city and patronage of the king. Not surprisingly, therefore, a common subject of royal propaganda was the ability of the kings, as patron of the cult, to "cause the gods to dwell" in the city or the city-temple.

163. *KTU* 1.4.VII.51-52.
164. So Briggs, *The Book of Psalms* II, 472.

In the Aramaic inscription of Panammū I of Ya'diya (8th century B. C. E.), the king indicated that he was commissioned by the gods to build. And so he erected the statue of Hadad and the "place"--i.e., the sanctuary (*mqm*).[165] He caused his god to dwell in the sanctuary (*hšbt bh 'lhy*).[166] The gods had stood with him from his youth, he claimed, and they had given him greatness and "a surety" (*'mn*).[167]

In the Phoenician version of the bilingual inscription from Karatepe, Azitawadda (late 8th century B. C. E.) boasts of his victory over his enemies, and the peace (*nḥt*) and prosperity that his rule brought.[168] In particular, he speaks of the city which he built and named after himself, and how he had caused the gods to dwell (*yšb*) in that city (*KAI* 26.A.II.17–III.2).

Similar themes occur in the Akkadian royal inscriptions.[169] In one text commemorating the inauguration of Dur-Šarrukīn (Khorsabad), Sargon II (722–705 B. C. E.) records that he ushered the gods to the city amid elaborate feasting and

---

165. *KAI* 214.14. For *mqm*, see A. Cowley, "The Meaning of מָקוֹם in Hebrew," *JTS* 17 (1916) 174–176. I take *pnmw br qrl* following *mqm* as starting a new sentence.

166. *KAI* 214.19.

167. *KAI* 214.1–3, 11–12. Cf. J. C. L. Gibson, *Textbook of Syrian Semitic Inscriptions* II (Oxford: Clarendon, 1975) 66–67, 71. Gibson reads: *w'mn . krt . by* "a sure covenant struck with me" and compares this with the Davidic covenant.

168. *KAI* 26. Although Azitawadda is not called "king" anywhere in the text, there is no doubt that he was the effective ruler (the regent), and the *form* of the inscription is still to be classified as a "royal inscription." See *KAI* 26.A.I.10–11. Cf. the discussion of the Phoenician and Luwian Hieroglyphic versions in J. Friedrich, "Zur Interpretation von Satz XVI der phönizisch-bildhethitischen Bilinguis von Karatepe," *Or* 31 (1962) 223–224.

169. Cf. H. Tawil, "Some Literary Elements in the Opening Sections of the Hadad, Zākir, and Nērab II Inscriptions in the Light of East and West Semitic Royal Inscriptions," *Or* 43 (1974) 40–55.

sacrificing.[170] In the famous Bull Inscription, he speaks of the completion of Dur Šarrukīn, and how the gods were ushered in and a banquet was held for them.[171]

Another example is a stela commissioned in the reign of Asshurnasirpal II (883–859 B. C. E.) to commemorate the completion of Kalḫu in (879 B. C. E.).[172] Like Jerusalem, the city is said to have been captured with divine help, made a capital, and presented to the king's patron god (ll. 4–40). Then, Asshurnasirpal invited Aššur and the other gods into the city for a great banquet (ll. 104–140). Finally, the "happy people of all the lands" feasted for ten days. They were symbolically blessed and sent back to their homes "in peace and joy" (ll. 150–153).

Beyond the inscriptions, R. D. Barnett points to the depiction of similar processions on monuments from Northern Syria and Southern Anatolia.[173] He observes that the theme of a procession of the gods into the city is common on the gateways of the region, indicating the public and propagandistic nature of the events. The reliefs variously show the participation of kings, priests, musicians and military personnel, often amid feasting and sacrificing, ushering the

---

170. H. Winckler, *Die Keilschrifttexte Sargons* I (Leipzig: Pfeiffer, 1889) 146, ll. 44–45. Cf. D. D. Luckenbill, *Ancient Records of Assyria and Babylonia* II (Chicago: University of Chicago, 1927) 44.

171. D. G. Lyon, *Keilschrifttexte Sargons Königs von Assyrien* (Assyriologische Bibliothek 5; Leipzig: Hinrichs, 1883) 46, ll. 101–102; cf. Luckenbill, *Ancient Records of Assyria and Babylonia* II, 47.

172. D. J. Wiseman, "A New Stela of Aššur-naṣir-pal II," *Iraq* 14 (1952) 24–44, pl. vii–xi.

173. "Bringing the God into the Temple," in *Temples and High Places in Biblical Times* (ed. A. Biran;, Jerusalem: Nelson Glueck School of Biblical Archaeology, 1977) 10–17; cf. also M. Mellink, "Hittite Friezes and Gate Sculptures," in *Anatolian Studies Presented to Hans Gustav Güterbock* (ed. K. Bittel, Ph. H. J. ten Cate, and E. Reiner; Istanbul: Nederlands historisch-archaeologisch Instituut, 1974) 201–214.

gods into the city. Among the examples cited by Barnett is a series of reliefs from the gates of the citadel at Karatepe which show a procession moving toward an enthroned and feasting deity.[174] These are particularly intriguing in light of the bilingual inscriptions of Azitawadda found in the vicinity.[175]

In sum, the historical cultic referent of Psalm 132 is the procession of the ark into Jerusalem. As in comparable rituals from elsewhere in the ancient Near East, the procession was conducted in joy by priests and other cultic participants. It culminated in a feast celebrating the occasion and symbolizing the deity's acceptance of the city as the new divine abode from which blessings would be dispensed to the multitudes.

The psalm concludes with a promise by the deity:

שם אצמיח קרן לדוד
ערכתי נר למשיחי
אויביו אלביש בשת
ועליו יציץ נזרו
(Ps 132:17–18)

There I will cause a horn to sprout for David;
I will prepare a lamp for my anointed.
His enemies I will clothe with shame,
But on him his crown will gleam.

---

174. Barnett, "Bringing the God into the Temple," 15.

175. This is not to suggest, however, that the inscriptions and reliefs are to be dated to the same period, although some scholars have placed both in the 9th century. So, for instance, D. Ussishkin, "The Date of the Neo-Hittite Enclosure in Karatepe," *AnSt* 19 (1969) 121–137. I am inclined to think that the inscription was put on the 9th century reliefs in the 8th century, Azitawadda's intent being a statement of his fidelity to the traditional acts of the ancient kings. Cf. J. B. Peckham, *The Development of the Late Phoenician Scripts* (HSS 20; Cambridge, Massachusetts: Harvard University, 1968) 117 n. 11.

This text has traditionally been interpreted messianically, that is, as the promise of a future king who will be a scion of David.[176] One reason for this interpretation is the similarity of v 17a to Jer 23:5 (הקמותי לדוד צמח צדיק "I will raise up for David a legitimate scion") and Jer 33:5 (אצמיח לדוד צמח צדקה "I will cause a legitimate scion to sprout forth for David").[177] The noun צמח, of course, came to refer to a future Davidic king in late Israelite prophecy.[178] But in Psalm 132 it is not צמח "sprout" that is the object of the verb, but קרן "horn," which is never used figuratively for progeny anywhere in the Hebrew Bible.[179] Rather, קרן is always a metaphor of power or authority and is usually associated with divine deliverance from one's enemies. Not surprisingly, therefore, the term is used of the deity as a divine warrior who is called upon to deliver his king from distress.[180] In the Akkadian inscriptions one finds the personal names [d]*Adad-qar-na-a-a*, [d]*Adad-qar-na-ia* "Adad is my Horn" and *SI-Adad* "Adad is (my) Horn."[181] In Amorite onomastica we find the names *Qar-ni-li-im; qar-na-na, qar-na-nu-num.*[182]

In the Song of Hannah, which is probably dated to the early monarchy, the king's horn is said to be exalted through YHWH (1 Sam 2:1). The context is, again, deliverance from enemies, for the poet goes on to gloat over the enemies and rejoice in the salvation which the deity brought. At the conclusion of the poem, we find a prayer for the king, who is called God's anointed, as in Psalm 132:

---

176. So recently, Kraus, *Psalmen* II, 1065.

177. Cf. Zech 3:8; 6:12; cf. *ṣmḥ* in *KAI* 43.11; 162.2; 163.3. Thus, Briggs (*The Book of Psalms* II, 467–469, 475), who dated the psalm to the Hellenistic period, concluded that "the glossator had these texts in mind."

178. See Zech 3:8; 6:12.

179. Nor are its cognates in West Semitic inscriptions or Akkadian texts so used.

180. Ps 18:3 // 2 Sam 22:3.

181. See *CAD* 13, 140.

182. Gelb, *Computer-Aided Analysis of Amorite*, 342.

יהוה ידין אפסי־ארץ
ויתן־עז למלכו
וירם קרן משיחו
(1 Sam 2:10b–c)

YHWH will judge the extremities of the earth.
May he grant his king strength;
And may he raise the horn of his anointed.

The parallelism leaves no doubt as to the meaning of the horn in this archaic poem: it is synonymous with power.[183] To raise the horn, then, is to grant or increase power.[184] But the closest parallel to our text is found in Ezek 29:21: ביום ההוא אצמיח קרן לבית ישראל "on that day, I will cause a horn to sprout for the house of Israel." Here the imagery is again of YHWH's deliverance from enemies,[185] and has nothing to do with succession. The meaning of the imagery is clarified in the next line: ולך אתן פתחון־פה בתוכם וידעו כי־אני יהוה "and to you I will give opening of mouth in your midst, that they will know that I am YHWH." (v 21).[186] So Ps 132:17 is not about descendants *per se*, but power and security for the Davidides.[187] Thus it belongs with the promise of YHWH's blessing in v 15 as a fitting conclusion for the procession of the ark. One must again compare the closing line of Psalm 29, which follows the enthronement of the deity over Flood: יהוה עז לעמו יתן // יהוה יברך את עמו בשלום "May YHWH give his people strength // May YHWH bless his people with peace" (Ps 29:11).

Nevertheless, the issue of the enduring Davidic line is not forgotten. The text says that YHWH will prepare a נר for the

183. Cf. further, Ps 89:18, 20ff.; 92:11; 112:9; Mic 4:13.

184. Conversely, to lop off the horn is to diminish one's power. See Jer 48:25; Lam 2:3; Zech 2:4; Ps 148:14.

185. See Zimmerli, *Ezekiel* II, 120–121.

186. On the opening of mouth, cf. Ezek 16:63.

187. *Contra* Kruse, ""Psalm CXXXII and the Royal Zion Festival," 288–290.

anointed. P. D. Hanson has suggested that the word נר in this psalm may be a defective spelling for ניר, a cognate of Akkadian *nīru* "yoke."[188] The term in Akkadian is frequently used figuratively of authority or rule, as in the idioms *nīr bēlûti* "yoke of lordship," *nīru ša šarri* "yoke of the king," *nīr ili* "yoke of god."[189] So we note the occurrence of *nīru* in the context of triumph over one's enemies: *šar Akkadê nīršu išširma ayyābīšu qāssu ikaššad* "the king of Akkad, his yoke will prosper and his hand will conquer his enemies"[190] Furthermore, in an OB Hymn to Ištar, one reads: *napḫar lakīšunu dadmī taṣṣamissunūti anīrišu* "all the inhabited regions of the world, she yoked them to his yoke."[191]

In light of the association of Akkadian *nīru* with victory and dominion over the enemy, a cognate of it would, indeed, be a proper parallel term for קרן.[192] Yet, it must be admitted that the Akkadian parallels are not decisive, since the metaphor of the "lamp" apparently occurs in the Hebrew Bible in connection with the Davidic dynasty. Thus, after David's retainers rescued him from death in combat, they urged him, "Don't go out to battle with us anymore, lest you extinguish

188. "The Song of Heshbon and David's NÎR," *HTR* 61 (1968) 310-320, esp. 318 n. 29.

189. We may compare here the geographical names $^{uru}$*Aššur-ni-ir-šú-ú-rap-piš* "Aššur-Extended-His-Rule" and $^{uru}$*Aššur-ni-ir-ka-rap-piš* "Aššur-Extend-Your-Rule." See Borger, *Die Inschriften Asarhaddons*, 107, §68, l. 34.

190. See R. C. Thompson, *The Report of the Magicians and Astrologers of Nineveh and Babylon in the British Museum* (London: Luzac, 1900) 49.2.

191. *RA* 22, 172.52. For further examples, see Hanson, "The Song of Heshbon and David's NÎR," 312f-313; *CAD* 11/II, 260-264.

192. Dahood (*Psalms* III, 248) compares Akkadian *qarnu* which is used of horn-shaped containers, suggesting that the "horn" here may be "a lamp in the shape of an animal." But the horn metaphor occurs regularly in royal psalms for deliverance from enemies (Pss 89:18, 20ff.; 18:3 // 2 Sam 22:3; 1 Sam 2:1, 10).

the lamp of Israel!" (2 Sam 21:17). Here the use of the verb כבה "quench, extinguish" leaves no doubt that the lamp metaphor is intended.[193] Moreover, the use of the verb ערך in Ps 132:18 would also indicate that "lamp" is intended, for the same verb is used in Lev 24:4 for the preparation of lamps (נרות) in the tabernacle.[194] The traditional rendering "lamp" is correct; the question is what the metaphor means.

It is necessary here to also consider the noun ניר, apparently a biform of נר.[195] The former occurs most frequently in connection with the continuity of the Davidic dynasty in Jerusalem, the disintegration of the Davidic empire notwithstanding.[196] The issue is not progeny *per se*, however, but continuity of power.[197]

The verb ערכתי is, of course, related to the participle ערוכה used of the eternal covenant in the so-called "last words of David" (2 Sam 23:5). The poet of Psalm 132 thus returns to the issue raised implicitly at the beginning of the psalm (v 1), and explicitly at the beginning of Part B (v 11), namely, God's covenant with David. I would interpret the end of the psalm, then, as a final response to the petition to remember *for the sake of David* (v 1). The very mention of לדוד in v 17 recalls the לדוד in vv 1 and 11, the beginnings of Parts A and B, respectively. By the same token, למשיחו in v 17 recalls the petition in v 10 not to reject the anointed

---

193. Cf. the quenching (כבה) of lamp(s) in 1 Sam 3:3; Prov 31:18; 2 Chron 29:7.

194. One may also note the expression נרות המערכה in Exod 39:37.

195. In Ugaritic, too, *nr* and *nyr* are both found, always meaning "lamp." See R. E. Whitaker, *A Concordance of Ugaritic Literature* (Cambridge, Massachusetts: Harvard University, 1972) 448.

196. 1 Kgs 11:36; 15:4; 2 Kgs 8:19; 2 Chron 21:7.

197. So Targ. has מלכו "rule" in 2 Kgs 8:19. See M. Cogan and H. Tadmor (*II Kings* [AB 11; New York: Doubleday, 1988] 95) for a possible Akkadian parallel for the metaphor.

(משיחך). YHWH will indeed remember the covenant לדוד, for it is YHWH who will cause the horn to sprout forth לדוד (*for David's sake*) and to prepare the lamp for the sake of the anointed.

Specifically, the promise will be effected in Jerusalem. This is the relevance of the adverb שם "there" at the beginning of v 17, which picks up on פה "here" in v 14. The Davidic line will continue "there"--in Jerusalem--despite the apparent threat of disintegration. The promise is then clarified in v 18: whereas the unnamed enemies of the anointed will be clothed in shame, the diadem (נזר), which is the sign of YHWH's consecration, will gleam on the head of the Davidic king. This concluding promise is the answer to the insecurity of the Davidides: YHWH will, indeed, remember for David's sake!

## C. SUMMARY OF RESULTS

Containing archaic liturgical material from the Davidic period, Psalm 132 provides some insights on the political significance of David's procession of the ark. The ritual demonstrated in a public manner the piety of the king and, hence, his acceptability to the populace as a leader who would bring about divine presence in the land. The procession was itself propagandistic in that it publicized at once the successes of David and the failures of Saul. The ark had fallen into oblivion in the days of Saul, and the cult was neglected. But through the pious initiative and commitment of David, publicly demonstrated in the procession, the ark was given its due place of prominence.

Parallels from Mesopotamia suggest that the ritual is comparable to the return of the divine statue and, thus, Psalm 132 cannot to be separated from the procession of 2 Samuel 6. The procession dramatized the return of the divine warrior to claim kingship in his new abode of rest from which he would demonstrate his beneficence. The association of the procession with mythological combat is evident in the Akkadian inscriptions, as it is in the procession of the ark in 2 Samuel 6. As in the procession of the divine statues in Mesopotamia, the procession of the ark dramatized the accession of the deity as king in the divine council. Furthermore, as in 2 Samuel 6, the procession of the ark, according to Psalm 132, resulted in the manifestation of the deity's blessings for his people. The people of the city would be satiated with food, even as Ba'l satiated the multitudes upon his claim of kingship in his newly won mount. Finally, the procession also dramatized the favor which the deity showed the king and the capital city which the king had established. Like the ushering in of the gods elsewhere in the ancient Near East, David's procession of the ark was a religio-political drama of great political significance for him.

But the significance of David's procession extended beyond his reign. Subsequent generations of Davidides remembered his act as a turning point in history. It is possible that the procession might have been repeated regularly by the Davidic kings, as Mowinckel and others have argued, although that is difficult to demonstrate. Psalm 132 cannot be used to show that there was a periodic procession of the ark. Nevertheless, the psalm shows the enduring political significance of David's procession for the Davidic kings. My contention is that Psalm 132 was composed in the aftermath of the political split between north and south, following the death of Solomon. In the face of the political crisis, the poet of Psalm 132 invoked the memory of that historic procession in a bipartite composition which has as its core ancient liturgical material (probably vv 3–9, 11b–15 are archaic) which had been used for the procession of the ark into Jerusalem. The apologist thus composed a poem about two oaths, the one of David to YHWH (vv 1–10) and the other of YHWH to David (vv 11–18), emphasizing the bond between the deity and the anointed. That bond was established because David carried out his oath to YHWH to establish a place for the deity, which he did by inviting the deity to the (royal) "resting-place"--that is, by bringing the ark in procession to Jerusalem. That event resulted in the establishing of a place for David, namely, in the promise of an enduring dynasty for David and the election of Zion as YHWH's abode. "Here" (פה, v 14) the deity chose to be enthroned and "there" (שׁם, v 17) the descendants of David would have their eternal reign.

# CONCLUSION

In order to discern the significance of the procession of the ark, this study began by examining the "mythological heritage" of the ark, as it is revealed in the traditions associated with two sanctuaries that housed the ark before Jerusalem, namely, Shiloh and Qiryat-Ye'arim. Such an investigation was prompted by the assumption that historians of Israelite religion usually make about the significance of the transferral of the ark: that Judean dynastic ideologies were shaped by the dynamic encounter of Israelite traditions associated with the ark and Jebusite traditions associated with the cult of 'Ēl 'Elyôn in Jerusalem.

On the one hand, it is universally accepted that the ark carried with it certain traditions from its connections with the central sanctuary of the league at Shiloh. Curiously, nothing is ever said about the possible contribution of Qiryat-Ye'arim to the tradition, even though the ark had been kept there for some two decades, and the city apparently had connections with the traditions of Ba'l. At the same time, the Israelite traditions from Shiloh have never been clearly defined, apart from vague allusions to the epithets "YHWH of Hosts" and "the one who sits enthroned upon the cherubim," both of which are generally believed to have been firmly established in the Shiloh cultus.

On the other hand, most scholars suppose that the sensational capture of the hitherto impregnable fortress of Jerusalem and the procession of the ark into that city inspired a new fusion of traditions, as it were. Out of this dynamic encounter of cultures and traditions, it is believed, came a new synthesis of old and new ideologies, of Israelite and Canaanite theologies. The Israelite notions of divine presence that were associated with the ark were radically reshaped and otherwise influenced by the putative Canaanite traditions associated especially with 'Ēl 'Elyôn, which scholars conclude was the mainstay of Jebusite religion. This conclusion is drawn from the brief and enigmatic reference to a certain Melkiṣedeq, the high priest of 'Ēl 'Elyon in Jerusalem, whom Abram encountered (Gen 14:18-22).

An investigation of the Shiloh cultus, however, reveals that YHWH was already identified with 'Ēl at that central sanctuary. This is evident in the divine epithets associated with the ark, namely, יהוה צבאות and ישב הכרבים, even as Cross and Mettinger have demonstrated. These epithets suggest the role of the deity as the victorious warrior-king and creator of the universe. Elistic personal names of worshippers at Shiloh, especially Elqanah, Yeroḥam (=Yeraḥme'el), and Samuel, suggest that the Israelite deity was identified with 'Ēl, not just because these names have 'Ēl as a theophoric element, but because they express traits and characteristics that were typically attributed to 'Ēl. The character of the deity as 'Ēl is further borne out by the stories of the deity's encounter with human beings: how he gave fecundity to the barren (as 'Ēl did to Kirta and Danel), how he appeared in dreams and communicated the divine will through intermediaries--as 'Ēl does in Ugaritic mythology. As in the Canaanite traditions about 'Ēl, the abode of the deity at Shiloh is depicted as both a permanent structure (היכל // בית) and a tent (משכן // אהל). Like the Canaanite high god 'Ēl, the deity at Shiloh was worshipped as the supreme god of the divine council. This is indicated not only by the epithets יהוה צבאות and ישב הכרבים, but also in the name of the high priest, 'Ēlî, which is ultimately derived from a designation of the god as the Most High of the divine council. The related divine title 'Elyôn is linked with the northern tribes in some of the oldest Israelite traditions, and, together with the name 'Ēl, it is connected in Psalm 78 with the cult of Shiloh before its destruction by the Philistines. Given the identification of YHWH with 'Ēl at Shiloh, the old assumptions about the Jebusite origin of the worship of YHWH as 'Ēl 'Elyôn in Jerusalem must be abandoned. Even if one grants that 'Ēl 'Elyôn was worshipped in pre-Israelite

Jerusalem, an assumption that is built on remarkably slim evidence that originated only *after* the entry of the ark into that city, one cannot legitimately speak of the Jebusite origin of the idea. YHWH was identified with 'Ēl, indeed, 'Ēl the Most High, already at Shiloh.

There is no smooth transition, however, from the worship of YHWH as 'Ēl at Shiloh to the theology of monarchical Jerusalem. The sanctuary of Shiloh came to an ignominious end at the hands of the Philistines following the battle near Ebenezer and Aphek in the eleventh century. Israelite traditions remembered the devastation of the sanctuary, and recent archaeology has confirmed it. The ark, which symbolized the presence of YHWH in holy war, was captured by the Philistines. It was later returned to the Israelites and kept at the neutral and relatively obscure site of Qiryat-Ye'arim. The reason for its apparently voluntary return is lost to the historian, although a few scholars have suggested that it was somehow connected with an actual plague that struck the region in the early Iron Age. Our only source about the ark is the narrative of 1 Samuel 4-6, which probably originated at Qiryat-Ye'arim, no doubt to explain and justify the presence of the ark there, but also to give an account of the deity's status vis-à-vis the gods of Israel's enemies. The story of the ark in 1 Samuel 4-6 begins with the ark's capture and the deity's apparent demise, but it ends with the triumph of YHWH over Dagon of the Philistines. In its movement from demise to ultimate victory, the story mirrors the myth of Ba'l. Like Ba'l, YHWH is, in the ark narrative of 1 Samuel, the feisty warrior fighting for dominion in the arena of divine combat. The defeat of Ba'l prompted the questions, *'iy 'al'iyn b'l // 'iy zbl b'l 'arṣ* "where is Mighty Ba'l? Where is the Prince, Lord of the Earth?" So the capture of the ark prompted the naming of an infant, *'y kbwd* "Where is Glory?" But as Ba'l eventually destroyed his enemies, so YHWH ultimately dismembered Dagon. Plagues and pestilence served as YHWH's weapons against his enemies, even as they are part of the divine warrior's entourage in Canaanite mythology.

The structure of the whole story from the apparent defeat of the deity to his ultimate triumph is built on the myth of Ba'l. There is no hint of the notion of divine kingship and unquestioned supremacy of the deity that is evident in the cult of Shiloh. Rather, the picture is of a god in the process of gaining dominion against his enemies.

It is not surprising that the *hieros logos* of the sanctuary at Qiryat-Ye'arim should have developed on the model of the feisty god, Ba'l. The city was, after all, variously called Qiryat-Ba'l ("City of Ba'l"), Ba'lah, Ba'lah of Judah, and Mount Ba'lah. Moreover, the myth of Ba'l obviously reflected the socio-political realities for the Israelites better than the images of 'Ēl at that juncture of their history. YHWH was not the triumphant divine king at a central sanctuary where he was worshipped as the Most High god of the universe. Rather, YHWH was more like Ba'l--a god for whom kingship was a status to be gained through the eventual defeat of the enemies. Like Ba'l, YHWH at Qiryat-Ye'arim was a god on the rise.

With the capture of Jerusalem and the decisive defeat of the Philistines, the myth of Ba'l's ascendency was given historical and political substance. The divine warrior had ultimately triumphed over his enemies and could move to claim his place in his newly won domain. The myth of the divine warrior was, of course, already known at Qiryat-Ye'arim ( = Qiryat-Ba'l )--the *hieros logos* of the ark at Qiryat-Ye'arim (1 Samuel 4-6) was essentially built on that myth. Its connection with the procession of the ark is suggested in the narrative of the victories over the Philistines at Ba'l Peraṣim. Continuing the traditions at Qiryat-Ye'arim, YHWH is identified as *ba'al pĕrāṣîm* "Ba'l/Lord of the Breakings." The defeat of the enemies is likened to the "breaking of Waters," that is, the smiting of the unruly waters in the myth of the divine warrior. This is the earliest example of the so-called *Völkerkampf* that became prominent in the Zion tradition, where the enemies of Israel who surrounded Zion were likened to the unruly waters of mythology.

So the entire myth of the divine warrior's accession was acted out in the religio-political drama that was the procession of the ark into Jerusalem. Despite its long literary history, 2 Samuel 6 preserves the sequence of that drama. The victory was celebrated in joy, as Ba'l's victory was joyously celebrated in the Ugaritic myth. There was probably a mock battle at a threshing floor where the defeat of Ba'l's enemies was acted out, although that sham battle is now obscured somewhat by the narrator's reworking. As expected, the victory in combat was followed by the march of the warrior, which was accompanied by the attendant convulsion of nature, dramatized by the participants in animal dances. The accession of the warrior was dramatized by the ascension to Jerusalem, YHWH's mount of victory and, probably, symbolized by the placing of the ark in its resting place. Finally, the divine banquet that in mythology is the climax of the celebration of the divine warrior's accession is symbolically carried out in David's distribution of food to the multitudes. David's procession of the ark, then, was a cultic performance of the myth of the divine warrior's rise. As such it dramatized at once the transitions that Israel experienced with the rise of David. Like Ba'l, YHWH had indeed defeated his enemies and risen to claim his new "place" among the gods. With the decisive victory over the Philistines, Israel was ready to move beyond the ignominy of defeat to claim its place as a new state. So the ark symbolically journeyed from the relatively obscure sanctuary of Qiryat-Ye'arim to the new abode of the deity in the newly won mount, Jerusalem. YHWH had risen to take his rightful place.

The investigation in the third chapter supports the traditional association of Psalm 132 with the procession of the ark. I do not believe, however, that the psalm was composed in its entirety for an annual procession. Rather, the poem is the work of a pro-Davidic apologist in the early days of the divided monarchy, whose purpose was to legitimate the Davidic dynasty. The composer does so by appealing to David's procession of the ark as the occasion for the establishment of the Davidic covenant. But since the apologist quotes from an ancient liturgical composition that was used in conjunction with David's procession of the ark, the psalm sheds light on the nature and significance of the procession itself. Thus, Psalm 132 shows that David's procession of the ark was a pivotal event in the history of Israelite religion and politics. For David, as well as for his descendants, the procession marked a turning point in history. David had succeeded in establishing a place for YHWH and, in doing so, had assured a place for himself and his posterity.

# SELECTED BIBLIOGRAPHY


Aartun, K. "Beiträge zum ugaritischen Lexikon." *WO* 4 (1968) 278-299.

Abou-Assaf, A., Bordreuil, P., and A. R. Millard. *La statue de Tell Fekheryé et son inscription bilingue assyro-araméenne.* Études Assyrologiques 7. Paris: Recherche sur les civilisations, 1982.

Abramsky, S. "The Woman Who Looked Out the Window." *Beth Mikra* 25 (1980) 114-124.

Ahlström, G. "*KRKR* and *ṮPD.*" *VT* 28 (1978) 100-102.

_________. *Psalm 89. Eine Liturgie aus dem Ritual des leidenden Königs.* Lund: Gleerup, 1959.

_________. "The Travels of the Ark: A Religio-Political Composition." *JNES* 43 (1984) 141-149.

Aistleitner, J. "Studien zur Frage der Sprachverwandtschaft des Ugaritischen, II: Vergleich des Ugaritischen mit dem Altmesopotamisch-Westsemitischen." *Acta Orientalia Academiæ Scientiarum Hungaricæ* 7 (1957) 286-307.

_________. "Zu Ps 68." *BZ* 19 (1931) 29-41.

Albright, W. F. *Archaeology and the Religion of Israel.* Baltimore: Johns Hopkins, 1942.

_________. "A Catalogue of Early Hebrew Lyric Poems (Psalm LXVIII)." *HUCA* 23 (1950) 1-39.

_________. "Contributions to Biblical Archaeology and Philology." *JBL* 43 (1924) 363-393.

_________. "Notes on Psalms 68 and 134." *NorTT* 56 (1955) 1-12.

_________. "The Old Testament and Canaanite Language and Literature." *CBQ* 7 (1945) 5-31.

_________. "The Oracles of Balaam." *JBL* 43 (1944) 207-233.

_________. "Review of B. N. Wambacq, *L'épithète divine Jahvé Ṣĕbā'ôt.*" *JBL* 67 (1948) 377-387.

_________. "Some Remarks on the Song of Moses in Deuteronomy XXXII." *VT* 9 (1959) 339-346.

_________. "The Song of Deborah in the Light of Archaeology." *BASOR* 62 (1936) 26-31.

_________. *Yahweh and the Gods of Canaan.* Garden City, New York: Doubleday. Reprinted. Winona Lake, Indiana: Eisenbrauns, 1968.

Allen, L. C. *Psalms 101-150.* WBC 21. Waco, Texas: Word, 1983.

Alt. A. *Essays on Old Testament History and Religion.* Trans. R. A. Wilson. Garden City, New York: Doubleday, 1968.

Al-Yasin, I. *The Lexical Relation Between Ugaritic and Arabic.* Shelton Semitic Monograph Series I. New York: Shelton College, 1952.

Anderson, G. A. *Sacrifices and Offerings in Ancient Israel: Studies in their Social and Political Significance.* HSM 41. Atlanta: Scholars, 1987.

Arnold, W. R. *Ephod and Ark.* HTS 3. Cambridge, Massachusetts: Harvard University, 1917.

Astour, M. C. "Some New Divine Names from Ugarit." *JAOS* 86 (1966) 277-284.

Attridge, H. W., and R. A. Oden. *Philo of Byblos: The Phoenician History*. CBQMS 9. Washington, D. C.: Catholic Biblical Association, 1981.

Avigad, N. "The Contribution of Hebrew Seals to an Understanding of Israelite Religion and Society." In *Ancient Israelite Religion. Essays in Honor of Frank Moore Cross*, ed. P. D. Miller, P. D. Hanson and S. D. McBride, pp. 195–208. Philadelphia: Fortress, 1987.

________. "Excavations in the Jewish Quarter of the Old City of Jerusalem, 1971." *IEJ* 22 (1972) 193–200.

________. *Hebrew Bullae from the Time of Jeremiah: Remnants of a Burnt Archive*. Jerusalem: Israel Exploration Society, 1986.

Avishur, Y. "*KRKR* in Biblical Hebrew and Ugaritic." *VT* 26 (1976) 257–261.

Bakon, S. "How David Captured Jerusalem." *Dor le Dor* 15 (1986/87) 43–44.

Bar-Magen, M. "The Shiloh Sanctuary." *Beth Mikra* 29 (1983/84) 149–153.

Barnett, R. D. "Bringing the God into the Temple." In *Temples and High Places in Biblical Times*, ed. A. Biran, pp. 10–20. Jerusalem: Hebrew Union College--Jewish Institute of Religion, 1981.

________. "Homme masqué ou dieux-ibex?" *Syria* 43 (1966) 259–276.

Barr, J. "Ugaritic and Hebrew 'šbm'?" *JSS* 18 (1973) 17–39.

Ben-Tor, A. "Cult Scenes on Early Bronze Age Cylinder Seal Impressions from Palestine." *Levant* 9 (1977) 90–100.

Bentzen, A. "The Cultic Use of the Story of the Ark in Samuel." *JBL* 67 (1948) 37–53.

Benz, F. L. *Personal Names in the Phoenician and Punic Inscriptions: A Catalog, Grammatical Study and Glossary of Elements.* Studia Pohl 8. Rome: Pontifical Biblical Institute, 1972.

Berger, P. L. *The Sacred Canopy: Elements of a Sociological Theory of Religion.* Garden City, New York: Doubleday, 1967.

Biran, A. "The Dancer from Dan, the Empty Tomb and the Altar Room." *IEJ* 36 (1986) 168–187.

__________. "Tel Dan, 1981." *IEJ* 32 (1982) 138–139.

Bisi, A. M. *Le stele puniche.* Studi Semitici 27. Rome: Università di Roma, 1967.

Blenkinsopp, J. *Gibeon and Israel. The Role of Gibeon and the Gibeonites in the Political and Religious History of Early Israel.* SOTSMS 2. Cambridge: Cambridge University, 1972.

Bloch, M. "Symbols, Song, Dance and Features of Articulation: Is Religion an Extreme Form of Traditional Authority?" *European Journal of Sociology* 15 (1974) 55-81.

Blommerde, A. C. M. *Northwest Semitic Grammar and Job.* BibOr 22. Rome: Pontifical Biblical Institute, 1969.

Boecker, H. J. *Redeform des Rechtslebens im Alten Testament.* WMANT 14. Neukirchen-Vluyn: Neukirchener, 1964.

Boehl, F. "Ältteste keilinschriftliche Erwähnungen der Stadt Jerusalem und ihrer Göttin?" *AcOr* 1 (1923) 76–80.

Boling, R. G., and G. E. Wright. *Joshua.* AB 6. Garden City, New York: Doubleday, 1982.

Borger, R. *Die Inschriften Asarhaddons Königs von Assyrien.* 2d ed. AfO Beiheft 9. Graz: Weidner, 1967.

Brekelmans, C. "Psalm 132: Unity and Structure." *Bijdragen* 44 (1983) 262–265.

Briggs, C. A., and E. G. Briggs. *A Critical and Exegetical Commentary on the Book of Psalms.* 2 Volumes. ICC. Edinburgh: T. & T. Clark, 1906–1907.

Brunet, G. "David et le *ṣinnôr.*" In *Studies in the Historical Books of the Old Testament,* ed. J. A. Emerton, pp. 73–86. VTSup 30. Leiden: Brill, 1979.

Budd, P. J. *Numbers.* WBC 5. Waco, Texas: Word, 1984.

Buren, E. D. van. "Mountain Gods." *Or* 12 (1943) 79–80.

Buss, M. J. "The Psalms of Asaph and Korah." *JBL* 82 (1963) 382–392.

Buttenweiser, M. *The Psalms.* 2d ed. Chicago: University of Chicago, 1938.

Campbell, A. F. *The Ark Narrative (1 Sam 4–6; 2 Sam 6): A Form Critical and Traditio-Historical Study.* SBLDS 16. Missoula: Scholars, 1975.

________. "Psalm 78: A Contribution to the Theology of Tenth Century Israel." *CBQ* 41 (1979) 51–79.

________. "Yahweh and the Ark: A Case Study in Narrative." *JBL* 98 (1979) 31–43.

Caquot, A. "Nouvelle inscriptions araméens de Hatra." *Syria* 40 (1963) 1–16.

________. "Observations sur la première tablette magique d'Arslan Tash." *JANES* 5 (1973) 45–51.

_________. "La prophétie de Nathan et ses échos lyriques." In *Congress Volume, Bonn* pp. 213–224. VTSup 9. Leiden: Brill, 1963.

_________. "Sur quelques démons de l'Ancien Testament (Reshep, Qeṭeb, Deber)." *Sem* 6 (1956) 53–68.

_________, and A. Lemaire. "Les textes araméens de Deir 'Alla." *Syria* 54 (1977) 189–208.

Caquot, A., and M. Sznycer. *Ugaritic Religion.* Iconography of Religions 15/8. Leiden: Brill, 1980.

Caquot, A., Sznycer, M., and A. Herdner. *Textes ougaritiques, I: Mythes et légendes.* Littératures anciennes du Proche-Orient 7. Paris: Cerf, 1974.

Cassuto, U. *Biblical and Oriental Studies.* 2 Volumes. Trans. I. Abrahams. Jerusalem: Magnes, 1973–1975.

_________. *The Goddess Anath.* Trans. I. Abrahams. Jerusalem: Bialik, 1971.

Childs, B. S. *The Book of Exodus. A Critical, Theological Commentary.* OTL. Philadelphia: Westminster, 1974.

Cintas, P. "Le sanctuaire punique de Sousse." *Revue Africaine* 91 (1947) 1–80.

Clapham, L. R. "Sanchuniathon: The First Two Cycles." Unpublished Ph.D. Dissertation. Harvard University, 1969.

Clements, R. E. *God and Temple.* Oxford: Blackwell, 1965.

Clifford, R. J. *The Cosmic Mountain in Canaan and the Old Testament.* HSM 4. Cambridge, Massachusetts: Harvard University, 1972.

_________. "In Zion and David a New Beginning: An Interpretation of Psalm 78." In *Traditions in Transformation. Turning Points in Biblical Faith.*, ed. B. Halpern and J. D. Levenson, 121-141. Winona Lake, Indiana: Eisenbrauns, 1981.

_________. "Psalm 89: A Lament Over the Davidic Ruler's Continued Failure." *HTR* 73 (1980) 35-47.

_________. "The Tent of El and the Israelite Tent of Meeting." *CBQ* 33 (1971) 221-227.

Cobb, W. F. *The Book of Psalms.* London: Methuen, 1905.

Cogan, M. *Imperialism and Religion: Assyria, Judah and Israel in the Eighth and Seventh Centuries B.C.E.* SBLMS 19. Missoula, Montana: Scholars, 1974.

_________, and H. Tadmor. *II Kings.* AB 11. New York: Doubleday, 1988.

Conrad, L. I. "The Biblical Tradition for the Plague of the Philistines." *JAOS* 104 (1984) 281-287.

Coogan, M. D. "Canaanite Origins and Lineage: Reflections on the Religion of Ancient Israel." In *Ancient Israelite Religion. Essays in Honor of Frank Moore Cross,* ed. P. D. Miller, P. D. Hanson and S. D. McBride, pp. 115-124. Philadelphia: Fortress, 1987.

Cooper, A. "The Life and Times of King David According to the Book of Psalms." In *The Poet and the Historian. Essays in the Literary and Historical Biblical Criticism,* ed. R. E. Friedman, pp. 117-131. HSS 26. Chico, California: Scholars, 1983.

_________. "Ps 24:7-10: Mythology and Exegesis." *JBL* 102 (1983) 37-60.

Cowley, A. *Aramaic Papyri of the Fifth Century B.C.* Oxford: Clarendon, 1923.

_________. "The Meaning of מָקוֹם in Hebrew." *JTS* 17 (1916) 174–176.

Craigie, P. "Helel, Athtar, and Phaeton (Jes 14:12–15)." *ZAW* 85 (1973) 223–224.

_________. *Psalms 1–50*. WBC 19. Waco, Texas: Word, 1983.

Cross, F. M. *Canaanite Myth and Hebrew Epic*. Cambridge, Massachusetts: Harvard University, 1973.

_________. "The Cave Inscription from Khirbet Beit Lei." In *Near Eastern Archaeology in the Twentieth Century. Essays in Honor of Nelson Glueck*, ed. J. A. Sanders, pp. 299–306. Garden City, New York: Doubleday, 1970.

_________. "The Development of the Jewish Scripts." In *The Bible and the Ancient Near East. Essays in Honor of William Foxwell Albright*, ed. G. E. Wright, pp. 133–202. Garden City, New York: Doubleday, 1961. Reprinted. Winona Lake, Indiana: Eisenbrauns, 1979.

_________. "The Divine Warrior in Israel's Early Cult." In *Biblical Motifs. Origins and Transformations*, ed. A. Altmann, pp. 11–30. Philip W. Lown Institute of Advanced Judaic Studies, Brandeis University. Studies and Texts 3. Cambridge, Massachusetts: Harvard University, 1966.

_________. "אֵל *'ēl*." *TDOT* I, ed. G. J. Botterweck and H. Ringgren, pp. 242–261. Trans. J. T. Willis. Revised. Grand Rapids, Michigan: Eerdmans, 1977.

_________. "A New Qumran Biblical Fragment Related to the Original Hebrew Underlying the Septuagint." *BASOR* 132 (1953) 15–26.

_________. "The Priestly Tabernacle." In *Biblical Archaeologist Reader* I, ed. D. N. Freedman and G. E. Wright, pp. 201–221. Garden City, New York: Doubleday, 1961.

_________. "The Priestly Tabernacle in the Light of Recent Research." In *Temples and High Places in Biblical Times*, ed. A. Biran, pp. 169–180. Jerusalem: Hebrew Union College-Jewish Institute of Religion, 1981.

_________. "Yahweh and the God of the Patriarchs." *HTR* 55 (1962) 255–259.

_________, and D. N. Freedman. *Studies in Ancient Yahwistic Poetry*. SBLDS 21. Missoula, Montana: Scholars, 1975.

Crüsemann, F. *Der Widerstand gegen das Königtum: Die antiköniglichen Texte des Alten Testaments und der Kampf um den frühen israelitischen Staat*. WMANT 49. Neukirchen-Vluyn: Neukirchener, 1978.

_________. "Zwei alttestamentliche Witze. I Sam 21, 11–15 und II Sam 6, 20–23 als Beispiel einer biblischen Gattung." *ZAW* 92 (1980) 215–227.

Culican, W. "The Iconography of Some Phoenician Seals and Seal Impressions." *AJBA* 1 (1968) 50–103.

_________. "Malqart Representations on Phoenician Seals." *AbrN* 2 (1960) 41–54.

Cunchillos, J. L. *Estudio del Salmo 29: Canto al Dios de la fertilidad-fercundidad. Aportación al conocimiento de la Fe de Israel a su entrada en Canaán*. Valencia: Soler, 1976.

Cutler, B. and J. MacDonald. "Identification of the *na'ar* in the Ugaritic Texts." *UF* 8 (1976) 27–35.

Dahood, M. "Ancient Semitic Deities in Syria and Palestine." In *Le Antiche Divintà Semitiche*, ed. S. Moscati, pp. 65–94. Studi Semitici 1. Rome: Università di Roma, 1958.

________. "The Divine Name 'Ēlî in the Psalms." *TS* 14 (1953) 452–457.

________. "Hebrew-Ugaritic Lexicography II." *Bib* 45 (1964) 393–412.

________. "Hebrew-Ugaritic Lexicography IV." *Bib* 47 (1966) 403–419.

________. *Psalms.* 3 Volumes. AB 16, 17, 17A. Garden City, New York: Doubleday, 1966–1970.

________. "Ugaritic Lexicography." In *Mélanges E. Tisserant* I, pp. 81–104. Studi e Testi 231. Vatican City: Pontifical Biblical Institute, 1964.

________. "Ugaritic Studies and the Bible." *Greg* 43 (1962) 55–79.

Davies, G. H. "The Ark in the Psalms." In *Promise and Fulfillment. Essays Presented to Professor S. H. Hooke in Celebration of His Ninetieth Birthday,* ed. F. F. Bruce, pp. 51–61. Edinburgh: T. & T. Clark, 1963.

________. "The Ark of the Covenant." *ASTI* 5 (1966/67) 30–47.

Davies, P. R. "Ark or Ephod in 1 Sam. XIV.18?" *JTS* 26 (1975) 82–87.

Day, J. "New Light on the Mythological Background of the Allusion to Resheph in Habakkuk III 5." *VT* 29 (1979) 353–355.

________. "Pre-Deuteronomic Allusions to the Covenant in Hosea and Psalm LXXVIII." *VT* 36 (1986) 1–12.

Delcor, M. "Jahweh et Dagon ou le Jahwisme face à la religion Philistins, d'après 1 Sam. V." *VT* 14 (1964) 136–154.

Delitzsch, F. *Biblical Commentary on the Psalms*. 3 Volumes. Trans. F. Bolton. Edinburgh: T. & T. Clark, 1877–1888.

Demsky, A. "Geba, Gibeah, and Gibeon--an Historico-Geographic Riddle." *BASOR* 212 (1973) 26–31.

Dhorme, É. P. *A Commentary on the Book of Job*. Trans. H. Knight. New York: Nelson, 1984.

__________. *Les livres de Samuel*. Études Bibliques. Paris: Gabalda, 1910.

Dibelius, M. *Die Lade Jahves*. FRLANT 8. Göttingen: Vandenhoeck & Ruprecht, 1906.

Dietrich, M., and O. Loretz. "*šb, šbm* und *udn* in Kontext von KTU 1.3 III 35b–IV 4 und KTU 1.82.8." *UF* 14 (1982) 77–81.

__________. "Der Vertrag eines *mrzḥ*-Klubs in Ugarit zum Verständnis von KTU 3.9." *UF* 14 (1982) 71–76.

Dijkstra, M., and J. C. de Moor. "Problematical Passages in the Legend of Aqhâtu." *UF* 7 (1975) 171–215.

Donner, H., and W. Röllig. *Kanaanäische und aramäische Inschriften*. 3 Volumes. 4th. ed. Wiesbaden: Harrassowitz, 1979.

Driel, G. van. *The Cult of Aššur*. Studia Semitica Neerlandica 13. Assen: van Gorcum, 1969.

Driver, G. R. "Problems in 'Proverbs'." *ZAW* 50 (1932) 141–148.

Driver, S. R. *Notes on the Hebrew Text and the Topography of the Books of Samuel*. 2d ed. Oxford: Clarendon, 1913.

Ebeling, E. *Die akkadische Gebetsserie Šu-ila "Handerhebung" vom neum Gesammelt und Herausgegeben.* VIO 20. Berlin: Akademie, 1953.

_________. "Enki (EA)." *RLA* II, ed. E. Ebeling and R. Meisner, pp. 374–379. Berlin: de Gruyter, 1938.

_________. *Parfümrezepte und kultische Texte aus Assur.* Rome: Pontifical Biblical Institute, 1950.

Ehrlich, E. L. *Der Traum im Alten Testament.* BZAW 73. Berlin: Töpelmann, 1953.

Eiler, D. L. "The Origin and History of Zion as a Theological Symbol in Ancient Israel." Unpublished Th.D. Dissertation. Princeton Theological Seminary, 1968.

Eilers, W. "Zur Funktion von Nominalformen: Ein Grenzgang zwischen Morphologie und Semasiologie." *WO* 3 (1964) 80–145.

Eissfeldt, O. *Kleine Schriften.* 6 Volumes. Ed. R. Sellheim and F. Maass. Tübingen: Mohr, 1962–1979.

_________. *Das Lied Moses Deuteronomium 32,1–43 und das Lehrgedicht Asaphs Psalm 78 samt einer Analyse der Umgebung des Moses-Leides.* Berichte über die Verhandlungen der Sächischen Akademie der Wissenschaft zu Leipzig. Phil.-hist. Klasse, 104/5. Berlin: Akademie, 1958.

Emerton, J. A. "New Light on Israelite Religions: The Implications of the Inscriptions from Kuntillet 'Ajrud." *ZAW* 94 (1982) 2–20.

_________. "The Riddle of Genesis XIV." *VT* 21 (1971) 403–439.

Engnell, I. *Studies in Divine Kingship in the Ancient Near East.* 2d ed. Oxford: Blackwell, 1967.

Epstein, C. "Early Bronze Age Seal Impressions from the Golan." *IEJ* 22 (1972) 209–217.

Fabry, H.-J. "הָדֹם *hᵃdhōm*." In *TDOT* III, ed. G. J. Botterweck and H. Ringgren. Trans. J. T. Willis, G. W. Bromiley, and D. E. Greene, pp. 325–334. Grand Rapids, Michigan: Eerdmans, 1978.

Falkenstein, A., and W. von Soden. *Sumerische und akkadische Hymnen und Gebete*. Die Bibliothek der alten Welt. Reihe der alte Orient. Zürich/Stuttgart: Artemis, 1953.

Faulkner, R. O. "Egyptian Military Organization." *JEA* 39 (1953) 32–47.

Fensham, F. C. "Remarks on Keret 54–59." *JNWSL* 3 (1974) 26–33.

__________. "Remarks on Keret 136(b)–153." *JNWSL* 13 (1987) 49–57.

Ficker, R. *Komposition und Erzählung: Untersuchungen zur Ladeerzählung 1 Sam 4–6; 2 Sam 6 und zur Aufstieg Davids 1 Sam 15–2 Sam 5*. D.Theol. Dissertation. University of Heidelberg, 1978.

Finkelstein, I. *The Archaeology of the Israelite Settlement*. Jerusalem: Israel Exploration Society, 1988.

__________, Bunimovitz, S., and Lederman, Z. "Excavations at Shiloh 1981-84. Preliminary Report." *Tel Aviv* 12 (1985) 123–180.

Fisher, L. R. "From Chaos to Cosmos." *Encounter* 26 (1965) 183–194.

__________, and F. B. Knutson. "An Enthronement Ritual at Ugarit." *JNES* 28 (1969) 157–167.

Fisher, L. R. *et. al.* (eds.). *Ras Shamra Parallels. The Texts from Ugarit and the Hebrew Bible.* 3 Volumes. AnOr 49–51. Rome: Pontifical Biblical Institute, 1972–1981.

Fitzmyer, J. A. *The Aramaic Inscriptions of Sefîre. BO* 19. Rome: Pontifical Biblical Institute, 1967.

Flanagan, J. "Social Transformation and Ritual in 2 Samuel 6." In *The Word Shall Go Forth. Essays in Honor of David Noel Freedman in Celebration of His Sixtieth Birthday*, ed. C. L. Meyers and M. O'Connor, pp. 361–372. Winona Lake, Indiana: Eisenbrauns, 1983.

Frankfort, H. *Kingship and the Gods. A Study of Ancient Near Eastern Religion as the Integration of Society and Nature.* Chicago: University of Chicago, 1948.

Freedman, D. N. "Divine Names and Titles in Early Hebrew Poetry." In *Magnalia Dei: The Mighty Acts of God. Essays on the Bible and Archaeology in Memory of G. Ernest Wright*, ed. F. M. Cross, W. E, Lemke, and P. D. Miller, pp. 55–107. Garden City, New York: Doubleday, 1976.

__________. "Psalm 113 and the Song of Hannah." *EI* 14 (1975) 56–69.

Fretheim, T. E. "The Cultic Use of the Ark of the Covenant in the Monarchial Period." Unpublished Th.D. Dissertation. Princeton Theological Seminary, 1967.

__________. "Psalm 132: A Form-Critical Study." *JBL* 86 (1967) 289–300.

Friedrich, J. "Zur Interpretation von Satz XVI der phönizisch-bildhethitischen Bilinguis von Karatepe." *Or* 31 (1962) 223–224.

Fulco, W. J. *The Canaanite God Rešep.* AOS 8. New Haven: American Oriental Society, 1976.

Gadd, C. J. "The Harran Inscriptions of Nabonidus." *AnSt* 8 (1958) 35-92.

Gaster, T. H. "A Canaanite Ritual Drama: The Spring Festival at Ugarit." *JAOS* 66 (1946) 49-76.

Geertz, C. *The Interpretation of Cultures. Selected Essays.* New York: Basic, 1973.

Gefter, I. "Studies in the Use of YHWH *ṣĕḇāʾôṯ* in Its Variant Forms." Unpublished Ph.D. Dissertation. Brandeis University, 1977.

Gelb, I. J. *Computer-Aided Analysis of Amorite.* AS 21. Chicago: Oriental Institute, 1980.

Gelb, I. J., Purves, P. M., and A. A. McRae. *Nuzi Personal Names.* OIP 57. Chicago: University of Chicago, 1943.

Gese, H. "Der Davidsbund und die Zionserwählung." *ZTK* 61 (1964) 10-26.

Gevirtz, S. *Patterns in the Early Poetry of Israel.* SAOC 32. Chicago: University of Chicago, 1963.

Gibson, J. C. L. *Textbook of Syrian Semitic Inscriptions.* 3 Volumes. Oxford: Clarendon, 1971-82.

Ginsberg, H. L. *The Legend of King Keret: A Canaanite Epic of the Bronze Age.* BASORSup 2-3. New Haven: American School of Oriental Research, 1946.

__________. "Psalms and Inscriptions of Petition and Acknowledgement." In *Louis Ginzberg Jubilee Volume* I, pp. 159-171. New York: American Academy for Jewish Research, 1945.

Globe, A. "The Text and Literary Structure of Judges 5,4-5." *Bib* 55 (1974) 167-178.

Gnuse, R. K. *The Dream Theophany of Samuel: Its Structure in Relation to Ancient Near Eastern Dreams and Its Theological Significance.* New York: University Press of America, 1984.

Görg, M. "זָהַר *zāhar*; זֹהַר *zōhar*." *TDOT* IV, ed. G. J. Botterweck and H. Ringgren, pp. 41–46. Trans. D. E. Greene. Revised. Grand Rapids, Michigan: Eerdmans, 1980.

Goetze, A. "The City Khalbi and the Khabiru People." *BASOR* 79 (1940) 32–34.

_________. "Remarks on Some Names Occurring in the Execration Texts." *BASOR* 151 (1958) 28–33.

Good, R. M. "Some Ugaritic Terms Relating to Draught and Riding Animals." *UF* 16 (1984) 77–81.

Gordis, R. *The Book of Job.* Moreshet 2. New York: Jewish Theological Seminary, 1978.

Gray, J. "A Cantata of the Autumn Festival: Psalm LXVIII." *JSS* 22 (1977) 2–26.

_________. "The Goren at the City Gate." *PEQ* 85 (1953) 118–125.

_________. *I & II Kings.* 2d ed. OTL. Philadelphia: Westminster, 1970.

_________. *The Krt Text in the Literature of Ras Shamra: A Social Myth of Ancient Canaan.* Documenta et Monumenta Orientis Antiqui 5. 2d ed. Leiden: Brill, 1964.

_________. *The Legacy of Canaan: The Ras Shamra Texts and their Relevance to the Old Testament.* VTSup 5. 2d ed. Leiden: Brill, 1965.

Grayson, A. K. "Assyrian Royal Inscriptions: Literary Characteristics." In *Assyrian Royal Inscriptions: New Horizons in Literary, Ideological and Historical Analysis*, ed. F. M. Fales, pp. 35–47. Orientis Antiqui Collectio 17. Rome: Instituto per l'Oriente, 1981.

Gröndahl, F. *Die Personnennamen der Texte aus Ugarit*. Studia Pohl 1. Rome: Pontifical Biblical Institute, 1967.

Gruber, M. I. *Aspects of Nonverbal Communication in the Ancient Near East*. 2 Volumes. Studia Pohl 12. Rome: Pontifical Biblical Institute, 1980.

———. "Ten Dance-Derived Expressions in the Hebrew Bible." *Bib* 62 (1981) 328–346.

Habel, N. *Yahweh Versus Baal: A Conflict of Religious Cultures*. New York: Bookman, 1964.

Hackett, J. A. *The Balaam Text from Deir 'Allā*. HSM 31. Chico, California: Scholars, 1984.

Hallo, W. H. "The Cultic Setting of Sumerian Poetry." In *Actes de la XVII[e] Rencontre assyriologique internationale*, pp. 116–134. Études recuéilles par André Finet. Ham-sur-Heure: Comité belge de recherches en Mésopotamie, 1970.

Halpern, B. *The Constitution of the Monarchy in Israel. HSM* 25. Chico, California: Scholars, 1981.

Hanson, P. D. "The Song of Heshbon and David's NÎR." *HTR* 61 (1968) 297–320.

Haran, M. "The Ark and the Cherubim: Their Symbolic Significance in Biblical Ritual." *IEJ* 9 (1959) 30–38, 89–94.

———. "Shiloh and Jerusalem: The Origin of the Priestly Tradition in the Pentateuch." *JBL* 81 (1962) 14–24.

_________. *Temples and Temple Services in Ancient Israel. An Inquiry into the Character of Cult Phenomena and the Historical Setting of the Priestly School.* Oxford: Clarendon, 1978.

_________. "ZBḤ YMM in the Karatepe Inscription." *VT* 19 (1969) 372–373.

_________. "Ze<u>b</u>aḥ Hayyamîm." *VT* 19 (1969) 11–22.

Hartmann, R. "Zelt und Lade." *ZAW* 37 (1917/18) 209–244.

Harvey, D. W. "Rejoice Not, O Israel!" In *Israel's Prophetic Heritage. Essays in Honor of James Muilenburg,* ed. B. W. Anderson and W. Harrelson, pp. 116–127. New York: Harper and Row, 1962.

Haupt, P. "Der Name Jahwe." *OLZ* 12 (1909) 211–214.

Hawkins, J. D., and A. M. Davies. "On the Problems of Karatepe: The Hieroglyphic Text." *AnSt* 28 (1978) 103–119.

Hayes, J. H. "The Tradition of Zion's Inviolability." *JBL* 82 (1963) 419–426.

Hempel, J. "Zu IVQ Deut.32:8." *ZAW* 74 (1962) 70.

Hendel, R. S. "'The Flame of the Whirling Sword': A Note on Genesis 3:24." *JBL* 104 (1985) 671–674.

Herdner, A. "Nouveaux textes alphabétiques de Ras Shamra XXIV^e campagne, 1966." In *Ugaritica* VII, pp. 44–60. MRS 18. Paris: Mission archéologique de Ras Shamra, 1978.

Hertzberg, H. W. *I & II Samuel.* Trans. J. S. Bowden. OTL. Philadelphia: Westminster, 1964.

Hidal, S. "Some Reflections on Deuteronomy 32." *ASTI* 11 (1977/78) 15–21.

Hiebert, T, *God of My Victory: The Ancient Hymn of Habakkuk 3*. HSM 38. Atlanta: Scholars, 1986.

Hillers, D. R. "A Convention in Hebrew Literature: The Reaction to Bad News." *ZAW* 77 (1965) 86-90.

__________. *Covenant: The History of a Biblical Idea*. Baltimore: Johns Hopkins, 1969.

__________. "*Mškn* 'temple' in Inscriptions from Hatra." *BASOR* 207 (1972) 54-56.

__________. "The Ritual Procession of the Ark and Ps 132." *CBQ* 30 (1968) 48-55.

Hitzig, F. *Die Psalmen*. 2 Volumes. Heidelberg/Leipzig: Winter, 1863-65.

Hoffner, H. A. "The Elkunirsa Myth Reconsidered." *RHA* 23 (1965) 5-16.

Hoftijzer, J., and G. van der Kooij. *Aramaic Texts from Deir 'Alla*. OrAnt 19. Leiden: Brill, 1976.

Holladay, J. S. "Assyrian Statecraft and the Prophets of Israel." *HTR* 63 (1970) 29-51.

Houk, C. B. "Psalm 132, Literary Integrity, and Syllable Word Structures." *JSOT* 6 (1978) 41-46.

Huffmon, H. B. *Amorite Personal Names in the Mari Texts: A Structural and Lexical Study*. Baltimore: Johns Hopkins University, 1965.

Humbert, P. "Qânâ en hébreu biblique." In *Festschrift für Alfred Bertholet zum 80. Geburtstag*, ed. W. Baumgartner, et. al., 259-266. Tübingen: Mohr, 1950.

__________. *La "Terou'a." Analyse d'un rite biblique*. Recueil de travaux publié par la Faculté des Lettres 23; Neuchâtel: Université de Neuchâtel, 1946.

Huwiler, E. F. "Patterns and Problems in Psalm 132." In *The Listening Heart. Essays in Honor of Roland E. Murphy*, ed. K. G. Hoglund, et. al., pp. 199-212. Sheffield: JSOT, 1987.

Hvidberg, H. H. *Weeping and Laughter in the Old Testament: A Study of Canaanite-Israelite Religion*. Leiden: Brill, 1962.

Ingholt, H. "Inscriptions and Sculptures from Palmyra, I." *Berytus* 3 (1936) 83-127.

Ishida, T. *The Royal Dynasties in Ancient Israel. A Study of the Formation and Development of Royal-Dynastic Ideology*. BZAW 142. Berlin/New York: de Gruyter, 1977.

Jackson, J. J. "The Ark Narratives: An Historical, Textual, and Form-Critical Study of I Samuel 4-6 and II Samuel 6." Unpublished Th.D. Dissertation. Union Theological Seminary, New York, 1962.

Jacobsen, T. "Religious Drama in Ancient Mesopotamia." In *Unity and Diversity. Essays in the History, Literature, and Religion of the Ancient Near East*, ed. H. Goedicke and J. J. M. Roberts, pp. 65-97. JHNES 7. Baltimore/London: Johns Hopkins University, 1975.

Johnson, A. R. *Sacral Kingship in Ancient Israel*. 2d ed. Cardiff: University of Wales, 1967.

Kapelrud, A. "אָבִיר *'ābhîr*; אַבִּיר *'abbîr*." In *TDOT* I, ed. G. J. Botterweck and H. Ringgren, 42-44. Trans. J. T. Willis. Revised. Grand Rapids, Michigan: Eerdmans, 1977.

Kautzsch, E. "Die ursprüngliche Bedeutung des Namens יהוה צבאות." *ZAW* 6 (1886) 17-22.

Kittel, R. *Die Psalmen*. KAT. 2d ed. Leipzig: Scholl, 1929.

Kloos, C. *Yhwh's Combat with the Sea: A Canaanite Tradition in the Religion of Ancient Israel.* Leiden: Brill, 1986.

Knudtzon, J. A. *Die El-Amarna Tafeln.* 2 Volumes. VAB 2. Leipzig: Hinrichs, 1915. Reprinted. Aalen: Zeller, 1964.

Koehler, L. "Äschpar Dattelkuchen." *TLZ* 4 (1948) 397-398.

_________. "Loch- und Ringbrot." *TLZ* 4 (1948) 154-155.

Koch, K. "אֹהֶל *'ōhel*; אָהַל *'āhal.*" *TDOT* I, ed. G. J. Botterweck and H. Ringgren, pp. 118-130. Trans. J. T. Willis. Grand Rapids, Michigan: Eerdmans, 1977.

Kraus, H.-J. *Die Königsherrschaft Gottes im Alten Testament. Untersuchungen zu den Liedern von Jahwes Thronbesteigung.* BHT 13. Tübingen: Mohr, 1951.

_________. *Psalmen.* 2 Volumes. *BKAT* 15. 5th ed. Neukirchen-Vluyn: Neukirchener, 1978.

_________. *Worship in Israel: A Cultic History of The Old Testament.* Trans. G. Buswell. Richmond: Knox, 1966.

Kristensen, A. L. "Ugaritic Epistolary Formulas: A Comparative Study of Ugaritic Epistolary Formulas in the Context of the Contemporary Akkadian Formulas in the Letters from Ugarit and Amarna." *UF* 9 (1977) 143-158.

Kruse, H. "Psalm cxxxii and the Royal Zion Festival." *VT* 33 (1983) 279-297.

Lack, R. "Les origines de 'ELYON, le Très-Haut, dans la tradition cultuelle d'Israel." *CBQ* 24 (1962) 44-66.

Lambert, W. G. "Enmeduranki and Related Matters." *JCS* 21 (1967) 126-138.

_________. "The Great Battle of the Mesopotamian Religious Year: The Conflict in the Akītu House." *Iraq* 25 (1963) 189–190.

Langdon, S. *Die neubabylonischen Königsinschriften.* VAB 4. Leipzig: Hinrichs, 1912.

Langlamet, F. *Gilgal et les récits de la traversé du Jourdain (Jos., III–IV).* CahRB 11. Paris: Gabalda, 1969.

Legrain, L. *Ur Excavations III: Archaic Seal Impressions.* Oxford: Oxford University, 1936.

Lemaire, A. *Inscriptions hébraïques I: Les ostraca.* Littératures anciennes du Proche-Orient. Paris: Cerf, 1977.

Levenson, J. D. "The Davidic Covenant and Its Modern Interpreters." *CBQ* 41 (1979) 205–219.

_________. *Sinai and Zion: An Entry into the Jewish Bible.* Minneapolis/Chicago/New York: Winston, 1985.

Levine. B. A. *In the Presence of the Lord. A Study of Cult and Some Cultic Terms in Ancient Israel.* SJLA 5. Leiden: Brill, 1974.

Lewy, J. "The Šulmān Temple in Jerusalem." *JBL* 59 (1940) 519–522.

L'Heureux, C. E. *Rank Among the Canaanite Gods: El, Ba'al, and the Repha'im.* HSM 21. Missoula, Montana: Scholars, 1979.

Lichtheim, M. *Ancient Egyptian Literature.* 3 Volumes. Berkeley/Los Angeles/London: University of California, 1973–1980.

Lind, M. C. *Yahweh is a Warrior: The Theology of Warfare in Ancient Israel.* Scottsdale, Pennsylvania: Herald, 1980.

Lipiński, E. "Juges 5.4-5 et Psaume 68.8-11." *Bib* 48 (1967) 185-206.

_________. *La royauté de Yahwé dans le poésie et le culte de l'ancien Israël.* Brussels: Paleis der Academiën, 1965.

_________. "Yāhweh mâlāk." *Bib* 44 (1963) 405-460.

Livingstone, A. *Mystical and Mythological Explanatory Works of Assyrian and Babylonian Scholars.* Oxford: Clarendon, 1986.

Loewenstamm, S. E. "Anat's Victory over Tunnanu." *JSS* 20 (1975) 22-27.

_________. "The Making and Destruction of the Golden Calf." *Bib* 48 (1967) 481-490.

_________. "The Trembling of Nature during the Theophany." In *Comparative Studies in Biblical and Ancient Oriental Literatures,* pp. 173-189. AOAT 204. Neukirchen-Vluyn: Neukirchener, 1980.

Loretz, O. *Psalm 29. Kanaanäische El- und Baaltraditionen in jüdischer Sicht.* UBL. Altenberge: CIS, 1984.

_________. *Die Psalmen II: Beitrag der Ugarit-Texte zum Verständnis von Kolometrie und Textologie der Psalmen. Psalm 90-150.* AOAT 202/2. Neukirchen-Vluyn: Neukirchener, 1979.

_________. "Der Torso eines kanaanäisch-israelitischen Tempelwiehespruches in 1 Kg 8, 12-13." *UF* 6 (1974) 478-480.

Luckenbill, D. D. *Ancient Records of Assyria and Babylonia.* 2 Volumes. Chicago: University of Chicago, 1926-27.

_________. *The Annals of Sennacherib*. OIP 2. Chicago: University of Chicago, 1924.

Lyon, D. G. *Keilschrifttexte Sargons Königs von Assyrien (722-705 v. Chr.)*. AB 5. Leipzig: Hinrichs, 1883.

McBride, S. D. "The Deuteronomic Name Theology." Unpublished Ph.D. Dissertation. Harvard University, 1969.

McCarter, P. K. "Aspects of the Religion of the Israelite Monarchy: Biblical and Epigraphic Date." In *Ancient Israelite Religion. Essays in Honor of Frank Moore Cross*, ed. P. D. Miller, P. D. Hanson, and S. D. McBride, pp. 137-156. Philadelphia: Fortress, 1987.

_________. "The Balaam Texts from Deir ʿAllā: The First Combination." *BASOR* 239 (1980) 49-60.

_________. *I Samuel*. AB 8. Garden City, New York: Doubleday, 1980.

_________. *II Samuel*. AB 9. Garden City, New York: Doubleday, 1984.

_________. "The Ritual Dedication of the City of David in 2 Samuel 6." In *The Word of the Lord Shall Go Forth. Essays in Honor of David Noel Freedman in Celebration of His Sixtieth Birthday*, ed. C. L. Meyers and M. O'Connor, pp. 273-278. Winona Lake, Indiana: Eisenbrauns, 1983.

McCarthy, C. B. "Psalm 132: A Methodological Analysis." Unpublished Ph.D. Dissertation. Marquette University, 1968.

McCarthy, D. J. "*bᵉrît* in Old Testament History and Theology." *Bib* 53 (1972) 110-121.

MacDonald, J. "The Role and Status of the *Ṣuḫāru* in the Mari Correspondence." *JAOS* 96 (1976) 57-68.

Maier, J. *Das altisraelitische Ladeheiligtum.* BZAW 93. Berlin: Töpelmann, 1965.

Mann, T. W. *Divine Presence and Guidance in Israelite Traditions: The Typology of Exaltation.* JHNES 9. Baltimore/London: Johns Hopkins University, 1977.

Margalit, B. "Lexicographical Notes on the *Aqht* Epic (Parts I- II: KTU 1.17-18/19)." *UF* 15 (1983) 65-103.

_________. *A Matter of Life and Death: A Study of the Baal-Mot Epic (CTA 4-5-6).* AOAT 206. Neukirchen-Vluyn: Neukirchener, 1980.

_________. "Studia Ugaritica II: 'Studies in Krt and Aqht'." *UF* 8 (1976) 137-192.

Mazar, B. "The Early Israelite Settlement in the Hill Country." *BASOR* 241 (1981) 75-85.

_________. ( = Maisler) "Das vordavidische Jerusalem." *JPOS* 10 (1930) 181-191.

Meier, S. A. *The Messenger in the Ancient Semitic World.* HSM 45. Atlanta: Scholars, 1988.

Mellink, M. "Hittite Friezes and Gate Sculptures." In *Anatolian Studies Presented to Hans Gustav Güterbock on the Occasion of his 65th Birthday,* ed. K. Bittel, Ph. ten Cate and E. Reiner, pp. 201-214. Istanbul: Nederlands historisch-archaeologisch Institut, 1974.

Mendenhall, G. E. "Samuel's 'Broken *Rîb*': Deuterorony 32." In *No Famine in the Land. Studies in Honor of John L. McKenzie,* ed. J. W. Flanagan and A. W. Robinson, pp. 63-74. Missoula, Montana: Scholars, 1975.

Meshel, Z. "Did Yahweh Have a Consort? The New Religious Inscriptions from the Sinai." *BAR* 5 (1979) 24-31.

———. *Kuntillet 'Ajrud: A Religious Centre from the Time of the Judaean Monarchy on the Border of Sinai.* Israel Museum Catalogue 175. Jerusalem: Israel Museum, 1978.

———, and C. Meyers. "The Name of God in the Wilderness of Zin." *BA* 29 (1976) 6-10.

Mesnil du Buisson, R. du. *Nouvelles études sur les dieux et les mythes de Canaan.* Études préliminaires aux religions orientales dans l'empire romain. Leiden: Brill, 1973.

Mettinger, T. N. D. *The Dethronement of Sabaoth. Studies in the Shem and Kabod Theologies.* ConBOT 18. Lund: Gleerup, 1982.

———. "Fighting the Powers of Chaos and Hell--Towards the Biblical Portrait of God." *ST* 39 (1985) 21-38.

———. *In Search of God: The Meaning and Message of the Everlasting Names.* Trans. F. H. Cryer. Philadelphia: Fortress, 1988.

———. *King and Messiah. The Civil and Sacral Legitimation of the Israelite Kings.* ConBOT 8. Lund: Gleerup, 1976.

———. "YHWH Sabaoth--The Heavenly King on the Cherubim Throne." In *Studies in the Period of David and Solomon and Other Essays*, ed. T. Ishida, pp. 109-138. Tokyo: Yamaka-Shuppansha, 1982.

Metzger, M. "Himmlische und irdische Wohnstatt Jahwes." *UF* 2 (1970) 139-158.

Milgrom, J. *Studies in Levitical Terminology, I: The Encroacher and the Levite.* University of California Near Eastern Studies 14. Berkeley/Los Angeles/London: University of California, 1970.

Miller, P. D. "Animal Names as Designations in Ugaritic and Hebrew." *UF* 2 (1970) 177-186.

__________. *The Divine Warrior in Early Israel.* HSM 5; Cambridge, Massachusetts: Harvard University, 1973.

__________. "El, the Creator of the Earth." *BASOR* 239 (1980) 43-46.

__________. "El the Warrior." *HTR* 60 (1967) 411-431.

__________. "Fire in the Mythology of Canaan and Israel." *CBQ* 27 (1965) 256-261.

__________. "Vocative Lamed in the Psalter: A Reconsideration." *UF* 11 (1979) 617-637.

__________, and J. J. M. Roberts. *The Hand of the Lord. A Reassessment of the "Ark Narrative" of 1 Samuel.* JHNES 8. Baltimore: Johns Hopkins, 1977.

Moor, J. C. de. *An Anthology of Religious Texts from Ugarit.* NISABA 16. Leiden: Brill, 1987.

__________. "Contributions to the Ugaritic Lexicon." *UF* 11 (1979) 639-653.

__________. "El, the Creator." In *The Biblical World. Essays in Honor of Cyrus H. Gordon,* ed. G. Rendsburg, et. al., pp. 171-187. New York: KTAV, 1980.

__________. *New Year with the Canaanites and Israelites.* 2 Volumes. Kampers Cahiers 21-22. Kampen: Kok, 1972.

__________. *The Seasonal Pattern in the Ugaritic Myth of Ba'lu According to the Version of Ilimilku.* AOAT 16. Neukirchen-Vluyn: Neukirchener, 1971.

__________. "Studies in the New Alphabetic Texts from Ras Shamra I." *UF* 1 (1969) 167-188.

———— and K. Spronk, "Problematical Passages in the Legend of Kirtu (I–II)." *UF* 14 (1982) 153–190.

Moran, W. L. "Review of G. W. Ahlström, *Psalm 89." Bib* 42 (1961) 238–239.

Morgenstern, J. "The Ark, the Ephod and the Tent of Meeting." *HUCA* 17 (1942–43) 155–171.

————. "A Chapter in the History of the High-Priesthood." *AJSL* 55 (1938) 1–24, 183–197, 360–377.

————. "The Etymological History of the Three Hebrew Synonyms for 'to Dance,' ḤGG, ḤLL, and KRR, and their Cultural Significance." *JAOS* 36 (1916) 321–332.

Mowinckel, S. *Der achtundsechzigste Psalm*. Avhandlinger utgitt av Det Norske Videnskaps-Akademi i Oslo, II. Hist.-Filos. Klasse 1. Oslo: Dybwad, 1953.

————. *Psalmenstudien II. Das Thronbesteigungsfest Jahwäs und der Ursprung der Eschatologie*. Skrifter utgitt av Det Norske Videnskaps-Akademi i Oslo, II. Hist.-Filos. Klasse 6. Oslo: Dybwad, 1922.

————. *The Psalms in Israel's Worship*. 2 Volumes. Trans. D. R. Ap-Thomas. New York: Abingdon, 1967.

————. *Zum israelitischen Neujahr und zur Deutung der Thronbesteigungspsalmen*. Avhandlinger utgitt av Det Norske Videnskaps-Akademi i Oslo, II. Hist.-Filos. Klasse 2. Oslo: Dybwad, 1953.

Mullen, E. T. *The Divine Council in Canaanite and Early Hebrew Literature*. HSM 24. Chico, California: Scholars, 1980.

Negbi, O. *Canaanite Gods in Metal: An Archaeological Study of Syro-Palestinian Figurines*. Tel Aviv University Institute of Archaeology 5. Tel Aviv: Peli, 1976.

Noth, M. *Die israelitischen Personennamen im Rahmen der gemeinsemitischen Namengebung*. BWANT 3/10. Reprinted. New York: Olms, 1980.

__________. "Jerusalem and the Israelite Tradition." In *The Laws in the Pentateuch and Other Studies*, pp. 132–144. Trans. D. R. Ap-Thomas. Philadelphia: Fortress, 1966.

Nyberg, H. S. "Studien zum Religionskampf im Alten Testament." *ARW* 35 (1938) 329–387.

O'Callaghan, R. T. "The Word *ktp* in Ugaritic and Egypto-Canaanite Mythology." *Or* 21 (1951) 37–45.

Ockinga, B. G. "An Example of Egyptian Royal Phraseology in Psalm 132." *BN* 11 (1980) 38–42.

O'Connor, M. "Yahweh the Donor." *Aula Orientalis* 6 (1988) 47–60.

Olávarri, E. "El calendrio cúltico de Karatepe y el Zebaḥ Hayyamym en I Sam." *EstBîb* 29 (1970) 311–325.

Ollenburger, B. C. *Zion, the City of the Great King: A Theological Symbol of the Jerusalem Cult*. JSOTSup 41. Sheffield: JSOT, 1987.

Olmo Lete, Del G. "Notes on Ugaritic Semantics V." *UF* 14 (1982) 55–69.

Olyan, S. M. *Asherah and the Cult of Yahweh in Israel*. SBLMS 34. Atlanta: Scholars, 1988.

Oppenheim, A. L. *Ancient Mesopotamia: Portrait of a Dead Civilization*. Chicago/London: University of Chicago, 1964.

Orlinsky, H. "*Hā-rōqdīm* for *hā-rēqīm* in II Samuel 6:20." *JBL* 65 (1946) 25–35.

Otten, H. "Ein kanaanäischer Mythus aus Boğazköy." *MIO* 1 (1953) 125–150.

Otto, E. *Das Mazzotfest in Gilgal*. BWANT 107. Stuttgart/Berlin: Kohlhammer, 1975.

Pardee, D. "Will the Dragon Never be Muzzled?" *UF* 16 (1984) 251–255.

Parnas, M. "*'Ēdût, 'Ēdôt, 'Ēdwôt* in the Bible, against the Background of Ancient Near Eastern Documents." *Shnaton* 1 (1975) 235–246.

Parrot, A. "De la Méditerannée à l'Iran: masques énigmatiques." In *Ugaritica* VI, pp. 409–418. MRS 17. Paris: Mission archeologique de Ras Shamra, 1969.

Patai, R. "Hebrew Installation Rites." *HUCA* 20 (1947) 143–225.

Peckham, J. B. *The Composition of the Deuteronomistic History*. HSS 35. Atlanta: Scholars, 1985.

————. *The Development of the Late Phoenician Scripts*. HSM 20. Cambridge, Massachusetts: Harvard University, 1968.

Perles, F. *Analekten zur Textkritik des Alten Testaments*. Munich: Ackerman, 1895.

Perlitt, L. *Bundestheologie im Alten Testament*. WMANT 36. Neukirchen–Vluyn: Neukirchener, 1969.

Pope, M. "A Divine Banquet at Ugarit." In *The Use of the Old Testament in the New and Other Essays. Studies in Honor of William Franklin Stinespring*, ed. J. M. Efird, pp. 170–203. Durham, North Carolina: Duke University, 1972.

————. *El in the Ugaritic Texts*. VTSup 2. Leiden: Brill, 1955.

_________. *Job*. AB 15. Garden City, New York: Doubleday, 1965.

_________. "The Status of El at Ugarit." *UF* 19 (1987) 219-230.

_________. "Marginalia to M. Dahood's *Ugaritic-Hebrew Philology*." *JBL* 85 (1966) 455-466.

Porter, J. R. "The Interpretation of 2 Samuel VI and Psalm CXXXII." *JTS* 5 (1954) 161-174.

Poulssen, N. "De Mikalscène 2 Sam 6, 16.20-23." *Bijdragen* 39 (1978) 32-58.

Prausnitz, M. "Note on a Cylinder Seal Impression." *'Atiqot* 1 (1955) 139.

Propp, W. H. *Water in the Wilderness: A Biblical Motif and Its Mythological Background*. HSM 40. Atlanta: Scholars, 1987.

_________. "On Hebrew *śāde(h)*, 'Highland'." *VT* 37 (1987) 230-234.

Rabe, V. W. "Israelite Opposition to the Temple." *CBQ* 29 (1967) 228-233.

Rabin, C. "BĀRI$^{A}$Ḥ." *JTS* 47 (1946) 38-41.

Rad, G. von. *Der heilige Krieg im alten Israel*. 5th ed. Göttingen: Vandenhoeck & Ruprecht, 1969.

_________. *The Problem of the Hexateuch and Other Essays*. Trans. E. W. T. Dicken. New York: McGraw-Hill, 1966. Reprinted. London: SCM, 1984.

Rainey, A. F. "The Ancient Hebrew Prefix Conjugation in the Light of Amarnah Canaanite." *Hebrew Studies* 27 (1986) 4-19.

———. "The Military Personnel of Ugarit." *JNES* 24 (1965) 17–27.

———. "The Toponymics of Eretz Israel." *BASOR* 231 (1978) 1–17.

Ravn, O. E. *A Catalogue of Oriental Cylinder Seals and Seal Impressions in the Danish National Museum*. Copenhagen: Danish National Museum, 1960.

Rawlinson, H. C. *The Cuneiform Inscriptions of Western Asia*. 5 Volumes. London: Bowler, 1861–1891.

Rendtorff, R. "The Background of אל עליון in Gen 14." In *Fourth World Congress of Jewish Studies* I, pp. 167–170. Jerusalem: Magnes, 1967.

———. "El, Ba'al und Jahwe: Erwägungen zum Verhältnis von kanaanäischen und israelitischen Religion." *ZAW* 78 (1966) 277–292.

———. *Studien zur Geschichte des Opfers im alten Israel*. WMANT 24; Neukirchen–Vluyn: Neukirchener, 1967.

Reymond, P. *L'eau, sa vie, et sa signification dans l'Ancient Testament*. VTSup 6. Leiden: Brill, 1958.

Riesener, I. *Der Stamm עבר im Alten Testament. Eine Wortuntersuchung unter Berücksichtigung neuer sprachwissenschaftlicher Methoden*. BZAW 149. Berlin/New York: de Gruyter, 1979.

Roberts, J. J. M. "The Davidic Origin of the Zion Tradition." *JBL* 92 (1973) 329–344.

———. *The Earliest Semitic Pantheon: a Study of the Semitic Deities Attested in Mesopotamia before Ur III*. Baltimore/London: Johns Hopkins University, 1972.

———. "The Hand of Yahweh," *VT* 21 (1971) 244–251.

———. "The Religio-Political Setting of Psalm 47." *BASOR* 221 (1976) 129-132.

Robertson, D. A. *Linguistic Evidence in Dating Early Hebrew Poetry*. SBLDS 3. Missoula, Montana: Scholars, 1972.

Robinson, A. "Do Ephrathah and Jaar Really Appear in Psalm 132, 6?" *ZAW* 86 (1974) 220-222.

Rohland, E. *Die Bedeutung der Erwählungstraditionen Israels für die Eschatologie der alttestamentlichen Propheten*. D.Theol. Dissertation. University of Heidelberg, 1956.

Rosen, H. B. "Arawna--nom Hittite?" *VT* 5 (1955) 318-320.

———. "Early Israelite Cultic Centres in the Hill Country." *VT* 38 (1988) 114-116.

Rosenberg, R. A. "The God Ṣedeq." *HUCA* 36 (1965) 161-177.

Ross, J. P. "Jahweh *ṣ$^{e}$ḇā'ôṯ* in Samuel and Psalms." *VT* 17 (1967) 76-92.

Rost, L. "Königsherrschaft Jahwes in vorköniglicher Zeit?" *TLZ* 85 (1960) 721-724.

———. *The Succession to the Throne of David*. Historic Texts and Interpreters in Biblical Scholarship 1. Trans. M. D. Rutter and D. M. Gunn. Sheffield: Almond, 1982.

Rudolph. W. *Chronikbücher*. HAT 1/21. Tübingen: Mohr, 1955.

Ryckmans, G. *Les noms propres sud-sémitiques*. 2 Volumes. Bibliothèque du Muséon 2; Louvain: Muséon, 1934.

Sachs, C. *World History of the Dance*. Trans. B. Schönberg. New York: Norton, 1965.

Sakenfeld, K. D. *The Meaning of Ḥesed in the Hebrew Bible.* HSM 17. Missoula, Montana: Scholars, 1978.

Salonen, A. "Prozessionwagen der babylonischen Götter." *StudOr* 13 (1946) 3–10.

Sanmartín, J. "Glossen zum ugaritischen Lexikon (IV)." *UF* 12 (1980) 335–344.

Sarna, N. M. "The Divine Title *'abhir ya'aqobh.*" In *Essays on the Occasion of the Seventieth Anniversary of the Dropsie University,* ed. A. I. Katsch and L. Nemoy, pp. 389–396. Philadelphia: Dropsie University, 1979.

Sasson, J. M. "The Worship of the Golden Calf." In *Orient and Occident. Essays Presented to C. H. Gordon on the Occasion of His Sixty-Fifth Birthday,* ed. H. A. Hoffner, pp. 151–159. AOAT 22. Neukirchen-Vluyn: Neukirchener, 1973.

Sauren, H. and Kestemont, G. "Keret, roi de Ḫubur." *UF* 3 (1971) 181–221.

Schaeffer, C. F. A. "Les fouilles de Minet el-Beida et de Ras Shamra, quatrième campagne (printemps 1932)." *Syria* 14 (1933) 93–127.

———. "La stèle de l'hommage du dieu El (?)" *Syria* 18 (1937) 128–134.

Schicklberger, F. *Die Ladeerzählungen des ersten Samuel-Buches. Eine literaturwissenschaftliche und theologiegeschichtliche Untersuchung.* FB 7. Würzburg: Echter, 1973.

Schmid, H. "Jahwe und die Kulttraditionen von Jerusalem." *ZAW* 67 (1955) 168–197.

Schmidt, W. H. *Königtum Gottes in Ugarit und Israel: Zur Herkunft der Königsprädikation Jahwes.* BZAW 80. Berlin: Töpelmann, 1966.

________. "Kritik am Königtum." In *Probleme Biblischer Theologie. Gerhard von Rad zum 70. Geburtstag*, ed. H. W. Wolff, pp. 440-461. Munich: Kaiser, 1971.

Schmitt, J. J. "Pre-Israelite Jerusalem." In *Scripture in Context: Essays on the Comparative Method*, ed. C. D. Evans, W. H. Hallo, and J. B. White, pp. 101-121. PTMS 34. Pittsburgh: Pickwick, 1980.

Schmitt, R. *Zelt und Lade als Thema alttestamentlicher Wissenschaft. Eine kritische forschungsgeschichtliche Darstellung*. Gütersloh: Mohn, 1972.

Schottroff, W. *'Gedenken' im alten Orient und im Alten Testament. Die Wurzel zākar im semitischen Sprachkreis*. WMANT 15. Neukirchen-Vluyn: Neukirchener, 1964.

Schreiner, J. *Sion-Jerusalem: Jahwes Königssitz. Theologie der heiligen Stadt im Alten Testament*. SANT 7. Munich: Kösel, 1963.

Schulz, A. *Die Bücher Samuel*. 2 Volumes. EHAT 8/1. Münster: Aschendorff, 1919-1920.

Scippa, V. "Davide Conquista Gerusalemma." *Bibbia et Oriente* 27 (1985) 65-76.

Seow, C. L. "The Designation of the Ark in Priestly Theology." *HAR* 8 (1985) 185-198.

________. "The Syro-Palestinian Context of Solomon's Dream." *HTR* 77 (1984) 141-152.

Seybold, K. "Der Redaktion der Wallfahrtspsalmen." *ZAW* 71 (1979) 247-268.

________. *Die Wallfahrtspsalmen: Studien zur Entstehungsgeschichte von Psalm 120-134*. BTS 3. Neukirchen-Vluyn: Neukirchener, 1978.

Seyrig, H. "Bas-reliefs monumentaux du temple de Bêl à Palmyre." *Syria* 15 (1934) 159-165.

Seyring, F. "Der alttestamentliche Sprachgebrauch inbetreff des Namens der sogen. 'Bundeslade.'" *ZAW* 11 (1891) 114-125.

Shiloh, Y. *Excavations at the City of David* I. Qedem 19. Jerusalem: Institute of Archaeology, 1984.

Silverman, M. *Religious Values in the Jewish Proper Names at Elephantine*. AOAT 217. Neukirchen-Vluyn: Neukirchener, 1985.

Skehan, P. "A Fragment of the 'Song of Moses' (Deut 32) from Qumran." *BASOR* 136 (1954) 12-15.

Smelik, K. A. D. "De intocht van de Ark in Jeruzalem." *Amsterdamse Cahiers* 4 (1983) 26-36.

Smend, R. *Yahweh War and Tribal Confederation: Reflections upon Israel's Earliest History*. Trans. M. G. Rogers. Nashville: Abingdon, 1970.

Smith, S. "The Babylonian Ritual for the Consecration and Induction of a Divine Statue." *JRAS* 57 (1925) 37-60.

Smith, W. Robertson. *Lectures on the Religion of the Semites*. Fundamental Institutions, First Series. Edinburgh: Black, 1889.

Soggin, J. A. "'Wacholderholz' 2 Sam VI 5a gleich 'Schlaghölzer,' 'Klappern'?" *VT* 14 (1964) 374-377.

Steinherr, F. "Die phönizisch-hethitischen Bilinguen von Karatepe." *Münchener Studien zur Sprachwissenschaft* 32 (1974) 103-148.

Steinkeller, P. "The Date of Gudea and His Dynasty." *JCS* 40 (1988) 47-53.

Stern, E. "Phoenician Masks and Pendants." *PEQ* 108 (1976) 110–118.

Stolz, F. *Das erste und zweite Buch Samuel*. ZBAT 9. Zürich: Theologischer, 1981.

__________. *Jahwes und Israels Kriege: Kriegestheorien und Kriegserfahrungen im Glaube des alten Israel*. ATANT 60. Zürich: Theologischer, 1972.

__________. *Strukturen und Figuren im Kult von Jerusalem: Studien zur altorientalischen vor- und frühisraelitischen Religion*. BZAW 118. Berlin: de Gruyter, 1970.

Streck, M. *Assurbanipal und die letzen assyrischen Könige bis zum Untergang Ninevehs*. 2 Volumes. VAB 7. Leipzig: Hinrichs, 1916.

Strivoski, A. "The History of the Name Ṣĕḇā'ôṯ in the Book of Samuel." *Beth Mikra* 49 (1972) 183–192.

Stummer, F. *Sumerisch-akkadische Parallelen zum Aufbau alttestamentlicher Psalmen*. Paderborn: Schöningh, 1922.

Tadmor, H. "Autobiographical Apology in the Royal Assyrian Literature." In *History, Historiography, and Interpretation. Studies in Biblical and Cuneiform Literatures*, ed. H. Tadmor and M. Weinfeld, pp. 36–57. Jerusalem/Leiden: Magnes/Brill, 1983.

Tallqvist, K. L. *Akkadische Götterepitheta*. StudOr 7. Helsinki: Academic Bookshop, 1938.

__________. *Assyrian Personal Names*. Acta Societas Scientiarum Fennicæ 63; Helsingfors, 1918.

Talmon, S. "הַר *har*; גִּבְעָה *gibh'āh*." In *TDOT* III, ed. G. J. Botterweck and H. Ringgren. Trans. J. T. Willis, G. W. Bromiley, and D. E. Greene, pp. 427–447. Grand Rapids, Michigan: Eerdmans, 1978.

Tarragon, J.-M. *Le culte à Ugarit d'après les textes de la pratique en cunéiformes alphabétiques.* CahRB 19. Paris: Gabalda, 1980.

__________. "David et l'arche: II Samuel, vi." *RB* 86 (1979) 514-523.

Tawil, H. "Some Literary Elements in the Opening Sections of the Hadad, Zākir, and Nērab II Inscriptions in the Light of East and West Semitic Royal Inscriptions." *Or* 43 (1974) 40-65.

Thompson, R. C. *The Report of the Magicians and Astrologers of Nineveh and Babylon in the British Museum.* 2 Volumes. Luzac's Semitic Text and Translation Series 6-7. London: Luzac, 1900.

Tournay, R. J. *Voir et entendre Dieu avec les Psaumes, ou La liturgie prophétique du second temple à Jérusalem.* CahRB 24. Paris: Gabalda, 1988.

Tsevat, M. "Alalakhiana." *HUCA* 29 (1958) 109-134.

__________. "Studies in the Book of Samuel, 4." *HUCA* 36 (1965) 49-58.

__________. *A Study of the Language of the Biblical Psalms.* SBLMS 9. Philadelphia: Society of Biblical Literature, 1955.

Ullendorf, E. "Ugaritic Marginalia." *Or* 20 (1951) 271-272.

Ulrich, E. C. *The Qumran Text of Samuel and Josephus.* HSM 19. Missoula, Montana: Scholars, 1978.

Ussishkin, D. "The Date of the Neo-Hittite Enclosure in Karatepe." *AnSt* 19 (1969) 121-137.

Vannutelli, P. *Libri Synoptici Veteris Testamenti.* Rome: Pontifical Biblical Institute, 1931.

Vattioni, F. "Il dio Resheph." *AION* 15 (1965) 39-74.

Vaux, R. de. "Arche d'alliance et tente de réunion." In *Bible et Orient*, pp. 262-265. Paris: Cerf, 1967.

———. "Les cherubins et l'arche d'alliance, les sphinx gardiens et les trones divins dans l'ancien orient." In *Bible et Orient*, pp. 231-259. Paris: Cerf, 1967.

———. "Jerusalem et les prophètes." *RB* 73 (1966) 481-509.

Vawter, B. "Yahweh: Lord of the Heavens and the Earth." *CBQ* 48 (1986) 461-467.

Veijola, T. *Die ewige Dynastie. David und die Enstehung seiner Dynastie nach deuteronomisticher Darstellung*. Annales Academiæ Scientiarum Fennicæ, Sarja-Ser. B 193. Helsinki: Suomalainen Tiedeakateneia, 1975.

———. *Verheissung in der Krise. Studien zur Literatur und Theologie der Exilszeit anhand des 89. Psalms*. Annales Academiæ Scientiarum Fennicæ, Sarja-Ser. B 220. Helsinki: Suomalainen Tiedeakateneia, 1982.

———. "Zu Ableitung und Bedeutung von *hē'id* I in hebräischen: Ein Beitrag zur Bundesterminologie." *UF* 8 (1976) 343-351.

Vida, G. L. della "El 'Elyôn in Gen 14 13-20." *JBL* 53 (1944) 1-9.

Vogt, E. "Benjamin geboren 'eine Meile' von Ephrata." *Bib* 56 (1975) 30-36.

Volkwein, B. "Masoretisches *'ēdût, 'ēdwôt, 'ēdôt*-'Zeugnis' oder 'Bundesbestimmungen'?" *BZ* 13 (1969) 18-40.

Volz, P. *Die Neujahrsfest Jahwes*. Sammlung gemeinverständlicher Vorträge und Schriften aus dem Bebiet der Theologie und Religionsgeschichte 67. Tübingen: Mohr, 1912.

Wambacq, B. N. *L'épithète divine Jahvé Ṣĕbā'ôt. Étude philologique, historique et exégétique*. Rome: de Brower, 1947.

Wanke, G. *Die Zionstheologie des Korachiten in ihrem traditionsgeschichtlichen Zusammenhang*. BZAW 97. Berlin: Töpelmann, 1966.

Ward, W. A. "Comparative Studies in Egyptian and Ugaritic." *JNES* 20 (1961) 31-40.

Waschke, E.-J. "Das Verhältnis alttestamentlicher Überlieferungen im Schnittpunkt der Dynastiezusage und die Dynastiezusage im Spiegel alttestamentlicher Überlieferungen." *ZAW* 99 (1987) 157-179.

Weil, H. "Exégèse du Psaume 68." *RHR* 117 (1938) 75-89.

Weinfeld, M. "The Covenant of Grant in the Old Testament and in the Ancient Near East." *JAOS* 90 (1970) 184-203.

________. "Zion and Jerusalem as Religious and Political Capital: Ideology and Utopia." In *The Poet and the Historian. Essays in Literary and Historical Biblical Criticism*, ed. R. E. Friedman, pp. 75-115. HSS 26. Chico, California: Scholars, 1983.

Weippert, M. "'Heiliger Krieg' in Israel und Assyrien: Kritische Anmerkungen zu Gerhard von Rad's Konzept des 'Heilige Krieges im alten Israel'." *ZAW* 84 (1972) 460-493.

Weiser, A. "Die Legitimation des Königs David." *VT* 16 (1966) 325-354.

———. *The Psalms*. OTL. Trans. H. Hartwell. Philadelphia: Westminster, 1962.

Wellhausen, J. *Die Composition des Hexateuchs und der historischen Bücher des Alten Testaments*. 4th ed. Berlin: de Gruyter, 1963.

———. *Prolegomena to the History of Ancient Israel*. Trans. Black and Menzies. Cleveland: Meridian, 1965. Reprint. Gloucester, Massachusetts: Smith, 1973.

———. *Der Text der Bücher Samuelis*. Göttingen: Vandenhoeck und Ruprecht, 1871.

Wesselius, J. W. "Three Difficult Passages in Ugaritic Literary Texts." *UF* 15 (1983) 312-314.

Westphal, G. "צבא השמים," In *Orientalische Studien Theodore Nöldeke zum 70. Geburstag*, ed. G. Bezold. Giesen: Töpelmann, 1906.

Wildberger, H. *Jesaja*. 3 Volumes. BKAT 10. Neukirchen-Vluyn: Neukirchener, 1972-1982.

Willis, J. T. "An Anti-Elide Narrative Tradition from a Prophetic Circle at the Ramah Sanctuary." *JBL* 90 (1971) 288-308.

Winkler, H. *Die Keilschrifttexte Sargons*. 2 Volumes. Leipzig: Pfeiffer, 1889.

Wiseman, D. J. "A New Stela of Aššur-nasir-pal II." *Iraq* 14 (1952) 24-44.

Wright, G. E. "The Lawsuit of God: A Form-Critical Study of Deuteronomy 32." In *Israel's Prophetic Heritage. Essays in Honor of James Muilenberg*, ed. B. W. Anderson and W. Harrelson, pp. 26-67. New York: Harper and Row, 1962.

Wyatt, N. "'Araunah the Jebusite' and the Throne of David." *ST* 39 (1985) 39–53.

———. "The Stela of the Seated God from Ugarit." *UF* 15 (1983) 271–277.

Zimmerli, W. *Ezekiel*. 2 Volumes. Hermeneia. Trans. J. D. Martin. Fortress: Philadelphia, 1979–1983.

## INDEX A: TEXTS CITED

### 1. Biblical and Jewish Sources

#### Scripture and Apocrypha

2. West-Semitic Sources

Ugaritic

4. Mesopotamian Sources



5. Egyptian Sources



6. Greek Texts

## INDEX B: WORDS and ROOTS

## INDEX C: SUBJECTS